If I Lived My Life Again

by

the Right Hon. Sir Winston S. Churchill

Compiled and edited
by

Jack Fishman

D0487494

W. H. Allen · London
A division of Howard & Wyndham
1974

PRINTED AND BOUND IN GREAT BRITAIN BY
BUTLER & TANNER LTD, FROME & LONDON
FOR THE PUBLISHERS W. H. ALLEN & CO. LTD
44 HILL STREET, LONDON WIX 8LB

ISBN 0 491 01901 7

If I Lived My Life Again

Books by Jack Fishman include:

The Seven Men of Spandau
My Darling Clementine

Contents

CONTENTS

THIS BOOK IS produced with the authority of the Churchill Centenary Trust, and proceeds from the sale will go to Churchill College, Cambridge, and the Winston Churchill Memorial Trust, the two principal national memorials established to commemorate the life of my husband.

Clementine S. Churchill

CHURCHILL COLLEGE, CAMBRIDGE, was founded by Sir Winston to promote the teaching and learning of Science and Technology at the exceptionally high level needed by Britain and the world in the modern age. The College, which includes women amongst its members, has already produced strikingly successful results in this country, in the Commonwealth and in America. It attracts eminent scholars from all over the world and it is the repository of Sir Winston's own archives.

The other memorial is the Winston Churchill Memorial Trust which, every year, sends abroad some one hundred men and women with grants to study and explore carefully selected social, industrial, scientific, ecological, or recreational subjects. The studies open to them are greatly varied and those who have received these grants are already making a valuable contribution to the country and to international understanding. For the hundred places offered every year several thousand people apply. Further funds are needed to enable the Trust to increase the numbers and wide benefits which result from its programme; and the total royalties from this book will be contributing to the Trust as well as assisting other worthy work.

John Colville

JOHN COLVILLE
Chairman, Churchill Centenary Trust

Acknowledgments

My SINCERE APPRECIATION is due to all who granted copyright clearances; co-operated; advised on research, in particular Sir Max Aitken, Chairman of Beaverbrook Newspapers; Jack Barnett; Bernard M. Baruch; John Colville; Peter Eastwood, Managing Director, and Maurice Green, Editor, of the Daily Telegraph; General Dwight D. Eisenhower; Howard French, Editorial Director of Harmsworth Publications; C. D. Hamilton, Chairman and Editor-in-Chief of Times Newspapers; General Lord Ismay; Rupert Murdoch, Chairman and Managing Director of News International; Lord Normanbrook; Gerald O'Brien of the Conservative and Unionist Central Office; Sir Tom O'Brien; General Sir Frederick Pile; Lord Robens; Percy Roberts, Managing Director of the International Publishing Corporation; Mrs Eleanor Roosevelt; Michael Shields, Managing Director of Associated Newspapers; Lord Thomson, Chairman of the Thomson Organisation; Evelyn Walkden; Colonel Barlow Wheeler, Sir Winston's constituency agent; John G. Winant; Charles Wintour, Editor of the Evening Standard.

Acknowledgments and thanks are also due to Crowell Collier-Macmillan Co. of New York; Edinburgh University; the Jewish Chronicle; the London School of Economics; Macmillan & Co. for the brief 'Action This Day' book quote from Lord Normanbrook used in the Preface; the New Commonwealth Society; the Pilgrims' Society; the University of Oxford and Clarendon Press; the Royal College of Physicians; the Royal Society of St George.

Above all, I am deeply grateful to Baroness Spencer Churchill for her co-operation, and to Winston S. Churchill, M.P., and John Colville, Chairman of the Churchill Centenary Trust, who worked closely with Sir Winston for many years, for approving publication of the book. I am happy that the total proceeds will be shared between Churchill

ix

College, Cambridge, the Churchill Memorial Trust and Churchill Fellowships; and mentally handicapped children. It is a privilege to be associated with the Centenary Trust and Baroness Spencer Churchill in presenting this treasure of wisdom from her husband, who so many of us miss, whose words we still need, and who the new generations should understand, remember, and profit from his legendary magnificence.

Preface

'WHEN I LOOK around me in my family and in the home I have built for myself by my own work and, in part, by my own hand, I feel deeply thankful for the many blessings which Providence bestowed upon me in this uncertain world.

'My pen makes me entirely independent. I have no need to enter business. I have the study of history and the amusement of painting to afford my mind agreeable occupation. Having served nearly all my grown-up life in the great offices of State, I find freedom and leisure very pleasant.

'I mean to devote the rest of my public life to giving the best advice I can and the fruits of my experience to my fellow countrymen, and to say what I think and feel without, as the saying goes, "Fear, favour, or affection."

'It surely is a good thing that there should be some people thus situated when political organisation and machinery are growing so much stronger than any individuals.'

These are Sir Winston Churchill's words, and he is the author of this book. Other than this introduction and the acknowledgments, every word, including the title and its relevant chapter (which was mostly written in 1931), are his.

Much of the wisdom this book contains is available for the first time, and I feel I should explain how it came about, and where the materials came from.

I am fortunate in possessing one of the most extensive files on the Churchills outside the official Churchill archives themselves. It is a vast treasury of facts and stories about them and by them; public and private speeches; comprehensive notes of their discussions and interviews with all manner of people in many parts of the world. The file also contains obscure or long-forgotten articles by Winston Churchill dating from his earliest journalistic days and covering an incredible range of subjects.

This file, collected over a period of thirty years, was the foundation of My Darling Clementine, the book I wrote about Lady Churchill and published in 1963. My Churchill file comprises well over 600,000 words of notes. I used some 200,000 in my tribute to Lady Churchill, but most of the material by Winston was inappropriate to her book.

Towards the close of 1973, I started to revise and extend My Darling Clementine for a new edition. One evening, during a break in the work, I happened to see a miners' union leader on television threatening to destroy the Government and help bring about revolution. I returned to my desk and my Churchill files, picked up a document, and found myself gazing at the words – 'It's no use arguing with a Communist.' It was a scathing attack by Winston on the dangers of Communism, and it was as if he were replying to the interview I had just witnessed on my television set.

I extracted from files Winston's words on a variety of subjects. The effect was startling. Here he was, commenting on today's great issues, in words written years ago: and what he had to say was still as pointed, still as dynamic, still as relevant as it had ever been.

Phrase-maker extraordinary, master of the English language, Winston Churchill, with his intimate knowledge of the virtues and failings of people, was well-equipped to pass judgment on them. When we were in dire peril, his opinions of men and events were accorded the full confidence of his nation and of other nations, and victory showed how well-placed had been that confidence. He will always be the voice of Britain and of freedom everywhere. To find anything that stands comparison with his inspiring words we have to go back to the great William Pitt's – 'I know that I can save my country and that nobody else can.'

The bulldoggedness, humour, and spirit of people found their own voice in his, and I felt it would do us good to listen to him again. No one has ever surpassed his gift for communication and – of great importance to democracy – for getting people to give the best of themselves. He didn't seek, as dictators do, to secure their blind faith. He only wanted to open their eyes. For great events have the effect of making imaginative men visionaries: that is, able to see the scheme, the tendencies, and truth in what is before them. Luckily for the world, Winston Churchill's record shows how unerring was his vision of the truth. Where others worked with their timidities, their habits, their prejudices, and their obsessions, he worked with imagination and all his strength and depth of insight, and no one doubts that he acted solely in the interests of his own country and of free-thinking peoples throughout the world. His courage and vision gave him a place in history second to none.

Great statesmen who sense where the future lies, should have the ability to galvanise people into working towards that future. Today's world statesmen desperately need Winston's flair for oratory, to persuade people to listen and see what has to be done. We still need his voice.

He was a realist who saw life as it is; who valued courage, resourcefulness, all kinds of achievement, and doing one's duty by one's country and by mankind. His inspiration was patriotism – according to many, an old-fashioned virtue today.

I felt this book was needed. I wrote to Baroness Spencer Churchill explaining my feelings and what I wanted to do. She replied by return of post suggesting that I explore the idea with Mr John Colville, Chairman of the Winston Churchill Centenary Trust. The result was my authorisation to proceed.

President Kennedy once said of Winston: 'He mobilised the English language and sent it into battle.'

This man who lived by words, and loved words, knew how to use them as weapons. No one could reach people – all kinds of people – with words as he could. As he said of himself: 'I have been a journalist, and half my lifetime I earned my living by selling words and, I hope, thoughts.' His speeches were literature, moreover. Of how many statesmen's words today could that be said?

The New York Times said of him in 1940:

'Seldom has the English-speaking world been so moved by public utterance as it is moved by the great speeches of Winston Churchill. Their candour, simplicity, and resolution give them stature. Men have come to feel that out of the crucible of experience in victory and defeat, of acclaim and bitter criticism, Mr Churchill emerged as the man fit to voice the dauntless spirit of a free people.'

And the Baltimore Sun added:

'You believed what he said, because you knew in your heart that he believed it himself – every solemn, measured word of it. There could be no doubt of that.'

London's street of ink and newspapers – Fleet Street – was where he learned his trade. Fleet Street and the House of Commons were the places he knew and liked best. For years he was a working journalist, and had an enormous respect for professionalism.

Unlike most politicians, he did not contribute to newspapers as an extension of his political platform. In the thirties, when he was ostracised politically for his views on the rearmament of Germany, he turned again to Fleet Street for his livelihood. It was not a new occupation for him. In 1897 the Daily Telegraph paid him £5 a column for his despatches from the North West Frontier. As a war correspondent during the Boer War he was captured when an armoured train in which he was travelling was ambushed. He escaped three weeks later.

At one time, he and I both wrote regularly for the same national newspaper and, on occasions, I found myself sub-editing his copy for print. Not that I was allowed to touch a single word. I just had to mark it typographically and double-check proofs. His words always fascinated me, and wherever possible, I kept copies of everything he wrote. We also sometimes met in the House of Commons which, for years, I attended at least twice a week. One day we discussed the career of journalism and writing. I asked whether he thought he had been wise to divide himself for so long between part-time journalism and part-time politics. 'Writing gave me a public voice when I had no political platform to speak from,' he replied. 'It also opened many doors that would otherwise have remained shut to me, and it was the school that taught me how to reach the public with words, so I suppose it was the most valuable thing I ever learned.

'I love journalism – earned most of my living from it. I pushed a pen in a lot of places – Egypt, India, South Africa, the United States.

'I was once asked whether I was sorry not to have given my life to literature, but I do not regret that. It was suggested to me that a great pen might do a greater lifework than an eloquent voice and a political genius.

'That may be true, but I am not prepared to admit that I have either the one faculty or the other in any high degree. If I were to pronounce one way or the other, I'd say I was much more at home with a pen than on a platform. To speak in public takes a great deal out of me. I never excelled as a platform speaker.'

In the crisis days before the outbreak of the last world war, I discussed with him at the House of Commons what he felt another war would be like. The following day he handed me a typescript of thoughts he had noted on this theme – in 1934. I incorporated some of these in the chapter of this book entitled 'War And Peace'.

Like most good journalists, he kept meticulous files of his writings, notes, and opinions on an extensive variety of topics, and from time to time he used these as a basis for newspaper and magazine articles or speeches. He was always ready with the right words at the appropriate moment, but they were not always as spontaneous as they sounded. They were largely the product of an enormous reading appetite, detailed research, careful thought, and shrewd analysis. He was, of course, a master of spontaneity too, but the fountain of his sparkling words sprang from a deep source. He never tried to conceal his preparations for a speech or an article. He took pride in them.

As Baroness Asquith once said of him: 'To Winston Churchill everything under the sun was new – seen and appraised as on the first day of creation. His approach to life was full of ardour and surprise. Even the eternal verities appeared to him to be an exciting personal discovery.'

He certainly had the seeing eye, and usually saw further and more clearly than almost anybody else.

He always had the urge to find out, and was never afraid to speak or write what was in his mind. He did not hide his opinions.

He never claimed to be wholly original – consciously or unconsciously he drew on the treasure-house of history and literature in which he steeped himself. But to everything he added himself – his style, his wit, his sharp cut and thrust.

He also loved to develop thoughts and ideas in private before a small audience – often at dinner. Dinner was always *the* occasion of the day in the Churchill homes when, after the meal was over and the port and brandy were being poured, Winston would expand on any subject that took his fancy. Close friends and associates such as Mrs Eleanor Roosevelt, General Lord Ismay, and that great American Statesman, Bernard M. Baruch, gave me accounts of some priceless dinner party discourses, and I have used extracts from them in several chapters. It was also Mrs Roosevelt and Bernard Baruch who led me to diaries and records that Winston had kept of some of his American travels, and on these I based the 'Transatlantic Travels And Thoughts' section of the book.

His writing method was to dictate and revise, and then revise again. Either he, or an editor, would suggest a subject, then he would develop it embodying key facts and arguments at suitable points, and reaching valid conclusions.

He would slot anything into a theme as long as it fitted the general framework of his narrative and thinking. He would walk up and down the room dictating the sweep of his thoughts to a secretary. He liked getting things down on paper and then modifying, drastically changing, or filling in gaps later.

I faithfully followed his own writing pattern to compile and create the chapters of this book. For each subject I found material from many sources and gave continuity without altering text or meaning. For example, the chapter 'The Right To Strike' was largely based on a feature of the same title which Winston wrote in 1919 for the Illustrated Sunday Herald, which later became the Sunday Graphic though it no longer exists. I added to this feature extracts from a commentary he wrote years later on 'The British Working Man', and I inserted comments he made privately on the same subject to Trade Union leaders and Members of Parliament, including former Socialist Minister Evelyn Walkden, Sir Tom O'Brien, and Alfred Robens (now Lord Robens). Yet another valuable contribution came from a Trade Union pamphlet.

I used essays; letters; interviews he gave at home and abroad; table talk with intimates; unpublished local constituency speeches – many of them made in his own constituency at Woodford, Essex; private after-dinner speeches; lectures he gave to such bodies as Edinburgh University; the Royal College of Physicians, Oxford University, or at his old school, Harrow.

I took material from his work for many now non-existent magazines and newspapers, including Strand Magazine, Answers, Pearson's; Nash's Pall Mall, the Sunday Chronicle, Sunday Graphic, Sunday Dispatch. Once purely local and ephemeral elements had been removed from the material, his assessments and advice sprang to life again, topical, timeless. Only a minor proportion of quotation is derived from his Parliamentary debating comments. The archives of the Conservative Party Central Office provided a further invaluable source of generally unknown speeches and writings. Many of the Central Office records and papers have been destroyed by fire, but I managed to trace rare copies elsewhere. Some of Winston's articles were published as limited edition booklets by private presses. For example, there was 'Mr Churchill and the Peers' – from a letter to his constituents, published in 1910 by the Liberal Publications Department; and for a shilling in 1910 you could also buy a little booklet by Winston expounding the cause of 'The People's Rights'.

He was an indefatigable reviser. Of this habit of his he would say:

'If I had known then what I know now, I should have written it differently.'

He would write an essay or a speech and, years later, revise and update it for another occasion, often repeating or slightly re-phrasing his earlier versions. He did this with speeches he gave to the Royal Society of St George on the theme of patriotism, and these gave me the basis of the chapter 'Is Patriotism Played Out?' Two of his asides on this topic I reluctantly had to exclude from the chapter. On one occasion he added:

'It is quite true that there are a lot of dull people about – that's the secret of Britain's greatness.'

And another time:

'I recall the notorious case in which a gentleman had been caught in a compromising situation with a lady in a London park. The circumstances were that the man was seventy-five and the month December, and there was five degrees of frost.

'It makes one feel proud to be an Englishman.'

The composition of a speech or an article was not a task he would ever skimp. He was never one for impromptu speeches. He might improvise briefly, but only to elaborate or clarify. Normally, though, he would adhere closely to what he had carefully prepared. 'Clarity and cogency can be reconciled with a greater brevity,' was one of his favourite admonitions; and another in the same vein was: 'It is slothful not to compress your thoughts.'

In spite of his speech impediment, he was often a great orator; his poetry and prose could be magnificent, moving, emotional, and he was never guilty of the sin of over-dramatisation. Nevertheless, though known the world over as a king of words, he was always nervous before making a speech – anxious for it to achieve the desired reaction and effect. Today, when reading his words, it is still possible to hear his voice.

In his early days he liked long words above everything, and revelled in producing unusual ones to puzzle Parliament. But when his greatest days arrived in the 1939-45 war, instinct told him to make his appeals in plain Anglo-Saxon terms: 'This was their finest hour' had a resonance that 'their noblest occasion' could never match.

As he grew old, he became increasingly convinced of the value and significance of the judgments of posterity. The pace of his work was slower, though he could still rise to great occasions or to the making of formidable speeches. But the difference was that now, when a speech was imminent, he seemed to feel a cloud hanging over his head for days beforehand, and he sometimes polished a text right up to the moment before delivering it.

After his illness in 1953, although he recovered, he remained unsteady on his feet and had what he described as 'a kick in his gallop.' He became increasingly apprehensive about his ability and physical fitness to carry out his duties to the full, and needed all the reassurance and moral support of his wife. Somehow, he overcame and was still able to show he was the master.

Lord Normanbrook, who was Secretary to the Cabinet at the time, recalls: 'In the daily round of his responsibilities he no longer had the necessary energy, mental or physical, to give to papers or to people the full attention which they deserved. But he was reluctant to take the final step of naming a date for his resignation. In part, I believe he was influenced by the thought that resignation from office would also mean the end of his connection with Parliament. But apart from his distaste for leaving the House of Commons, he was reluctant to abandon his special position of influence as Prime Minister.'

As the years roll on the old and the middle-aged who knew him, or saw him, or just heard him as a voice, will tell their stories. Then will come the younger generation – the girls and boys who stood with their parents in the streets, or watched his unforgettable funeral on television. Afterwards will come historians and legend-makers. Truly this was a man who raised life to a peak and guided countless generations. And the Man of the Century spoke words that still help guide us for the rest of this century, and in the centuries to come.

Through the personal papers and notes of private conversations; documents; essays and speeches – many hitherto unpublished or largely unfamiliar – his giant experience and far-sightedness incredibly, powerfully speak to us once more. He has found his voice again – the Voice of Yesterday talks pointedly and illuminatingly of To-day and To-morrow, shrewdly assessing matters that concern everyone, everywhere.

There was one chapter which I almost excluded from this book. It is entitled 'Great Fighters Of Lost Causes'. Although it contains moral points and principles applicable to current times, the essay upon which the chapter was based was mainly Winston revelling in ancient history, and the theme was not as strikingly topical as the general contents of the book. So why is it included?

I found a copy of the manuscript, written in 1933, at the British Museum. It was charred and burnt and too fragile even to photocopy.

As I fearfully turned the pages, they crumbled in my hands. It had been damaged in the early Blitz days of the last war. But the manuscript had, like Winston himself, defied bombs, fire, and Hitler, and refused to be vanquished. I had to include it.

So once more, it is Churchill the fighter, Churchill the champion of lost causes, Churchill the prophet speaking, and from now on, the words in this book are no longer mine. They are Winston Churchill's.

JACK FISHMAN

CHAPTER I

The Truth About Myself

As I KNOW a great deal about myself, at first sight you would think that to write the truth about myself would be easy. But, on the other hand, mine is a very simple tale to tell. Having been born and bred in a victorious country with a constitutional monarchy and a free Parliament, I have never been called upon to mingle in the ferocious convulsions of disaster and defeat which have gripped so many other countries. I have always been taught that 'One-man power' is odious to the British nation, and that ministers and functionaries of all kinds are the servants and not the masters of the State.

Under the well-proved laws established by our ancestors, and under the ancient monarchy which we all revere, an enormous measure of personal and political liberty is enjoyed by British men and women. We know that the fundamental institutions of the realm stand high above the conflicts of parties or the passions and ambitions of individuals. We loathe anything in the nature of totalitarian uniformity. The poorest man has the right to criticise the most powerful administration. Everyone is entitled to form his own opinion and express it to as many as care to listen.

Although we use a lot of hard language about each other – especially at election times – we recognise that no party or section has the monopoly of wisdom or virtue, and that not only the happiness but the dignity of a community depends upon free speech and writing, both in public and in private. It would be loathsome to me and the kind of people I have lived my life among to live in a State where it was a crime not to curry favour with the Government of the day, where all challenge to authority was forbidden and punished, where even private talk about politics might be made the basis of a criminal charge, and where everyone was looking over his shoulder for some spy or eaves-dropper. All this is the barbarism of the dark ages from which the genius and the intellect of man have steadily and valiantly emancipated themselves. On this personal freedom, on the right of the home to form and express its own opinions, depends to my mind everything that makes life worth living.

But if I would not like to live under such a regime as now prevails in so many populous countries, still less would I like to be one of the grim figures who enforce it. For years I sat in the Cabinets of Great Britain, and bore my part in many important decisions. No doubt it appeals to several sides of man's nature to be able to make good arrange-ments and help to steer the ship of State; but I cannot understand any-one wishing to purchase such privileges by violent deeds. Leaving moral questions on one side, the attraction of public office, the pomp of authority, the loud shouts of well-drilled crowds, would seem to me a poor, shabby recompense for inflicting misery and shedding human blood.

Therefore I present myself to you only as one who has lived the bulk of his life in the House of Commons and has never wished to exercise such direful sways. I thank God that this is so. I do not feel at all envious of these modern world-figures, and I hope while life beats within my breast to keep all Dictatorships away from our native land. I trust, indeed, that the British people will realise more clearly how much has been gained for them by the courage of their forebears, and how much they enjoy – as free as the air they breathe – which is denied to-day to a very great portion of educated mankind. Honour there is and long renown to be sought in our slowly-grown-up society, and surely it is splendid to dream that one may play a small but recognisable part in the unfolding of our history.

Therefore I have no lurid confessions to make. I have a heart devoid of hate and am content with the share I have had in our broad, decent, tolerant public life. It always gives me great pleasure to hear those lines:

> The nations not so blest as Thee
> Shall in their turn to tyrants fall,
> Whilst Thou shalt flourish great and free,
> The dread and envy of them all.

I often ask my public audiences where they come from, and quite a lot of people know that they are one of the verses of 'Rule, Britannia'. Perhaps nowadays the word 'dread' might be thought arrogant. I would be quite content to substitute the word 'hope'. Perhaps it would be truer, because certainly the kind of life we have built up and guarded during nearly a thousand years of independence embodies the greatest hope of the world. But I am afraid in the times in which we live one cannot altogether exclude the word 'dread', because it would be fatal for us to get into a condition where our rights and freedom could be trampled down by any of the various forms of oppression which now flourish so extensively. That is why I have always been an admirer of France. I recognise in the glint of those bright bayonets that made the French Revolution and opened the 'free career for talent' to all classes, one of the mainstays of human freedom.

But in thus revealing my feelings to you upon these great causes, I am perhaps straying too far from myself. Let me return, therefore, to the main topic. As a matter of fact I am a very modest man. The great Duke of Marlborough wrote to his wife that he never liked to see his name in print, and that he thought that a man, especially an officer, should live simply by the opinion of his fellows. I can hardly say that the same repugnance to publicity has been transmitted to his descendants; but I can assure you that it is only the solicitations of others which have induced me to write about my own personality. The best explanation is my kind-heartedness; for one ought always to try to meet other people's wishes as far as one can. Let me therefore begin by saying that not only am I a modest, but also an extremely benevolent man.

You would no doubt be surprised to know that I am also the most consistent of politicians. There are moments when I feel that I might make a case for being the *only* consistent politician. But then that would savour of vanity. In fact it seems to me that I have always pursued the same main objectives throughout my political life, and that it is the Parties and the occasions which have shifted and varied around me. For instance, it has fallen to my lot to fight in a Liberal Cabinet for a strong Navy and to fight in a Conservative Cabinet against large naval programmes. But is that inconsistency? It all depends upon the circumstances of the time. The highest consistency is to resist excessive tendencies, whether for disarmament or armament.

Still I should not go so far as to pretend that threading my course through this ever-changing world I have not leaned more than was reasonable now this way and now that. But here again one must consider the circumstances. Let anyone, above all let any politician, look back on the last twenty years and see how violently external affairs have forced him from the path he wished to tread.

Looking back with after-knowledge and increasing years, I seem to have been too ready to undertake tasks which were hazardous or even forlorn. Examples are endless, and it is the cheapest form of unintelligent political argument to hunt up back speeches and try to score a point by them.

I have seen the Conservative party espouse a cause; repudiate it; espouse it again, and repudiate it again, and finally achieve it. I have seen the Liberal party abominate conscription, and carry it. I have seen the Socialist Party quite ready to abandon in office all the root propositions they advocated in opposition, and then go back to them again when they were no longer responsible. I claim my own record is as good as any of these. But I have a tendency about which I should perhaps be on my guard; it is to swim against the stream. I feel myself often irritated by the over-statement of any particular view. I like Rudyard Kipling's lines about standing to 'jeer the fatted soul of things'. Also I am glad to think I react against the hounding-down of individual men and causes. When worshipful forces run in full cry together, my inclinations are to go the other way. I am sorry that it should be so. I must no doubt labour to correct myself. However, that is how I feel instinctively. Especially is this so when great men are hounded down and ill-used by the country they have served so faithfully. It was a blot upon the reputation of France that they should have treated Clemenceau so ill after his grand services, and a similar reproach lies upon our people because, after having exalted Mr Lloyd George above his deserts in the hour of need, they turned from him so ungraciously in the last fifteen years of his life.

Ever since I was about twenty-three I made speeches. I dare say I have made thousands. Isn't it awful? I also fought many elections. How would you like that experience? Politics is not a game. It is an earnest business, and a very good rule I was taught when I was a young man was – don't bring politics into private life.

I am supposed to be quite a good speaker: indeed, I am sometimes called an orator and all that. The truth is that I am not a good speaker, and I only learned to speak, somehow or other, with exceptional difficulty and enormous practise. I was not and have never been a naturally fluent speaker. I always relied on ideas and argument and trusted them to command attention. I have often sat amazed in admiration of those who are able to spin out of their heads without apparent effort animated, concise and pungent speeches, without the slightest sign of effort or trace of preparation.

When I first entered Parliament I had a very good memory, and even in those times the power to foresee and imagine, days and even weeks beforehand, the sort of conditions and situations which would arise when particular issues were debated. Guided by this light, I learnt my arguments so thoroughly that I knew them backwards and forwards, as well, for instance, as one knows the Lord's Prayer, and could within limits vary the sequence not only of the arguments but of the sentences themselves.

Thus, at the very outset and in the first month of my Parliamentary life, I, who could hardly string ten words together spontaneously, managed to engineer and deliver at least three speeches which held the attention and obviously commanded the interest of a none too friendly assembly. And not many people guessed how little spontaneity of conception, fulness of knowledge, or flow of language there was behind this fairly imposing facade. These methods are not to be recommended to those more brightly armed with natural gifts.

Public speaking is one of the most difficult of all the arts; for I never persevered in anything as I have in trying to convey my thought and feelings forcefully and easily, convincingly and persuasively to my fellow-men. My difficulty is not that I run short of ideas. It is the exact opposite. I see too many things at once and jumble them up together in a foolish fashion. If I could make speeches like I write – or rather dictate – quite slowly and steadily, and could think out exactly which way I mean to turn every phrase, I should be a very effective speaker. But speaking extempore to a public audience or to Parliament with a full mind on a very large question is a most exacting test and one in which, according to my own opinion and usually that of other people, I nearly always fail. Of course it is quite easy if you write it out beforehand and learn it off by heart, or read it from your notes. But then there is no fun in that. I always remember the late Lord Birkenhead's description of true spontaneous oratory. He said, 'I like to be on the unpinioned wing.' And nothing attracts and persuades the audience so much as when they feel that the thought is coming to them clothed in the right words straight from the human heart.

If I had to argue out a very important matter or defend myself, I would rather do it in writing than by speech. After all, no very high standard of thought can be reached while composing on one's legs, nor can there be any real finish and polish such as the famous orators of former times have taught us to admire. But when you come to write in the solitude of your own room and with full deliberation pick the best arguments and the aptest words you can command, then one ought to be capable of doing justice to the tale.

What the House of Commons likes is a good argument, well thought out, plainly and simply and, if possible, shortly stated. If the course of this argument can be relieved by happy turns of wit and fancy, and illuminated by flashing episodes of rhetoric, so much the better. But an argument sound, ingenious, or original would carry a man through, even in spite of commonplace language and halting elocution.

'I always liked to hear your father speak,' said an old Member to me when I first entered the House of Commons. 'He was always trying to prove something.'

'Unfold your case,' said another. And added: 'if you have got one.'

It is often said by my opponents that although I have a lot of ideas and sometimes put them quite well, it is my judgment that is faulty. I cannot feel that this is true. After years of the battle and the breeze, I feel great confidence in my judgment, once I can see the whole problem in my mind. In fact if I believed what these opponents say I should be broken-hearted. I would go out and feed the swans, or lay bricks, or paint pictures, and I would never offer you my advice again on public matters. But I believe most devoutly that my discernment of the truth, and my sense of proportion, are the best things I have. However, I must admit that I do not always reach the same conclusions as the majority. I do not move in unison with their thoughts. I am sometimes ahead of them, and very often I run counter to them. What most people call 'bad judgment' is judgment which is different from theirs at a particular moment.

But when I look back over my long life I feel that most of my mistakes have been due to allowing my judgment to be overruled or deflected by other people's stupid judgment. But what can you do when the other people have the power and you have to work with them? I whole-heartedly subscribe to a democratic system, and I must take the rough with the smooth.

To work from weakness and fear is ruin. To work from wisdom and power may be salvation.

The disappointment of my life was the Dardanelles. I saw this great hope much more clearly than I see my own salvation. Nowadays, instructed naval and military opinion sees, too, that it was right, that it was sure, that it touched the vital nerve centre of the world war. But I could never persuade anyone who mattered more than about three-quarters of the way. I was never able to make the plan in its integrity, and persevere to a conclusion. If I had been a better man, or a more adroit, or perhaps an older man, I might have succeeded. As it was I could only get the power to carry everything far enough to make a grievous failure.

This was a horrible experience to undergo. To see the truth shining clear and bright, and all the sombre, useless slaughter and muddle going on elsewhere; and here was the way out, the path to victory – and even more than victory – to early peace. They clobbered it all to the ground, and their children and their children's children rue the day!

The profound, almost mortal lesions which the Great War caused to the life of mankind came upon us only in the last two years of its fearful and needless prolongation. I make my testament that here was merciful escape.

Young men ought to be ambitious. In a free country everyone may nourish lawfully and rightfully a desire to guide the State. But such an experience as I have recorded is surely a cure for any form of personal ambition.

And here let me dispose of a few legends about myself which have gained a limited but an obstinate currency.

The first is about my hats. I am usually caricatured with a tiny hat on my head, and stories are written about the great number of hats that I delight in. All this arose from the fact that many years ago at Southport I picked up an uncommonly small hat, and walking with my wife on the sands was the victim of a snapshot. All the rest is harmless embroidery. I do not delight in hats.

Neither let me say do I delight in war. I have served in war; I have studied war; I have been concerned in preparations for war. And I have written histories of war. But it is my dearest wish that I may be suffered to live out my span without ever seeing this country, or indeed Europe, drawn into another hateful, squalid and devastating struggle. I shall always believe that if my proposal to the Germans in 1912 of a naval holiday had been accepted by the Emperor, it might have brought about an easement of the whole European situation, and set in train a series of negotiations which would have postponed, if they could not avert, the final catastrophe.

There is a regular tyranny of public opinion which demands smooth and comfortable assurances from public men. It is alike unfashionable and unpopular to dwell upon the seamy underside of things. The public like soft sawder; the language of Statesmen in all countries becomes increasingly urbane, and their sentiments ever more elevated. But when these Statesmen have finished making their public speeches, they go back to their offices or Cabinet councils and hold very different talk among themselves.

This gap between public professions and reality, between what the peoples are told and what the governments are doing, has become so wide that it is a positive duty to draw attention to it. It is folly to ignore facts.

We are no longer an island, and insidious propaganda gains much attention. Let us purchase the favours of the strong at the cost of the weak. Anything for a quiet life. Such is the hateful theme. Ministers of religion, philanthropists, satirists, and clever cartoonists, all inculcate the speedy surrender of the position which our ancestors gained for us among the nations.

To change from sane government would be like expecting a patient struggling through a serious illness, to make a satisfactory recovery if you kept changing the doctors and the treatment every five minutes. Or perhaps you might think of it as a Channel swimmer giving up within sight of Dover, and so losing the fruits of all the long effort from the French coast.

If you are going to make good in anything you must always swim your Channel.

I must avow myself in strong reaction against this powerful tide of insidious propaganda. I am proud to feel the glow of counter-attack.

Apart from abuse so persistently and freely directed against me by extremists, at both ends of politics, there has been nothing to which I could not reply. But abuse never does any man any harm as long as he feels strong enough to treat it with contempt.

But here once more I am straying from the personal topic which I was invited to enlarge upon. If I were to persist I should soon find myself making one of those political speeches of which there are so many of all kinds. Let me return to the strait path. I must confess to having a sanguine disposition. Although I see so harshly the dark side of things, yet by a queer contradiction I wake each morning with new hope and energy revived. I believe intensely that the British people are still masters of their own destinies and I have the feeling that time will be given to them to repair their past mistakes and negligence. I believe, moreover, that the heart of the nation is sound and that its mission is not yet exhausted. I mean to do my part in this while life and strength remain.

Now I have told you the truth about myself. But have I told you the whole truth? I am not so sure of that. There may be a few things I have overlooked! Besides, think of the space I should take up if I told you everything! I am often reminded that I have made many mistakes. I say with old Clemenceau when responding to a similar charge, 'perhaps I have made some mistakes that you have never heard of.'

CHAPTER 2

Is Patriotism Played Out ?

'PATRIOTISM IS OLD-FASHIONED, out of date,' say brainy persons in Britain and the Commonwealth, in America, in Europe, and in so many democratic Nations, who cherish freedom and pride in their country.

There are always people who wake up every morning and think – 'What is there we can find that belongs to our country that we can give away? – what is there that has made our country great that we can pull down?'

That is the question they ask themselves. Such people can be a nation's weakness. They do a very great deal of harm.

If on all sides – in Asia, in Europe, across the Atlantic – nations assert a more aggressive nationalism and we are paralysed by theoretical doctrines, then indeed all that the croakers predict will come true, and ruin will be swift and final.

But why break up a solid structure of power for dreams which are only dreams or maybe nightmares? We have not journeyed across the centuries, across oceans, across the mountains, across the prairies, because we are made of sugar-candy.

Shakespeare wrote the noblest tribute ever penned to England:

> 'This royal throne of kings, this sceptre'd isle,
> This earth of majesty, this seat of Mars,
> This other Eden, demi-paradise . . .
> This happy breed of men, this little world;
> This precious stone set in the silver sea . . .'

The words still thrill like the blast of a trumpet; thrill, I suspect, the Scots and Irish and Welsh among us as well as the English. They move us not only because they are beautiful, but because they are true – as true today, in the reign of Queen Elizabeth II, as they were under the first Royal Elizabeth.

I am a great admirer of the Scots. I am quite friendly with the Welsh. I must confess to some sentiment about Old Ireland. But there is a forgotten, nay, almost a forbidden word, which means more to me than any other.

That word is 'England'.

Once we flaunted it in the face of the whole world like a banner. It was a word of power. It humbled the pride of the tyrant, and brought hope and succour to the oppressed. To the lover of freedom it was the one sure rock amid shifting sand. But today we are scarcely allowed to mention the name of our country.

Usually we are told to call ourselves 'Britishers', a nasty word – coined, I believe, by our opponents at the time when the American Colonists went off and made such a success of everything. Or we are allowed to call ourselves 'citizens of the United Kingdom of Great Britain and Northern Ireland'. Or, perhaps, if we are good, we may be designated as 'persons dwelling in one of the Dominions of the British Commonwealth of Nations'.

I want to revive the grand old name of 'Englishman'.

Can you imagine what would happen if a Scot, or a Welshman, or an Irishman, were told that he must no longer keep alive that tradition of separate nationality to which he clings?

Why should we English alone of the great sister nations, be expected to subscibe to this self-denying ordinance?

The Royal Navy goes back to Alfred the Great, who was an English king.

It was another King of England who sent out the ship that discovered North America.

It was an Englishman who put Australia on the map.

Let us remember these things and the other great deeds and mighty adventures that star the pages of our English history, as Scots and Irish and Welsh recall with pride the storied past of the lands that gave them birth. They would tell us that patriotism begins at home. Let our patriotism begin at home also, and it is not enough to have the name of England once more upon our lips. We must also revive the old qualities – the old spirit.

11

I sometimes think that that spirit of chivalry, of adventure, of care for the weak and defiance of the mighty, if their power is founded in evil and oppression – finds its perfect expression in the old legend of St George and the Dragon. But I often wondered what would happen if that episode had been repeated under conditions existing in the years that followed the last war.

St George would have arrived in Cappadocia* accompanied, not by a horse, but by a secretariat. He would have been armed, not with a lance, but with several flexible formulae. He would have been welcomed by the local branch of the United Nations Association. He would have proposed a conference with the Dragon – a Round Table Conference, no doubt. That would be more convenient for the Dragon's tail.

He would have made a trade agreement with the Dragon, then lent the Dragon a lot of money. The maiden's release would have been photographed and referred to New York, the Dragon, meanwhile reserving all his rights.

It is a moving picture, but I doubt if we should think it worth while to engrave it on our coins for a thousand years. It is not really in keeping with the English spirit – or with English ways.

It is no part of my thought to exalt England at the expense of her partners, our fellow-subjects in this island or across the oceans. We need them all. But there are a few things which I will venture to say about England and her civilisation. They are written in no invidious sense.

The first is this:

England is not a bad country to live in. With all its faults, it is still the best country for the duke or the dustman.

Here it would hardly occur to anyone that the banks would close their doors against their depositors.

Here no one questions the fairness of the Courts of Law and Justice.

Here we do not persecute on account of religion or race.

Here everyone – except the criminal – looks on the policeman as the friend and servant of the public.

Here we provide for poverty and misfortune with more compassion – in spite of all our burdens.

Here we can assert the rights of the citizen against the State, or criticise the Government of the day without failing in our duty to the Crown or in our loyalty to the Sovereign.

* Cappadocia: an ancient region of Asia Minor – which would now be in Turkey. It was the home, legend says, of St George, who died in A.D. 303.

Within a 50-mile radius of the Houses of Parliament, in the heart of England, there dwell more people, except, perhaps, around New York, than in any other equal space. They form the freest and richest, the most prosperous, the most law-abiding, and the most good-natured community alive. The ancient and mighty City of London is still the financial centre of the world.

The genius of our people springs from every class and from every part of the land. You cannot tell where you will not find a wonder. The hero, the fighter, the poet, the master of science, the organiser, the artist, the engineer, the administrator, or the jurist – he may spring into fame. Equal opportunity for all, under free institutions and equal laws – there is the banner for which we do battle against all rubber-stamp bureaucracies or dictatorships. You can test our people as you would put a bucket into the sea, and always find it salt.

This land of ours draws its strength from many sources. And in the last century and a half she discovered fresh reserves of leadership in the classes created by the expansion of enterprise and wealth which followed the Industrial Revolution.

Without name or influence to help them, often with no money save what they won by their own efforts, these sons of merchants, and manufacturers, of doctors, lawyers, and clergymen, of authors, teachers, shopkeepers and labourers, made their way to the front rank in public life and to the headship of almost every great business by native worth alone.

Their contribution to government has been rich and varied. It is impossible, looking back, to imagine what we should have been without them. Blot them from the pages, and how much is left of the political history of the nineteenth and twentieth centuries?

We have qualities which no one should overlook. Like nature, we never draw a line without smudging it. We have our differences in this country, but there is an underlying spirit of neighbourliness. There is a strong common sense of national unity. Although that doesn't help with the small matters with which we have to deal day to day, it is our salvation in trouble.

Historians have noticed all down the centuries one peculiarity of our people which has cost them dear. We have always thrown away after victory the greater part of the advantages we gained in the struggle. So resolute, so dogged, so invincible in danger, we always collapse in spirit and action after danger has been warded off.

It was so after the wars of Marlborough; it was so after the triumphs of Chatham; it was so after the overthrow of Napoleon; it was so after the last war.

Across the gulf of centuries our hearts still beat faster to the lilt of 'an auld sang' and we recall with pride and a quickening of the pulses the deeds of our ancestors.

We have inherited so much, but inheritance carries with it responsibilities. We are in the position of trustees of the land of our forefathers. How are we discharging our stewardship?

In olden days very few people were able to build at all, but those who could had wealth and culture. While beautiful things were erected, no pains were taken about their preservation after their utility had departed. Now everybody can build in one way or another, and many exceedingly ugly structures deface the countryside. On the other hand, we have a corrective in a stronger public feeling. There is a desire to preserve what is beautiful, a growing power to deal with what is especially detestable. We have gained more than we have lost, and the period of greatest danger by acts of destruction of ancient relics and monuments and objects of curiosity and beauty is over.

One of the most efficient and powerful instruments by which this is accomplished is local patriotism. If each of us is jealous to safeguard the amenities of his own district, the country as a whole will take care of itself. There are other functions too, which local patriotism fulfills. It is the guardian, not only of the body of the country – its woods and fields and waters, and the old-world buildings which Time has weathered to a richer loveliness – but also of its soul.

It was once rightly said: 'Who can be proud of his own country who is not proud of his own county?'

There is much wisdom in that question. Many and various loyalties are required from us in this modern age. We have to do our duty to kith and kin, to home and county, in addition to being good patriots, and good citizens of the world. Those loyalties are not incompatible, and the task before us is not to choose one and reject the rest. The task is to reconcile them and to render each its due.

The strong life of local communities is important. To love the little platoon we belong to in society, is the first principle, the germ as it were, of public affections. It is the first step in the series by which we proceed to a love of country and of mankind.

There is nothing separative or destructive about county sentiment; on the contrary, the counties are essentially cohesive in character. The county bridges the immense gap between the individual and the national stage, and plays in the life of the State a part which is indispensable to the general welfare.

The worst difficulties from which we suffer do not come from without. They come from within, from a peculiar type of brainy people always found in our country who, if they add something to its culture, take much from its strength.

Our difficulties come from the mood of unwarrantable self-abasement into which we have been cast by a powerful section of our intellectuals.

They come from acceptance of defeatist doctrines by large proportion of politicians.

Religion, they tell us, has played its part except to teach us humbleness. Patriotism, they declare, is played out, except where paying Income Tax is concerned.

Our very clever talkers deride ancient themes. But what do they put in their place, but a vague internationalism, a squalid materialism, and the promise of impossible Utopias? That is all they offer us in a world where the struggle for national self-preservation is daily intensified.

They tell us that our day is done, our sun is set, and night is coming on. They declare – some with crazy exultation in their tones – that our decline and fall is at hand. If that be true, it will be our own fault. But we will never accept such a fate!

Our power is founded upon health, kindliness, and freedom. We are, as a race and society, perhaps more capable of bearing shocks and strains – especially long strains – than any other.

Our institutions are capable of changing with time and circumstances. We ought to weather any storm that blows at least as well as any other land under any other existing system of human government. We are more experienced.

Nothing can save a nation if she will not save herself. If we lose faith in ourselves, in our capacity to guide and govern, and lose our will to live, then indeed our story is told. But, it may well be that the most glorious chapters of our history are yet to be written. The very problems and dangers that encompass us and our country should make men and women of this generation glad to be here. We ought to rejoice in the responsibilities with which Destiny has honoured us.

The class of persons who are very much inclined to omit primary stages in their various loyalties, couple an expansive love for mankind as a whole with complete disdain for any particular race or country. Like Rousseau, they love their kind and hate their kin. They are the friends of every country but their own. They are so busy planning brilliant futures for the World State that they have no sympathy left for the ordinary men and women among whom they have been brought up.

These persons forget that world organisations can only be judged by, and indeed, only exist for, the nobility and well-being of individuals and the happiness and distinction of small societies. Moreover, the great World State can only be built up by the genius of great nations, and nations are not made by simply lumping together millions of individuals to make an arithmetical total because they happen to be situated in a geographical area.

If an artist were to attempt to paint a picture by mixing all the colours indiscriminately together and producing a muddy blur, one would think him crazy. Far more subtle, profound, and mysterious forces are at work in the structure of the life of nations.

Disraeli said: 'Nations can only be ruled by force or by tradition.'

We see many countries in the world today that are ruled by force. No country is more ruled by tradition than this island, and no country gains more by the influence – the gentle, modifying, softening, and controlling influence – of tradition than we do.

I confess myself to be a great admirer of tradition. The longer you can look back, the farther you can look forward. This is not a philosophical or political argument–any oculist will tell you this is true. The wider the span, the longer the continuity, the greater is the sense of duty in individual men and women, each contributing their brief life's work to the preservation and progress of the land in which they live, the society of which they are members, and the world of which they are servants.

Let us think of these things as well as the varied enchantments of our scenery and the great achievements of our people in war and peace, and pledge ourselves to do all that is in our power to strengthen the deep, unseen foundations without which our race and its fame cannot long preserve their position in the world.

Patriotic men and women in every land, especially those who understand the high causes in human fortunes at stake, must rise above the nation debasers; rise above fear; rise above inconvenience and, perhaps most difficult of all, above boredom.

CHAPTER 3

It's No Good Arguing With A Communist

I TELL YOU – it's no good arguing with a Communist. It's no good trying to convert a Communist or persuade him. You can only deal with them on the following basis . . . you can only do it by having superior force on your side on the matter in question – and they must also be convinced that you will use – you will not hesitate to use – those forces, if necessary, in the most ruthless manner. You have not only to convince the Soviet Government that you have a superior force – that they are confronted by superior force – but that you are not restrained by any moral consideration, if the case arose, from using that force with complete material ruthlessness. And that is the greatest chance of peace, the surest road to peace.

I once wrote a letter to a Communist. I said:

You invoke the time-honoured tradition of freedom of speech and opinion and in the same breath declare yourself a Communist.

Personally, I am in favour of the utmost freedom of thought and discussion. In the open clash of conflicting opinions in the political arena, the right of public meeting, and an unfettered and independent Press I see the surest guarantees of ordered progress. But the Communist seeks to abolish these things. The ideal is the totalitarian state, in which opposition is treason and criticism a crime. Freedom of thought is equally alien to the philosophy of Marx as it was to the creed of Hitler. In Russia the creation of opinion is a Government monopoly.

Communists discovered that truth does not matter so long as there is reiteration. They have no difficulty in countering a fact by a lie which, if repeated often enough and loudly enough, becomes accepted by the people.

From the infant school to the university the mind of youth is moulded to the pattern the Dictatorship has ordered. The deadly iteration of the loud-speakers destroys, little by little, the individuality of those who listen and builds up the mass mind in the adult population.

Stage and screen, literature and the Press, are all perverted to the same grim purpose. Education and recreation have become instruments of propaganda. Religion, if it is tolerated at all, must confine its teachings within the narrow limits of the State morality.

There is a fundamental antagonism between systems of this kind and the principles on which Western civilisation rests. The conception of the totalitarian state is, indeed, a challenge to all the old human values. For centuries we have been taught to regard freedom as the most precious of all things. The goal to which these new philosophies conduct alike their votaries and their victims is the goal of universal slavery.

Free men can be ruled by reason, but slaves must be kept in subjection by fear. Until such time as generations of intensive propaganda have produced a race of robots, discontent and disillusion must be reckoned with, and may take dangerous forms. Slaves have been known to rebel against their masters. These new slaves may rise in revolt against the State.

So terrorism becomes one of the bulwarks of government. An elaborate system of espionage is created, to poison every human relationship with distrust and suspicion. A careless word may lead to imprisonment.

Real friendship becomes impossible when every man and woman you meet may be a spy. Even within the doors of your own home it may be unsafe to speak your mind. Your own child may betray you and the unnatural act be acclaimed and rewarded as a public service.

Petty tyranny flourishes under conditions like these. No one dares to protest against even wanton oppression lest the action be interpreted as an attack on the regime. There is no check upon the exactions or the insolence of minor officials or of the members of the victorious 'Party'.

The Communists will denounce all these things, but the totalitarian state does not change its nature because the Swastika has been replaced by the Hammer and Sickle. These evils are inherent in Communism as in every system which deifies the State and abases the citizen.

The evils find their supreme expression in the sphere of economics. In factory, workshop, and office the fear of punishment replaces the incentive of reward. Men can no longer gain an honourable independence by their own enterprise and effort, as is possible, even in these days of large aggregations of capital, in this and other Western countries. They can be – and are – made scapegoats for the mistakes of others.

Communism created new crimes. Failures in business which, in a capitalist economy, would lead at the worst to bankruptcy or dismissal, become sabotage when every industry is a State monopoly. And the miscalculations of others, or the need to divert the public mind from inconvenient questionings, may result in an innocent man being imprisoned or exiled.

The Courts will not protect him. Under Communism the Courts are not concerned with such questions as the guilt or innocence of the accused, but with the political effect of verdict and sentence. Justice is an instrument of policy. We prefer to allow even those who plot against the State to employ, if they choose, the process of the Courts. If, in dealing with Communist activities, the authorities permit zeal to overcome discretion, and there is technical infringement of some ancient statute, even-handed British justice, careless alike of persons and opinions, will award damages to the aggrieved revolutionaries.

Such an attitude seems fantastic to those who live in lands where political freedom has ceased to exist. And Communism is something more than a political philosophy or a theory of economics. It is a technique of revolution, a plan of campaign for civil war.

But the democratic State does not rest upon the uneasy foundations of force and fear. Our citizens are partners in the government of their country, not slaves of a dictatorship. And if our tradition of free speech concedes to Communists the liberties they would deny to others, it is a price which we can afford to pay rather than set bounds to the thoughts of man and place the human mind in fetters.

The whole future of humanity, indeed, depends upon how far we can secure to men the opportunity of individual development, how far we can combine community life with richness and variety of personality.

If Communism or any similar system triumphs, and men are drilled and regimented and 'conditioned' until all individuality has been ironed out from among them, there is an end to human achievement. The onward, upward march will be checked and halted; the eternal quest abandoned, and in their place will be the aimless, sterile activities of the unchanging antheap.

The peril has been recognised as the gravest that now overhangs the world. In the Communist sect it is a matter of religion to sacrifice one's native land for the sake of the Utopia. People who, in ordinary life, would behave in a quite honourable manner, if they are infected with this disease of the mind, will not hesitate a moment to betray their country or its secrets.

Hatred of the Communists for the existing order of society; hatred of the existing order of society; hatred of the existing order, for they have effaced all laws, every tie between man and woman, every rule of civilised society and even the calculations of common prudence.

Everyone is of course familiar with their methods of propaganda. Poisonous doctrines are spread, germ cells are created in many walks of life. In every country they are linked to Moscow and thence controlled by discipline and funds.

What Rome is to Catholics, Moscow is to the Communists of every country; with the important difference that whereas devout Catholics contribute to the centre of their faith, it is Moscow which distributes money to foreign lands.

I saw quite plainly that this would be the peril civilisation would have to face after the defeat of Nazism and Fascism. When we thought we had finished with Nazism and Fascism, we had Communism looming up against us representing the former Hitler tyranny with an Asiatic guise.

Russia is a riddle wrapped in a mystery inside an enigma; but, perhaps there is a key. That key is national interest, for Russia pursues a cold policy of self-interest.

She has made herself an Ishmael among the nations, but she is one of the most titanic factors in the economy and diplomacy of the world. With her enormous, rapidly increasing armaments; with her limitless man-power and her corrosive hatreds, she weighs heavily upon a whole line of countries, some small, others considerable from the Baltic to the Black Sea, all situated adjacent to her territory. We must never forget that most of them have been carved, in whole or in part, out of the old Russian Empire of Peter the Great and Catherine the Great.

Here we have a State whose subjects are so happy that they have to be forbidden to quit its bounds under the direst penalties; whose diplomatists and agents sent on foreign missions have often to leave their wives and children at home as hostages to ensure their eventual return.

Sombre indeed would be the fortunes of mankind if some awful schism arose between the western democracies and the Soviet Union, if new cataclysms of inconceivable violence destroyed all that is left of the treasures and liberties of mankind.

During the war, Communism's past with its crimes, its follies and its tragedies, flashed away when I saw Russian soldiers standing on the threshold of their native land, guarding the fields which their fathers tilled from time immemorial. I saw them guarding their homes where mothers and wives prayed – ah yes, for there are times when all pray – for the safety of loved ones, the return of the breadwinner, of their champion, of their protector. I saw the ten thousand villages of Russia where the means of existence was wrung so hardly from the soil, but where there are still primordial human joys, where maidens laugh and children play. I saw advancing on this in hideous onslaught the Nazi war machine, with its clanking, heel-clicking, dandified Prussian officers, its crafty expert agents fresh from the cowing and tying-down of a dozen countries. I saw also the dull, drilled, docile, brutish masses of the Hun soldiery plodding on like a swarm of crawling locusts. I saw the German bombers and fighters in the sky, still smarting from many a British whipping, delighted to find what they believed an easier and a safer prey.

No government ever formed among men has been capable of surviving injuries so grave and cruel as those inflicted by Hitler upon Russia. But under the leadership of Stalin, and thanks to the stand by the British peoples when they were alone, and to abundant British and American ammunition and supplies of all kinds, Russia not only survived and recovered from these frightful injuries, but inflicted, as no other force in the world could have inflicted, mortal damage on the German army machine.

Therefore, any idea of Britain's pursuing an anti-Russian policy, or making elaborate combinations to the detriment of Russia, is utterly opposed to British thought and conscience. Nothing but a long period of very marked injuries and antagonisms could develop any such mood.

They tested us and provoked our patience time and time again. Fortunately, we have shown strength and there is nothing they admire so much as strength, just as there is nothing for which they have less respect than for military weakness.

In 1933 we hit back when they put on public 'trial' British engineers and Soviet employees of a British company.

What a trial! What principles of jurisprudence known to human reason did it represent? A band of wretched Russians employed by the Metropolitan-Vickers Company rounded up and harassed on scientific principles. Under threats of instant death and, alternatively, promises of food and freedom, they were made to spin their yarn. From the cells of an inquisition as cruel as the Spanish, but with the service of the Devil instead of God as its aim, emerged these pale phantoms to recite their pitiful confessions. It may well be that one or two of them were Ogpu agents planted into the Vickers' offices some time and reserved for such an occasion. Such was the evidence.

The British prisoners sustained something of the same ordeal, but were of tougher fibre. Whatever complaint there may be about the weakness of Britain in these modern days, the average Englishman, Scotsman, or Welshman hears echoing voices from the past. He cannot believe his country will desert him. He cannot forget that her heart is warm and her arm is long. 'Civis Romanus sum!' leaps to his lips. 'Do what you will to me, but don't forget that there is a small island lost among the northern mists of which men have sometimes heard.'

A few of the engineers broke down under the strain. Let those who have not felt it judge them indulgently. Although threatened by the Public Prosecutor in a court of pretended justice with being turned into manure for Socialist fields, they spoke like free men in a world of slaves. However, the Communists, having control of the radio, took good care that their words did not reach the servile millions.

We acted with vigour and decision against the Soviets. We used denial of trade as our sword, and there is no doubt that but for the promptitude with which the Embargo Bill was pressed into law, not only the liberty but the lives of those engineers in Moscow would have been in the greatest jeopardy.

The Bolsheviks were startled and astonished by the indignation which was aroused in Britain at their proceedings. They had not expected any such sharp and drastic reaction. To them the fate of a few men and the distress of a few families seemed a matter inconceivably trivial. They are accustomed to treat their own people as the cheapest raw material of their theories. The numerous executions by which their power is maintained, the immense number of penal slaves on which their timber industry was founded, and their whole system of thought and action had made them quite callous towards human suffering.

The sanctity of an individual life, the rights of a private citizen against the State are conceptions altogether beneath Communist mentality. The Bolsheviks take the traditional Asiatic view that subjects exist only to obey their rulers, and they are accustomed to destroy them with the automatic pistol or toil them to death in mines and forests with the composure of a Chinese mandarin. They were, therefore, genuinely puzzled as well as perturbed by what they regard as much ado about nothing.

That any Power should take so much trouble in such a matter appeared to them very odd. That Great Britain of all other Powers should do so was incomprehensible. Was she not the Power that cared most of all for money? Was she not the first of the capitalist States to tout upon them for trade favours? Did she not stand out before all the world to recognise them and their system and admit them to the comity of nations? Did she not do this after being cheated out of £1,250,000,000 in public loans and private property? To them Britain seemed at once the most money-grubbing and improvident power. Moreover, in England the Socialists were lately dominant. They could form Governments and make treaties; so that whether they regarded us as a capitalist State or as a quasi-Socialist community, the Bolsheviks felt themselves fairly safe.

But what happened? Of a sudden, this country they had thought so sordid and squalid kicked, and kicked hard. Apparently it had shown itself quite indifferent to all questions of profit and loss.

The Soviet knew that the British Government had recently extended to them £7,000,000 of additional credits, and they owed a further £3,000,000 to English firms besides all they had stolen in the past. Therefore, they thought they had the whip hand. Yet this most commercial of all nations had apparently thrown calculations to the winds, brushed aside material considerations, and brought its fist down with a bang upon the table – all on account of a handful of engineers.

Obviously, if the Soviet had realised what was going to happen they would not have had this trial. Why did they have it? It is very difficult for non-Communists to understand their modes of thought, but fairly practical explanations have been given. Their Five-Year Plan was breaking down. Its failure was becoming daily more unconcealable. Even the brutalised, down-trodden masses felt disaster in the air. Everywhere there was a shortage of food, and one of the greatest granaries in the world was ceasing to function. In whole districts there was famine. The bread carts had forgotten to call at the lunatic asylum.

The airy vision of scores of thousands of tractors ploughing up land superseding the primitive agriculture of the peasants and their landlords was dissolving. The tractors rusted in the fields. The spare parts had been forgotten. The great machines purchased from England and America, put together by Russians failed to work. From every quarter the tale of fiasco reached the Central Government. What to do?

Scapegoats had to be found. Russian scapegoats do not count for much. What was the use of turning all the hate propaganda, all the resources of radio and printing presses, on to batches of Russian scapegoats? That had been done too often before. The mass execution after a well-staged trial of a few score of Russians would make no impression on the people. They were used to that. They bow their heads beneath the yoke. They would feel it was only a case of turning the dung-heap over again. Some prey, novel, rare, and spicy, had to be found. Why not pillory, torment, or kill a few foreign engineers? That's the stuff to give the troops. But which foreigners to choose? Obviously Britons – fat, tame, sentimental Britons. Sob stuff. Shopkeeping Britain. The United States? That would hardly do; they had never recognised the Soviet, so they had to be treated with respect. Germany? The Germans were too near neighbours; they know too much about us. France? A very tough proposition; a capitalist State founded on a revolution with the land owned by the people! Nothing doing there. No! Britain – rich, vulnerable, and we have friends in her midst. Britain let it be.

The trial was an education to the British public. They understood, many of them for the first time, what Bolshevist government means. Some of us had tried to tell them for years. But now the moral struck home.

The nation supported the Government in any measures they thought necessary to curtail or terminate our trade with the Soviet. I said at the time that we had traded with cannibals under proper precautions, but that we should give credit and facilities to this regime which we denied civilised friendly countries or own Dominions, was something that should stop. Would we never learn?

The British Government's counter-action freed our engineers. We are highly respected for our vision and calm indomitable resolve.

We have no hostility to the Russian people and no desire to deny them their legitimate rights and security. We seek nothing from them but good will and fair play.

I watched with sorrow the long years of the cold war, and the withering of so many hopes. I played a part in awakening free Europe to the need to join together with the United States and the British Commonwealth to protect their freedom; but the cold war was none of my seeking and I never sought to perpetuate or prolong it.

In April 1945, as the victorious Western and Russian Forces were joining hands in victory, I wrote to Stalin: 'Do not, I beg you, my friend Stalin, underrate the divergencies which are opening up. There is not much comfort in looking into a future where you and the countries you dominate, plus the Communist parties in many other States, are all drawn up on one side, and those who rally to the English-speaking nations and their associations or Dominions are on the other.

'It is quite obvious that their quarrel would tear the world to pieces and that all of us leading men on either side who had anything to do with that would be shamed before history.

'Even embarking on a long period of suspicions, of abuse and counter-abuse, and of opposing policies, would be a disaster hampering the great developments of world prosperity for the masses which are attainable only by our working in trinity.'

Stalin did not listen.

Mr Khruschev referred to me as the author of the cold war, but my conscience was clear. I always sought, nothing but peace with the Russians, just as after the war I did my utmost to bring Germany back into the circle of the European family.

The Soviets hope that the doctrines of Karl Marx may eventually prevail. We on our side trust and believe that as the mild and ameliorating influence of prosperity begins at last to uplift the Communist world, so they will be more inclined to live at ease with neighbours.

This is our hope. We must not be rigid in our expression of it: we must make allowances for justifiable Russian fears: we must be patient and firm.

No one has been a more consistent opponent of Communism than I have. I will unsay no word that I have spoken about it. The Nazi regime was indistinguishable from the worst features of Communism. It is devoid of all theme and principle except appetite and racial domination. It excels all forms of human wickedness in the efficiency of its cruelty and ferocious aggression.

The Russian Communists have built up an empire far beyond the dreams of the czars, out of a war in which they would have been conquered or driven beyond the Ural mountains, in spite of the bravery with which the Russian army fought for its native soil. They would have been conquered or driven out but for the immense diversionary aid of Britain and the United States on land, sea, and, above all, in the air.

The men in the Kremlin who rule nearly 300,000,000 human beings with an arbitrary authority never possessed by any Tsar since Ivan the Terrible, and who now hold down nearly half Europe, dread the friendship of the free civilised world almost as much as they would its hostility. For the sake of their own interests and skins they cannot allow any intercourse or intermingling. Above all, they fear and hate the genial influences of free and easy democratic life, such as we have gradually evolved for ourselves in the Western world. It is part of the established technique of the Soviets that all men, whatever their occupation, be reduced to a level, so as to make it easy to govern them by commissars and masses of officials and police, all well trained and dependent for their very existence upon the satisfaction they give their superiors in the party hierarchy.

This is all set forth before our eyes as plainly as Hitler told us about his plans in 'Mein Kampf'.

Let them throw open their vast regions on equal terms to the ordinary travel and traffic of mankind. Let them give others the chance to breathe freely and let them breathe freely themselves. When they have done this, or even more of it, and given these proofs of good faith and given up what they had no right to take, then, indeed, it will be time to raise the question of putting away the one vast, and I believe, sure and overwhelming means of security which remains for protection and guards the progress of mankind.

What do you suppose would be the position if it had been Russia instead of free enterprise America which had created the atomic weapon?

Instead of being a sombre guarantee of peace and freedom it would have become an irresistible method of human enslavement.

The menace and aggression continues to spread throughout the world. The men in the Kremlin have a policy the aim of which we can see, but the execution and timing of their ambition for world government we cannot predict. They pay lip service to peace, but by peace they mean submission to their will and system.

Tyranny makes a demand on all free men to risk and do all in their power to withstand it.

I am not the enemy of any race or nation in the world. It is not against any race or nation that we range ourselves. It is against tyranny in all its forms, ancient or modern, new or old, that we stand upright and unflinching.

Tyranny is always the same whatever slogans it offers, whatever name it calls itself, whatever liveries it wears. If we are to achieve our supreme reward we must lay aside every impediment and conquer ourselves. We must rise to a level above the passions which laid nations in ruins. Old feuds must die, territorial ambitions must be set aside, national rivalries must be confined to proving who can render the truest service to the common cause.

The changes in Asia are immeasurable. Perhaps they were inevitable. The decline of British power has been accompanied by the rise and expansion of Soviet Russia. The ambitions of this mighty Empire and oligarchy go far beyond the dreams of Tsarist days. Domination of the whole of the Balkan Peninsula and the conquest and probable incorporation of Turkey, are two objects of Russian desire. Beyond these stretch the Arab world and the Nile Valley. But the world front that has been established and is being strengthened against this aggression, will I believe, preserve mankind from a disaster infinitely more fearful than any we have ever known or even dreamed in our wildest nightmares. None of the free countries now banded together must flinch or waver.

Why have the Russians deliberately acted so as to unite the free world against them? It is certainly not because there are not very able men among them. Why have they done it? I offer you my own answer to this conundrum. It is because they fear the friendship of the West more than its hostility. They cannot afford to allow free and friendly intercourse to grow up between the vast area they control and the civilisation of the West. The Russian people must not see what goes on outside, and the world must not see what goes on inside the Soviet domain. Thirteen men in the Kremlin, holding down hundreds of millions of people and aiming to rule the world, feel that at all costs they must keep up the barriers. Self-preservation, not for Russia, but for themselves, lies at the root and is the explanation of their sinister and malignant policy.

In consequence of their conduct the relations of Russia with other great powers of the world are without precedent in history. Measures and counter-measures have been taken on many occasions which in any previous period could only have meant armed conflict.

There has grown up throughout the English-speaking world a deep desire to be friends on equal and honourable terms with the mighty

Russian Soviet Republic, and to work with them, making allowance for our different systems of thought and government.

But if they are ever convinced that we are afraid of them and can be bullied into submission, then I should despair of our future relations with them and much else.

If there is to be a war of nerves let us make sure our nerves are strong and are fortified by the deepest convictions of our hearts. And let us beware that foolish visionaries or interested persons do not sap the pillars upon which our country stands and destroy our families, homes, and our happiness.

There is among us a small but highly intellectual school of thought which reaches its fullest expression in Russia, but also flourishes among some of our friends, which proclaims that it is better for a nation to go through the bankruptcy court and start business again. They would destroy to achieve their Utopia. But Communism is a ghoul descended from a pile of skulls. The American Constitution declares: 'All men are born equal'. The Communists add: 'All men must be kept equal'.

There is a noticeable division among Communists in different countries. Those who are paid by the Soviet or are still under the Moscow spell, conceive as their first duty the furtherance of Russian foreign policy and the maintenance of Russian national safety. The orthodox doctrinaires in whom resides the pure venom of the Leninic word regard these tendencies with fury and disgust. There is thus a rift throughout the whole Communist underworld.

Let me recapitulate the great resemblances of Fascism and Bolshevism. First, there is the worship one, the One-Man power. All the wisdom of our common ancestors, the main theme which made the Parliamentary system in Britain and framed the Constitution of the United States, was dominated by the conviction that the One-Man power was a thing odious, pernicious and degrading to the nature and stature of men.

This miserable, fetish worship and the setting up of a single individual, investing him with superhuman, almost godlike power, has always been a temptation to the weak and ignorant. It has always been obnoxious to the architects of English and American institutions.

What a contrast when we turn to the great democracies! Our Parliament pays the Leader of the Opposition an annual salary. The Bill providing for this salary was supported from the Ministerial side of the House of Commons, on the ground that the Leader of the Opposition has important and exacting duties to perform, and that he should be placed in a position of financial independence, so that he can devote his whole time to them. And what are these duties? Primarily to criticise every measure which the Government brings forward, every administrative act which appears open to question, and, all the time, to work to bring about the defeat of the Ministry at the polls when the next General Election takes place.

It is not only in Fascist and Communist States that this may seem Gilbertian fantasy.

But the most serious doubt expressed regarding this is that it may in some way limit or curtail the freedom and independence of the gentleman who is thus to be paid from public funds.

In both sides of this discussion we may see the high value that is placed on criticism and reasoned opposition as elements in government. In Dictator countries words are feared.

Such contrasts may be multiplied endlessly from the records of the Despotisms and Democracies. One more will suffice for the moment.

In the United States we see the Supreme Court guarding the edifice of the Constitution, interpreting the fundamental law of the Great Republic according to the conscience of its members, without regard to the convenience, the exhortations, or the threats of the President and his colleagues and supporters.

And although new blood may be introduced, although the Supreme Court of tomorrow may allow a greater flexibility to the Constitution, it is still upon legal grounds, with a full sense of judicial responsibility, and in the spirit of the oath that its members have taken, that its judgments will be given.

But when we turn to the State trials which have taken place in Moscow we see the judicial function degraded and perverted to an instrument of terror.

There are no judges, independent of the Government, doing equal justice between man and man, or between the State and the citizen. There are only agents of the Executive, decked with comical juristic trappings.

Always they have sought checks and counter-checks to the despot, or even to the concentration of power. Indeed, the division of power has been carried to the logical extreme in the American constitution, often beyond the point of convenience, and broad gulfs have been deliberately created between the Executive, the Legislature and the Judiciary. The next resemblance is the conception of a totalitarian state where no one is allowed to differ from or criticise the bosses who have collared the machine-guns and the radio.

Think of it! No one is allowed to say: 'This is unfair. This is untrue. That is not right. This is cruel. That is evidently stupid.' To utter such comments, even in your own home, is to run the risk of betrayal and severe punishment.

Betrayal opens up a new field. The child betrays its parent; the wife's lover betrays the husband, adding civic injury to sexual insult. The genial and engaging acquaintance turns out to be a police spy drawing you out and writing it all down afterwards to your undoing. The business rival, the other local greengrocer or garage-owner has the pull with the powers that be, is very punctual on the parades, and lets it be gradually known that he is doubtful whether you really think that Stalin was the finest thing ever seen on earth.

Not only the police, but overgrown, hobbledehoy schoolboys will beat up the man of learning and letters, flog the professor or the philosopher, drag the suspect – and very often his family, too – to the concentration camp and crush the life out of him with cold, hunger, toil, and a hateful kind of drill-sergeantism.

And all merely for criticising the Government! There is no freedom where governments cannot be criticised. And no government that is not criticised is ever healthy or clean or capable of progress. Even with the most fierce criticism governments tend to imagine themselves the masters instead of the servants of the people.

Imagine the state of Society which emerges from this eavesdropping, spying and private treachery! Every word has to be calculated, every thought is guarded at its inception. No one dare, except at grave hazard, confide even in his most trusted friend.

The new religions and new principles of statecraft are, indeed, but old barbarism writ large and armed with high explosive and poison gas. The great theories of government which the British race devised and which the English-speaking peoples have adopted, closely associated as they are with the system of Christian ethics, are the foundation upon which civilisation stands and without which it will fall.

Communism loses ground in all countries where free speech is allowed and parliamentary institutions thrive. But behind the sub-human chatter of Communist doctrinaires stands the armed might of the Kremlin oligarchy. Every step made towards closer European unity, for example, encountered vehement hostility of the Communist Party in every country, and the more we progressed, the more bitter became the Communist campaign of vilification.

The tyranny upon which Communism is founded would be directly threatened by the establishment of a united, peaceful and prosperous Europe. Unless a strong, united and valiant Europe can be created, there is little hope of peace, freedom or civilisation for the rest of mankind. We are united in our resistance to the hateful doctrines of Communism which have proved fatal in many parts of Europe to human rights as we understand and cherish them.

Every principle long held dear of personal liberty and the ordinary decencies of social life; every principle of religious freedom has been trampled down by the iron rule of Russian despots, so our policy must be peace through strength. Nothing could be more foolish than for us to bring about closer contacts with Soviet Russia by a break-up of the unity among themselves of the free nations.

I do not believe the Russians desire war. What they desire is the fruits of war and the indefinite expansion of their power and doctrines.

It would, I think, be a mistake to assume that nothing can be settled with Soviet Russia. We must work towards closer contact. It is the duty and also the interest of the Communist and free worlds that they should live in peace together, and strive untiringly to remove or outlive their differences.

It must be recognised that free and effective access to the oceans and broad waters of the world is a natural claim for so vast a land power as the Soviet Union. I have myself always favoured this aspiration. Russia is becoming a great commercial country. Her people experience every day in growing vigour those complications and palliatives of human life that will render the schemes of Karl Marx more out of date, and smaller in relation to world problems than they have ever been before.

By all means let us trade with her, by all means let our traders or merchants or business men make what bargains they can at their own risk, by all means let us free their trade and traffic from every obstacle; let no impediment be placed in their way, but do not let us go out of our way to show a special advantage, to show favour to a regime which is unquestionably one of the worst and meanest tyrannies.

If the Soviets really like being governed by officials in a sealed pattern, and so long as they do not endanger the safety and freedom of others, that, I feel, is a matter for them to decide for themselves. Nothing is final. Change is unceasing.

Whether it be true or not that opinions cannot be combated by force, it is certainly true that those who seek to propagate their opinions by force can be combated by force, and ought to be combated by force by every free and worthy citizen in every civilised State.

Where the doctrine is a doctrine of violence, even though it remains only in the intellectual form, it may produce in other persons overt action of such a deadly character that those who are the source and origin of the doctrine cannot expect to be immune from the counter-application of that same physical force on which they habitually rely.

Diseased persons contract or incubate their maladies as individuals; but it is realised that there are persons who work it up together among themselves by a form of associated effort, and that they are in sympathetic relationship with one another, although they may be separated by distance, by race, by class, and by language throughout the world.

When they obtain power in any country, they rigorously suppress all forms of opinion except their own. No newspapers but their own can be tolerated. No party is allowed except the Communist. And for all forms of criticism or protest the penalty of death and ruin to home and family stands ever ready. Communism possesses the science of civilisation without its mercy, the fanaticism of religion without God.

It was once pointed out to me that, although I may not like Communism, its creed is Russia's affair. Well, I would rather crush the egg of Bolshevism in Russia than have to chase the damned cockerel around the world.

CHAPTER 4

A Little Man, A Little Pencil, And A Little Bit of Paper

I LEARNED ONE great lesson from my father – never to be afraid of democracy.

How is the word 'democracy' to be interpreted? My idea of it is that the plain, humble, common man, just the ordinary man who keeps a wife and family, who goes off to fight for his country when it is in trouble, goes to the poll at the appropriate time showing the candidate he wishes to be elected to Parliament – he is the foundation of democracy.

And it is essential to this foundation that this man or woman should do this without fear, and without any form of intimidation or victimisation. He marks his ballot paper in strict secrecy, and then elected representatives meet and together decide what government, or even, in times of stress, what form of government they wish to have in their country.

That is democracy, I salute it. I espouse it.

The principle of 'one vote, one value' is an orthodox and unimpeachable principle of democracy. It is a logical, numerical principle. If the attempt be made to discriminate between man and man because one has more children and lives in the country, it would be arguable that we should discriminate because another man has more brains or more money, or lives in the town, or for any other of the many reasons that differentiate one human being from another. The only safe principle, I think, is that, for electoral purposes, all men are equal, and that voting power, as far as possible, should be evenly distributed among them.

People have the right to vote, and to deprive them of that right is to make a mockery of all the high-sounding phrases so often used. At the bottom of all the tributes paid to democracy is the little man, walking into the little booth, with a little pencil, making a little cross on a little bit of paper – no amount of rhetoric or voluminous discussion can possibly diminish the overwhelming importance of that point.

We must not forget what votes are. Votes are the means by which the poorest people in the country and all the people in the country can make sure that they get their vital needs attended to, and a democratic government is bound by the laws which it administers. It is not above the law.

All classes of people and almost every shade of political influence can be represented not merely in the sterile business of criticism, or in the arid work of political theorising, but in the actual control from day to day of the government which they themselves have returned in accordance with their choice. It is that fact which associates the whole people with the business of government.

It has been accepted generally that the best way of governing States is by talking. An assemblage of persons who represent, or who claim to represent, the nation meet together face to face and argue out our affairs. The public at large having perforce chosen these persons from among those who were put before them submits itself in spite of some misgivings and repinings to their judgment. The public are accustomed to obey their decisions and the rulers who rest upon a parliamentary majority are not afraid to use compulsion upon recalcitrants. Of this method the English may not be the inventors; but they are undoubtedly the patentees. Here in this island have sprung and grown all those representative and parliamentary institutions which so many countries new and old alike have adopted and which still hold the field in the more powerful communities of the world.

However, democracy has shown itself careless about those very institutions by which its own political status has been achieved. It sometimes seems ready to yield up the tangible rights hard won in rugged centuries to party organisations, to leagues and societies, to military chiefs or to dictatorships in various forms. Nevertheless, we may say that representative institutions still command a consensus of world opinion. In the United States representative institutions have expressed themselves almost entirely through the machinery of party; but here at home, although the party organisation is necessary and powerful, the parliamentary conception is still dominant.

I regard democratic institutions as precious to us almost beyond compare. They seem to give by far the closest association yet achieved between the life of the people and the action of the State. They possess apparently an unlimited capacity of adaptiveness, and they stand an effective buffer against every form of revolutionary or reactionary violence. It should be the duty of faithful subjects to preserve these institutions in their healthy vigour, to guard them against the encroachment of external forces, and to revivify them from one generation to another from the springs of national talent, interest, and esteem.

We must, however, recognise the great change which has come over our public life. Before, issues fought out in Parliament were political and social. Parties fought one another heartily in a series of well-known stock and conventional quarrels, and the life of the nation proceeded underneath this agitated froth. It is no longer a case of one party fighting another, nor of one set of politicians scoring off another set. It is the case of successive governments facing economic problems, and being judged by their success or failure in the duel. The nation has, in the main, got the political system it wants; what it now asks for is more money, better times, regular employment, expanding comfort, and material prosperity. It turns to Parliament asking for guidance. Its structure has stood the strain of the most violent contentions. Its long tradition, its collective personality, its flexible procedure, its social life, its unwritten inviolable conventions have made an organism more effective for the purpose of assimilation than any of which there is record.

The constitutional boa-constrictor which has already devoured and absorbed the donkeys of so many generations only requires reasonable time to convert to its own nourishment and advantage almost any number of rabbits. And similarly Parliament tames, calms, instructs, reconciles, and rallies to the fundamental institutions of the State all sorts and conditions of men and women.

Since the dawn of the Christian era a certain way of life has slowly been shaping itself among the western peoples, and certain standards of conduct and government have come to be esteemed. After many miseries and prolonged confusion, there arose into the broad light of day the conception of the right of the individual; his right to be consulted in the government of his country; his right to invoke the law even against the State itself, and democracy does not express itself in clever manoeuvres by which a handful of men survive from day to day, or another handful of men try to overthrow them. It is not a caucus obtaining a fixed term of office by promises, and then doing what it likes with the people. There ought to be a constant relationship between the rulers and the people, although under our representative institutions it is occasionally necessary to defer the opinions of other people.

In remarks I have made about democracy and the attitude I have taken throughout the time I was burdened with high responsibilities, and broadly I believe throughout my life, I stood upon the foundation of free elections, but I feel quite different about left wing democracy. It takes all sorts to make democracy, not only left wing, or even Communist, but I do not allow a party or a body to call themselves democrats who believe in the most extreme forms of revolution. I do not accept a party as necessarily representing democracy because it becomes more violent as it becomes less numerous. One must have some respect for democracy, and not use the word too lightly. Do not let us rate it as if it were merely grabbing power and shooting those who do not agree with you. That is the antithesis of democracy. It is not based on violence or terrorism, but on reason, on fair play, on freedom, on respecting the rights of other people.

Nothing, for example, can be more abhorrent to democracy than to imprison a person or keep him in prison because he is unpopular. This is really the test of civilisation.

Peaceful countries, which aim at freedom for the individual and abundance for the mass, start with a heavy handicap against a dictatorship whose sole theme is war, the preparation for war, and the grinding up of everything and everybody into its military machine.

If democracy and Parliamentary institutions are to triumph, it is absolutely necessary that Governments resting upon them shall be able to act and dare, that the servants of the people shall not be harassed by nagging and snarling, that enemy propaganda shall not be fed needlessly out of our own hands and our reputation disparaged and undermined throughout the world.

The choice is between two ways of life: between individual liberty and State domination: between concentration of ownership in the hands of the State and the extension of a property-owning democracy: between a policy of increasing restraint and a policy of liberating energy and ingenuity: between a policy of levelling down and a policy of finding opportunity for all to rise upwards from a basic standard.

Households which have possessions which they prize and cherish because they are their own, or even a house and garden of their own, investments that their thrift has bought, a little money put by for a rainy day, or an insurance policy, the result of forethought and self-denial which will be a help in old age or infirmity, or after their death for those they love and leave behind – that is what we mean by a property-owning democracy. And the more widely it is distributed and the more millions there are to share in it, the more will democracy continue to have the spirit of individual independence, and the more they will turn their backs on the delusion that one ought to be proud of being totally dependent on the State.

Democracy maintains that where you find that State enterprise is likely to be ineffective, then utilise private enterprises, and do not grudge them their profits. We certainly could never earn our living by world trade or even exist in this island without full recognition of all forms of exceptional individual contribution, whether by genius, contrivance, skill, industry or thrift. It is by many thousands of small individual enterprises and activities that the margin by which alone we can maintain ourselves has been procured.

At the head of our mainmast we, like the United States, fly the flag of free enterprise. We are determined that the native genius and spirit of adventure, or risk-taking in peace as in war, shall bear our fortunes forward, finding profitable work and profitable trade for people.

The idea that a nation can tax itself into prosperity is one of the crudest delusions which has ever fuddled the human mind.

What the average anti-capitalist really means when he speaks of 'Fair shares for all' is *equal* shares for all. Equal shares for those who toil and those who shirk. Equal shares for those who save and those who squander. No reward offered to the skilled craftsman. No incentive to the industrious and experienced piece-worker. No extra payment for overtime that is not taken back in taxation. No reward for enterprise, ingenuity.

I believe the strong should help the weak, but there are those who say that the strong should be kept down to the level of the weak in order to have equal shares for all. How small the share is does not matter so much, in their opinion, so long as it is equal. This is the philosophy of failure, the creed of ignorance, and the gospel of envy.

We seek a free and varied society, where there is room for many kinds of men and women to lead happy, honourable and useful lives. We are fundamentally opposed to all systems of rigid uniformity. We have grown great by indulging tolerance, rather than logic.

The concentration of all power over the daily lives of ordinary men and women in what is called 'the State' exercised by what is virtually single-chamber government, is a reactionary step contrary to the whole trend of democratic history and to the message it has given to the world.

State Management has proved, in every case where applied, to be cumbrous, wasteful, and incompetent. I do not believe in the capacity of the State to plan and enforce an active high grade economic productivity upon its members or subjects. No matter how numerous are the committees they set up, or the ever-growing hordes of officials they employ, or the severity of the punishments they inflict or threaten, they cannot approach the high level of internal economic production which, under free enterprise, personal initiative, competitive selection, the profit motive corrected by failure, and the infinite processes of good house-keeping and personal ingenuity, constitutes the life of a free society.

You may try to destroy wealth, and find that all you have done is to increase poverty. I think that private property has a right to be defended. Our civilisation is built up on private property, and can only be defended by private property.

A society in which property was insecure would speedily degenerate into barbarism; a society in which property was absolutely secure, irrespective of all conceptions of justice in regard to the manner of its acquisition, would degenerate, not into barbarism, but death.

The old Radical campaign against exploitation, monopolies, unfair rake-offs and the like, in which I took part in my young days, was a healthy and necessary corrective to the system of free enterprise. But it is in the nice adjustment of the respective ideas of collectivism and individualism that the problem of the world and the solution of that problem lies in the years to come.

When I see people denouncing capitalism in all its forms mocking with derision and contempt the tremendous free enterprise capitalist system on which, for example, the mighty production of the United States is founded, I cannot help feeling that we are not acting honourably or even honestly. The inherent vice of capitalism is the unequal sharing of blessings. The inherent virtue of Socialism is the equal sharing of miseries. In ordinary day-to-day affairs of life, men and women expect rewards for successful exertion, and this is right and reasonable.

We must draw a line below which we will not allow persons to live and labour, yet above which they may compete with all the strength of their manhood. We must have free competition upwards; we must decline to allow free competition to run downwards.

We seek to benefit private enterprise with the knowledge and guiding power of modern Government, without sacrificing the initiative and drive of individual effort under free, competitive conditions. The policy is based on the two main principles of fair play and adequate opportunity.

Toiling masses in every country have the opportunity of a fuller and less burdened life, Science is at hand to spread a more bountiful table than has ever been offered to the millions and to the tens of millions. Shorter hours of labour, greater assurances against individual misfortune, a wider if a simpler culture, a more consciously realised sense of social justice, an easier and more equal society – these are the treasures which, after all these generations and centuries of impotence and confusion, are now within the reach of mankind.

Many forms of government have been tried, and will be tried, in this world of sin and woe. No one pretends that democracy is perfect or all-wise. Indeed, it has been said that it is the worst form of government except all those other forms that have been tried from time to time; but there is the broad feeling that the people should rule, and that public opinion, expressed by all constitutional means, should shape, guide, and control the actions of ministers who are their servants and not their masters.

Democracy asserts that it is not Parliament that should rule; it is the people who should rule through Parliament.

Democracy does not proceed only by debate. It proceeds by debate and by division. It is only in this way that the majority can express its views. The majority can dismiss an administration at any time, unless of course the administration obtains a Dissolution from the Crown and finds itself sustained by the people. That is the way the Constitution works – and it is greatly admired in many countries – and it is a good thing always to keep that position in mind.

Party conflict and party government should not be disparaged. It is in time of peace, and when national safety is not threatened, one of those conditions of a free Parliamentary democracy for which no permanent substitute is known. Party government is not obnoxious to democracy. Indeed, democracy has flourished under party government. That is to say, it has flourished so long as there has been full freedom of speech, free elections, and free institutions. So we must beware of a tyranny of opinion which tries to make one side of a question the only one which may be heard. Everyone is in favour of free speech. Hardly a day passes without its being extolled, but some people's idea of it is that they are free to say what they like, but if anyone says anything back, that is an outrage.

Free speech carries with it the evil of all foolish, unpleasant and venomous things that are said: but on the whole we would rather lump them than do away with it.

We attach immense importance to the survival of democracy. We wish to see Parliament a strong, easy, flexible instrument of free debate. It is notable that Parliaments elsewhere have to a very large extent reproduced our Parliamentary institutions in their form as well as in their spirit.

We do not seek to impose our ideas on others; we make no invidious criticisms of other nations. All the same we hold none the less tenaciously to them ourselves. There are few things that cannot be done by a great and educated democracy if everybody acts together in good comradeship and good will.

We have reconciled democracy and tradition; for long generations, nay, over several centuries, no mortal clash or religious or political gulf has opened in our midst. We have found the way to carry forward the glories of the past through all the storms, domestic and foreign, that have surged about, and thus to bring the labours of our forebears as a splended inheritance for modern progressive democracy to enjoy.

Democracy incontinently cast aside treasures gained by centuries of struggle and sacrifice. With a savage shout, not only the old feudalism but all liberal ideals were swept away. Still it is one great system in which law is respected and freedom reigns, where the ordinary citizen may assert his rights fearlessly against the executive power or criticise its agents and policies. A Prime Minister of a democracy is liable to dismissal at a moment's notice by a simple vote. It is only possible for him to do what is necessary, and what has got to be done on occasion by somebody or other, if he enjoys support, and is refreshed and fortified from time to time, and especially in bad times, by massive and overwhelming majorities. Thus we arrive, by our ancient methods, at a practical working arrangement which shows that democracy can adapt itself to all situations and go out in all weathers.

Governments derive their just powers from the consent of the governed, says the Constitution of the United States, and this must never evaporate in swindles and lies propped up by servitude and murder. So our foreign policy too lets us strike continually the notes of freedom and fair play as we understand them.

The doctrine has its limits, but, generally speaking, given free institutions on a fair basis, the best side of men's nature will in the end surely come uppermost.

I have heard democracy defined as the association of us all through the leadership of the best. So if democracy is in danger, are we quite sure it is democracy which is at fault, or the leadership?

While a Government has to bear the responsibility and reality of actual power, other parties sometimes say to electors who complain of any trouble whatever: 'You sign the ballot paper and we'll do the rest.' That seems an easy way to get rid of the troubles and burdens of human life and to solve the insoluble problems of the State.

An opposition party engages in trying to make out that everything is as bad as it possibly could be. They declare that everything is going to rack and ruin whilst the other opposition party says it has already gone, and that the state of the country is the most horrible thing human virtue can conceive.

Under our system they are entitled to say what they like, for the right of public expression is one of the most valuable rights. Democracies have nothing in common with either Fascism or Bolshevism. For good or ill we dwell in a different atmosphere.

We have been reared in it. We are habituated to the parliamentary system. We believe in government by assemblies freely elected and by public opinion freely formed and freely expressed. We believe that it is the duty of the State to guard the rights of individuals. We hold that the State exists to give full expression to the family and the home. We are the opponents of totalitarianism in all its forms. We stand for tolerance.

We are the foes of racial and religious persecution. In Paris, in London, and in New York men may dwell at the heart of a society which, with all its obvious shortcomings, holds aloft a torch of freedom for the thinkers and toilers of every land. With all the many evils, abuses and shams, we can claim to have produced a greater measure of material well-being for the people, man for man, household for household, than can be shown elsewhere. With all its faults, our system carries within itself the faculty for almost unlimited self-improvement. We should value these treasures, true glories I call them, as we do our lives, and there should be no sacrifice we would not make, and no lengths to which we would not go, conformable with honour and justice, to hand them on unmutilated, unsmirched, to our children.

Is not our cause, 'The Better Way', worthy to be defended? Does not our system of free democracy embodying the law, the wit and wisdom of a thousand years, claim allegiance as faithful, a service as punctual, an ardour as valiant as Nazi-ism or Bolshevism? And ought we not to take all the measures necessary for the preservation of our way of life? Why should our faith, the result of so many centuries of patient building, not also be confident and capable of defending itself?

Why should we, who are marching on the true path of progress, even though the road be stony, halt abashed and humbled while error, oppression and scientific villainy are blatant and armed? Must the good cause always lack hearts as resolute, swords as sharp, as those who champion evil?

Free nations, the liberal and parliamentary democracies, great and small, on whichever side of the Atlantic Ocean they dwell, must continue to take all the necessary measures to place themselves in a state of security; must also be 'Cause conscious' and from a hundred angles, and upon a thousand occasions, endeavour to build up a broad security for those treasures of peace and freedom which our ancestors rescued for us from the long confusions of the past.

We must not forget the glories of the past, nor how many battles we have fought for the rights of the individual and for human freedom. So I stand for the sovereign freedom of the individual within the laws which freely elected Parliaments have freely passed. I stand for the rights of the ordinary man to say what he thinks of the Government of the day, however powerful, and to turn them out, neck and crop, if he thinks he can better his temper or his home thereby, and if he can persuade enough others to vote with him.

CHAPTER 5

A Crown Can Be Too Heavy

BY TRIAL AND error, and by perseverance across the centuries, we found a very good plan. It is: The Queen can do no wrong. Bad advisers can be changed as often as the people like to use their rights for that purpose. A great battle is lost: Parliament turns out the Government. A great battle is won – crowds cheer the Queen. What goes wrong is carted away with the politicians responsible.

In other countries, people are often disposed to imagine that progress consists in converting oneself from a monarchy into a republic. We have known the blessings of limited monarchy. Great traditional and constitutional chains of events have come to make an arrangement, to make a situation, unwritten, which enables our affairs to proceed on what I believe is a superior level of smoothness and democratic progress.

Whereas up to the middle of the nineteenth century the British monarchy seemed to many serious political thinkers to be fading with the trappings of the past – an institution medieval, obsolete, moribund, which had served its purpose and played its part – the new age has been astonished to find it revivified, fortified, glorified, indispensable. It has become at once the single golden link by which the loyalties of all are united and the practical mechanism by which the daily routine of all high constitutional business proceeds. This marks a prodigious, fortunate, and almost unforseseen political evolution.

The prerogatives of the Crown have become the privileges of the people.

It is natural for Parliament to talk and for the Crown to shine.

Being a strong monarchist, I am in favour of constitutional monarchies as a barrier against dictatorships, and for many other reasons. It would be a mistake for us to try to force our system on other countries.

Our ancient Monarchy renders inestimable services. Above the ebb and flow of party, the rise and fall of Ministries and individuals, the changes of public opinion or public fortune, the Monarchy presides, ancient, calm and supreme within its functions, over all the treasures that have been saved from the past and all the glories we write in the annals of the country.

There is no doubt that of all the institutions which have grown up among us over the centuries, or sprung into being in our lifetime, the constitutional monarchy is the most deeply founded and dearly cherished by the whole association of our peoples. It acquired a meaning incomparably more powerful than anyone dreamed possible in former times. The Crown became the mysterious link – I may say, the magic link – uniting our loosely bound but strongly interwoven Commonwealth of nations, states and races. Peoples who would never tolerate the assertions of a written constitution which implied any diminution of their independence, are the foremost to be proud of their loyalty to the Crown.

It is the golden circle of the crown which alone embraces the loyalties of so many. It is the symbol which gathers together and expresses those deep emotions and stirrings of the human heart which has made men travel far to fight and die together, and abandon possessions and enjoyments for the sake of abstract ideas.

In the Commonwealth we not only look out across the seas towards each other, but backwards to our own history, to Magna Carta, to Habeas Corpus, to the Petition of Right, to Trial by Jury, to the English Common Law and to Parliamentary democracy. These are the milestones and monuments that mark the path along which our people have marched to leadership and freedom. And over all this, uniting us all with our majestic past, is the golden circle of the Crown. What is within the circle? Not only the glory of an ancient unconquered people, but the hope, the sure hope, of a broadening life for hundreds of millions.

Soon after the first World War, the world read one of the most remarkable series of royal letters which have ever seen the light. They became known as the 'Willy-Nicky' correspondence. They were authentic letters between Kaiser Wilhelm and Tsar Nicholas II.

How did these men compare with the common run of us? They were both born to the throne, and both succeeded at a comparatively early age to power which no man should wield and responsibilities which no man can discharge. In reading these letters, everyone should ask himself whether he is quite sure that he possesses in his own nature the qualities which would have enabled him to avoid the crimes of the one or the errors of the other, and still more whether he possesses those supreme qualities which would have enabled him to steer the ponderous world aright. Confronted always with the greatest issues, taught almost from infancy to identify themselves with their nation, surrounded always by flatterers, untrained by the competition or opposition of equals, they suffered from many disadvantages and from an absence of those salutary checks which, except in most violent times, should always curb the human will.

In the main it seems probable that both these men in the supreme act of their lives conformed to deep and overpowering passions in the hearts of their respective nations. No two races ever drew the sword with greater ardour and alacrity than the Russians and the Germans in that fateful August of 1914. It is a mere pretence to deny this fact. The Slav race sprang to arms in an intense effort to assert its unity and greatness; and the Teuton, drawing his bright, well-sharpened sword, hastened blithely along a thousand roads to the conflict.

Russia had never known a national movement so intense and universal as that which bade her hurry to the rescue of the Serbian people; and Germany, when all is said and done, felt and responded to the passions, the ambitions, the vain glory and, it may be added, the apprehensions which were embodied and displayed so effectively by her Kaiser. It is to the credit of the German people that, although they changed their form of Government drastically and fundamentally, they did not try to curry favour with the victors at the expense of the ruler who so unwisely gratified their national lust.

Enough evidence has been made public to show that the Kaiser was a bad man – vain, excitable, fond of attitudes, unscrupulous and double-dealing not only in great but in small affairs. The Tsar was of the weak, honourable type, much swayed by the women of his family, who were themselves narrow and superstitious. Still, the Tsar had good impulses. The League of Nations which President Wilson presented to us in such fine language was after all only the successor and development of the Hague Tribunal which Nicholas II, by his own spontaneous effort, called into being years ago; and in the whole of Russia before the war there was nothing that foreign nations, friend or foe, could depend on comparable to the word of honour of this loyal gentleman.

Compare either of these men with an apparition like Lenin – seizing power by dark and violent means, using it with merciless ferocity not in accordance with the will of his own people but solely in gratification of his theories, committing more murders and cold-blooded executions in a month than Willy or Nicky in all their reigns, trampling on religion, tearing down every institution without regard to human sympathy or human decency, deserting his allies, betraying his country, and finally, to prolong his tyranny, abandoning to a large extent even the theories and doctrines for the sake of which all this bloodshed and misery was inflicted.

The view of the Kaiser as a kind of Titan-demon evolving from his own internal energies the world-wide catastrophe into which we plunged is beyond the truth. He had not the brains. He seems to have been a fairly ordinary man, with much superficial cleverness, whose head was turned by the adulation of which he had been the life-long object. We disputed his claims to a high seat in pandemonium. We think he will there be relegated to those humbler murky benches where the weak party leaders who dare not face or tell the truth, the fire-eating editors who prepare the atmosphere of wars, and the obstinate generals who push armies into hopeless offensives will be assembled. Lenin was of a different mould.

All tyrants are the enemies of the human race. All tyrannies should be overthrown. But what is a tyranny? Let us be clear on that.

We need not plunge into philosophical abstractions. A tyranny may be defined for practical purposes as the arbitrary rule of one man without regard to the wishes of millions. A tyrant is one who allows the fancies of his mind to count for more in deciding action than the needs, feelings, hopes, lives and physical well-being of the people over whom he has obtained control. A tyrant is one who wrecks the lives of millions for the satisfaction of his own conceptions. So far as possible in this world, no man should have such power, whether under an imperialist, republican, militarist, socialist or soviet form of Government.

The twentieth century has been destructive of monarchs, and few now remain. At the same time no proof has been given that the republican form of Government produces better results for the mass of the people. On the contrary, there are many instances which show that the cost of Government is greater under republics than under monarchies, that there is more corruption, less freedom and less progress, both physical and intellectual. There are, of course, exceptions, and it would be wrong to generalise. Every nation is entitled to the form of Government it chooses, and once the apparatus of monarchy has been overthrown in a country there are few precedents for its restoration. The fact remains, however, that it has been the experience of many nations to have dwelt more happily, more safely, more prosperously and more progressively under a monarchy than either an oligarchy or a republic.

It seems probable that on the whole the best arrangement that can be made for the Government of a State is the kind of Monarchy and Commonwealth which, by the patient and valiant efforts of so many centuries, we have achieved in Britain. We have the separation in our national life of what is permanent from what is temporary. We are able to divide what is the common inheritance of all from those matters which must necessarily be in dispute between classes and parties and factions. We have a Constitution which places the supreme position in the State beyond the reach of private ambition, but which at the same time assures to a political leader, in fulfilment of the wishes of the electors, a freedom and confidence of action unsurpassed in any land. Above all, we have that separation of pomp from power, which is perhaps one of the most important practical principles in the organisation of a political system. It is too much for one human being to unite in himself a great measure of executive power with the power of sovereignty. No one can be trusted to stand it, and no one ought to have it. All the splendour and tradition of the realm belong to the Crown; but the difficult, doubtful, disputable, day to day business is transacted by plain men who can be turned out and replaced if they do not give satisfaction, without any very serious consequences. This eminently practical method has been arrived at almost entirely through the genius of the English people, and wherever it has been imitated it has, with rare exceptions, been attended with a measure of success superior to that of any other form of Government. The limited or constitutional monarchy may well challenge comparison, judged by every test, with any and every form of modern Government that has been devised or put into practice in any country in the world.

The unfortunate Tsar was endeavouring to create within the brief span of his own life a parliamentary system in Russia. Had he or had the Kaiser succeeded to their thrones, under something like the British Constitution, and with the experienced political advisers at their side whom our constitutional system has always hitherto supplied, their families might both be reigning peacefully at the present moment, and the world would have been spared measureless calamities. A crown can be too heavy for some to wear.

We love 'the happy medium,' and we usually manage to get it. Other less fortunate or less sagacious peoples oscillate from one extreme to another, now reeling in the delirium of revolution, now gripped tight again under a military despotism. It is this knack of choosing a middle course in reconciling opposite systems and securing the advantages of both without the evils of either that constitutes the peculiar political aptitude of the British people.

Surveying the misfortunes and convulsions of so many nations, our hearts must go out in gratitude to that long line of wise statesmen and stout-hearted citizens who built up step by step, generation after generation, that wonderful constitutional instrument under which we progressed in peace and triumphed in war, which served as a model to many, which excites the envy of most and commands the respect of all.

How careful, yet how resolute, should be our steps along that middle path on which our forefathers have set us, leading through an ordered freedom to a progressive prosperity, avoiding on the one hand the criminal follies of a vain or incompetent autocrat, and on the other the swift alternations of anarchy and dictatorship.

In my own lifetime I saw the destruction and the overthrow of the Imperial houses of Brazil, China, Turkey, and, in Europe, of the Romanovs, the Hohenzollerns, and the Hapsburgs; and the abolition of the monarchies of Portugal, Greece, Spain, and all the German states.

These events were attributed not only to the fortunes of war and the errors of princes, but to the spread of democratic popular government based upon adult suffrage or successive approaches thereto. Political theorists and pedants considered that this process would continue invincibly until mankind was everywhere 'free' – that is to say, misruled and overtaxed by governments which had no crowned head.

The actual course of events was very different. Democracy, universally enfranchised and proclaimed the arbiter of all, seemed even more inclined to destroy parliaments than monarchies.

Under the pressures of Armageddon and its aftermath the urge of the multitude was towards dictatorships. Nearly all the parliaments on the English model so hopefully erected during the nineteenth century in Europe, and to some extent also in the Americas, disappeared, and were replaced by forms of Caesarism, with presidents or despots who maintained themselves against their rivals and contended against their many difficulties and perils by destroying old laws, rights, and liberties handed down from the past and enshrined in so many venerable constitutions.

The old kings, with their long record of legitimacy, were pulled down, and in their place fierce, audacious, capable adventurers set up as tyrants amid popular applause.

They did not call themselves kings, because their power was far greater than that of kings. They couldn't look forward to the future, because they could not look back upon the past. They lived in the present without scruple or pity, and were acclaimed because they acted with vigour, if not with wisdom or virtue, and seemed to grapple with the problems of a period of flux.

It is certain in nearly every case – though there were notable exceptions – that the peoples were no happier or better off under those who thus seized the machinery of state than they were under the parliaments or the hereditary kings. Indeed, they seemed to have lost, for the most part, the greater portion of those rights, liberties, and safeguards which, from the days of ancient Greece and Rome, had always been cherished or admired as the essentials of human dignity, culture, and progress.

Freedom of speech, the right of public meeting, the right to criticise and oppose the government of the day, the right of the individual as against the state, of the plain man against the policeman, the inviolability of the domicile ('the Englishman's home is his castle'), the impartiality of the courts of law, even freedom of thought and of creed – all these were assailed or trampled down.

In their place came processions, parades, demonstrations, banners, emblems, the blare of brass bands, and the wire-pulling of caucuses, the partisanship and ardour of party organisations. The Press, even when neither squashed nor squared, sang in chorus for 'the strong man'. The control of broadcasting by the men in power afforded new facilities for organised propaganda and oppression.

The world swung again full circle, and Personal Rule, with none of its former sanctions or restraints, with none of its old glamour, splendour, and stability, held sway over many of the mightiest states.

We escaped the worst of Continental tribulations. The wisdom of our ancestors led them, consciously or unconsciously, across three or four centuries, to aim at the separation of pomp from power.

The joining together in a single person of the headship of the State and the headship of the government, or any approach thereto, open or veiled, has always been odious in Great Britain. We have known how to preserve the old and glorious traditions of hereditary monarchy while slowly building up a parliamentary system which met the needs of a growing people and changing times.

This English conception of a limited monarchy, where the sovereign reigns but does not govern, still holds its own as a practical instrument and means of national self-preservation against every type of republic and every degree of dictatorship.

In the nineteenth century English parliamentary institutions – or British, as they had then become – were the ideal towards which the thinkers of many different races stretched out their hands. But when they gained what they sought, they knew not how to profit by it, and soon threw away all they had won.

One of the worst misfortunes and mistakes was the decision to drive out the legitimate reigning houses of Germany and Austria. Many steadying loyalties centred upon the Hohenzollerns and the Hapsburgs.

Although individual wearers of these crowns, by their association with War, rendered themselves obnoxious not only to their enemies, but to their own defeated subjects, there were other members of these royal families quite guiltless and free from all blame or responsibility for the world catastrophe. To ban the whole line of princes from the throne was a claim the victors should never have made upon the vanquished.

President Wilson and the United States played an overweening part in deciding this issue. The silly idea that republics are more free and better governed than monarchies dominated the treaty-makers at Paris. The governments of Germany and of the shattered Austro-Hungarian Empire were irresistibly thrust into the hands of the parties of the Left in these countries.

In Germany the strong national and patriotic elements, deprived by foreign intrusion of their reigning Houses, raised from the dust a new despotism, incomparably more dangerous to the world than the old could have been.

Russia is past praying for. The tyranny into which the Russian people fell was an impersonal one. Stalin, the all-powerful head of the Soviets, was not so much a personal ruler as the high priest of a new religion which embodied hatred instead of love, and unconsciously worshipped the Devil instead of God.

In Italy Mussolini preserved the Monarchy, adding the force ot tradition of an hereditary ruler to his own leadership.

The wisdom of our ancestors led us to an envied and enviable situation. We have the strongest Parliament in the world. We have the oldest, the most famous, the most honoured, the most secure, and the most serviceable, monarchy in the world. King and Parliament both safely and solidly based upon the will of the people.

Tremendous changes swept across the world; systems, manners, and outlook decisively altered; the knowledge, science, wealth, and power of mankind underwent great and rapid expansion, and the speed at which the evolution of society took place baffled all comparison. These shocks and disturbances were fatal to most of the empires, monarchies, and political organisations of Europe and Asia. Mighty nations which gained their liberties in the nineteenth century, and hopefully erected parliaments to preserve them, fell, or yielded themselves to the sway of dictatorships.

Still there was one great system in which law was respected and freedom reigned, where the ordinary citizen could assert his rights fearlessly against the executive power and criticise as he chose its agents and policies. There was one institution, among the most ancient and venerable, which, so far from falling into decay, breasted the torrent of events, and even derived new vigour from the stresses.

Unshaken by the earthquakes, unweakened by the dissolvent tides, the Imperial Monarchy of Britain stood firm. An achievement so remarkable, a fact so prodigious, a fact contrary to the whole tendency of the age, that it could not be separated from the personality of the good, wise and truly noble King George V whose reign will be regarded as one of the most important and memorable in the whole of our history.

The King's father died at a moment of severe political excitement and constitutional crisis. The Great Council, which at St James's Palace acclaimed George V as King, saw before them a man humble in the presence of responsibilities which the hereditary lawful succession of a thousand years had cast upon him. There were few who did not feel compassion and sympathy for the unproved inheritor of such anxious glories. Some there were who had misgivings. Yet at that moment no one could foresee the shattering catastrophes towards which the whole world was hurrying.

It was in these years that the institution of the Monarchy and the growing regard for the person of the King preserved unity, in measures of defence and foreign policy, in a nation otherwise torn by the fiercest political strife, and even, as it sometimes seemed, drawing near to the verge of civil war. Amid this domestic turbulence and growing foreign danger the King experienced his keenest anxieties and sorrows. He had not then the commanding influence which he had gathered to the Crown and to his person by the end of his long reign; but he adhered unswervingly to the Constitution.

He strove to mitigate the fury of parties and to preserve intact the grand common inheritance of the people. Quietly and patiently he strengthened himself, and steadily mounted in the esteem and confidence of all his subjects. Then, suddenly, out of what to ordinary folk, appeared to be a summer sky, rushed thunderbolts of world war.

We saw the King, using all the influence he had, make Britain united in an hour so big with fate. All stood firm, not a link in the chain broke; but the holding-ground in which all the anchors of strength were cast was the hereditary Sovereign and the function of Monarchy which he so deeply comprehended. Victory came at last. Victory absolute, final, unquestionable; a triumph in arms rarely surpassed in completeness. All the kings and emperors against whom he had warred, fled or were deposed. But the shadow of victory was disillusion. The reaction from extreme effort, prostration. The aftermath even of successful war is long and bitter. The years that followed, and such peace as the infuriated democracies would allow their statesmen to make, were years of turbulence and depression.

The Sovereign, uplifted above class-strife and party-faction, has a point of view unique in our society. To be the Sovereign of all the people can be his only ambition. He must foster every tendency that makes for national unity. All law-abiding subjects must have the chance, by the Constitutional process, to exercise the highest duties under the Crown.

Every political leader who commands a majority in the House ot Commons, or even through the diversion of other parties can maintain himself in that Assembly, is entitled to the fullest, most generous measure of the royal countenance and aid.

George V reconciled the new forces of Labour and Socialism to the Constitution and the Monarchy. This enormous process of assimilating and rallying the spokesmen of left-out millions will be intently studied by historians of the future. To the astonishment of foreign countries and of our American kinsmen, the spectacle was seen of the King and Emperor working in the utmost ease and unaffected cordiality with politicians whose theories at any rate seemed to menace all existing institutions. The result was to make a national unity from Constitutional fundamentals the wonder of the world. In the compass of his reign

George V revived the idea of Monarchy throughout the world. He drew upon himself and his country the envious admiration of many lands. He revivified national spirit, popularised hereditary kingship, and placed himself upon an eminence where, as a true servant of the State, he commanded not only the allegiance, but the affection, of all sorts and conditions of men.

In a world of ruin and chaos, he brought about a resplendent rebirth of the great office which fell to his lot.

The Anglo-Saxons proclaimed their Kings and Christianity grafted on to the pagan tradition the symbol of the consecrated oil, by virtue of which the prophet Samuel made David the shepherd the Lord's anointed.

All the essentials, to a considerable degree even the actual words of the ceremony, were already fixed and established before William of Normandy came to his stormy crowning.

Of the Kings under whom this ritual grew and took shape few ruled over more than a part of England. The earliest of them all were tribal chiefs, holding dominion only over London and the district immediately around it.

They knew nothing of the rest of the world beyond, perhaps, what some Phoenician trader had told them. In any case, the world that even the Phoenicians knew was small.

Today men come to a crowning from lands whose very existence was unguessed 500 years ago.

So the sap of this living present rises from roots deep-buried in the past. The supreme link between today and that long line of yesterdays is the Monarchy.

It is also the supreme link between the little island of Britain and the wide lands of the Commonwealth.

In the case of the great self-governing Dominions almost every other link has been severed. The Imperial Government no longer meddles with their affairs or seeks to hold their Parliaments in tutelage.

Gradually, little by little, over a period of years, it relinquished every right over them that it once claimed, abandoned every check upon their independence. They control, in the fullest possible sense, their own destinies.

I witnessed the Coronations of King George V's sons and grandchild. The Coronation of the Sovereign of Great Britain is, perhaps, the most impressive and spectacular of all the ceremonials that the modern world has inherited from the centuries of the past. It is no idle pageantry or antiquarian survival. There is in it no threat to the rest of the world, such as the marching multitudes and wheeling aircraft of a Fascist holiday or Communist anniversary may hold.

But a King over free men pledges faith to them, and they pledge faith to him, according to ancient rites that have an abiding significance and validity.

There have been many changes in our conception of monarchy since the first hallowing at Westminster of a King of England.

To our mail-clad ancestors the King was essentially the leader of his people in battle. His powers had no limit save that set by his own ability to enforce them. The idea of a constitutional King would have seemed as fantastic to our forefathers as absolutism appears to us today.

But to them, also, Kingship meant service, dedication to a task. And it is upon this that the emphasis is placed in the Coronation ritual.

The beginnings of that ritual go back to days before history began. Long before Caesar landed on the shores of Britain warriors met in a forest glade – perhaps on that very spot where Westminster Abbey now stands – to raise upon a shield, so that all might see and do homage to him, the man upon whom the uneasy lot of chieftainship had fallen.

They achieved full national status, and now stand beside the United Kingdom as equal partners in the dignities and the responsibilities of the British Commonwealth.

The change in the relationship between the Dominions and Great Britain was recognised in the Balfour Declaration of 1926, which thus defined the position of the Mother Country and her daughter-nations:

> They are autonomous Communities within the British Empire, equal in status, in no way subordinate one to another in any respect of their domestic or external affairs, though united by a common allegiance to the Crown, and freely associated as members of the British Commonwealth of Nations.

And the last vestiges of the old suzerainty were swept away by the Statute of Westminster, 1931.

This more direct relationship between the Sovereign and the nations of the British Commonwealth found appropriate expression at the Coronations of Queen Elizabeth II, and her father. For the first time in history the representatives of the Dominions attended by right and not by grace, at a crowning and played their part in the ancient ceremonial, which assumed new significance from their presence. That fact alone made the Coronations historic and marked yet another milestone in the development of the Monarchy.

Yet though here and there an alteration has been made in the ritual to emphasise the new position, the changes have been in no way considerable. The essentials of the ceremony remain unchanged. The Sovereign is set apart from the moment of his accession; but the Coronation emphasises his unique position, his dedication to the responsibilities and the loneliness of the Throne.

King George VI ascended the throne in unhappy circumstances which no one, perhaps, regretted more keenly than himself.

It is certain that, could any sacrifice of his have prevented King Edward's abdication he would gladly have made it. In relation to his brother he was always self-effacing.

Such was the central figure of that Coronation.

All the eyes of the world turned on one who had always shunned, rather than sought, the limelight. He took up, from a supreme sense of duty, a burden far greater than falls to a King who has succeeded to the Throne in the ordinary course of nature.

The dedication, which is the keynote of the Abbey service, was perhaps in his case peculiarly appropriate. He was already self-dedicated to duty.

It was notable, also, that for the first time for many long years, the Sceptre, which symbolises the club or mace of the ancient warleader – a weapon older than the Sword, which also figures in the ritual – was placed in the hand of a King who had seen active service in the largest of naval battles.

That Coronation was more splendid and impressive for the presence of a Queen Consort.

Like the King, Queen Elizabeth, daughter of the Earl of Strathmore, could claim to be a descendant of the Royal House of Stuart. In her veins also flows the blood of the ancient Kings of Scotland.

Her childhood home, Glamis Castle, was part of the dowry the Princess Jean, daughter of Robert II and great-grand-daughter of the Bruce, brought to Sir John Lyon.

Glamis was an ideal setting for the childhood of the future Queen. Innumerable are the tales of old romance associated with this, perhaps the oldest inhabited house in all Britain.

There is a legendary connection with Macbeth. There are links with Bonnie Prince Charlie and Claverhouse.

The fifth Earl of Strathmore was killed in battle in the rising of the

'Fifteen'. One wonders what the ghost of this staunch old Jacobite made of the marriage of a daughter of his house to the descendant of George I, or of the fact that, by the operation of the Act of Settlement, which he attempted to repeal by force of arms, she became Queen of England.

There are sombre threads in the tapestry. Glamis holds a grim secret, conjecture regarding which has given rise to many wild tales of the supernatural.

It may also be recalled that in the sixteenth century one of the ancestresses of the new Queen Elizabeth was accused of attempting to murder the Scottish King by witchcraft and burned on the Castle Hill at Edinburgh.

At the same time the family estates were declared forfeit to the Crown. The unhappy lady was proved innocent, even to the satisfaction of those dark times. She was not even, like so many 'witches', the dupe of her own imaginings. She had been falsely accused.

The informer on whose evidence she was condemned confessed his perjury before he died.

The Coronation is an ordeal to its central figures. At the crowning which I witnessed of King Edward VII, the aged Archbishop of Canterbury, Dr Frederick Temple, was a sick man. His hands trembled as he performed the prescribed rites. When the supreme moment came and St Edward's Crown was placed in his hands by that other ancient, the then Dean of Westminster, its weight seemed too much for him. With the greatest difficulty he raised it.

But there was one ghastly moment when it looked as if it were going to slip from his fingers and crash on the floor of the Abbey. It shook as he held it over the King's head. But at last he got it on.

True, it was back to front, but everyone was too much relieved to worry about that.

Four months afterwards the Archbishop died.

It is inevitable, of course, that the Archbishop of Canterbury, like the Judges in the Supreme Court in the United States, should be advanced in years.

The highest office in the Church can never fall to the lot of a young man.

But the right of crowning the Sovereign is one which no Primate will willingly consent to delegate.

Ralph d'Escures rose from a sick bed and was carried in a litter to Westminster Abbey on the Coronation Day of King Henry II.

Because of Ralph's age and infirmity it had been arranged that the Bishop of Salisbury should crown the King. But when he lifted the Crown from the High Altar the Archbishop snatched it from him. The effort was too great.

The most precious of the jewels of England slipped from his grasp. It seemed that nothing could save it, but the Bishop of Salisbury, hampered as he was by his robes, dived and caught the Crown before it shivered to fragments on the Abbey pavement.

We have grown more decorous. But if there was more likelihood of an unseemly squabble marring the solemnity of a medieval coronation the men of those days had at least one great advantage over those of the twentieth century.

Accustomed to wearing not only robes but armour, they found the coronation trappings lighter than their descendants.

A peer's robes and uniform may weigh from 14 lb. to 20 lb. By the end of the ceremony they seem many times heavier than that.

The Sovereign must endure not only the weight of sumptuous robes, but also, for a period, that of the Crown and the Insignia.

At one point in the ceremony, so great is the strain that the Sovereign's arm has to be supported in order to ease the burden.

And there is always the haunting fear of some unhappy accident which superstition may twist into an omen of evil to come.

At the Coronation of George III, for instance, a large diamond fell from the Crown while the King was wearing it.

The incident was regarded as ominous, and the forebodings seemed justified when, a score of years later, the American Colonies seceded from the Empire and the United States claimed its place among the nations.

No one, perhaps, could be blamed for the loss of the diamond, but from start to finish the arrangements for George's Coronation were bungled. Even the Sword of State was mislaid and could not be found when it was required.

There is little wonder that at last the Royal patience gave way and the King expressed his strong dissatisfaction to the Deputy Earl Marshal, the Earl of Effingham.

'It is true, sir,' said Effingham to the young King, 'that there has been some neglect, but I have taken care that the next Coronation shall be regulated in the best manner possible.'

The next Coronation, however, was to witness the culminating scene of the gravest scandal in the annals of the later Kings of England.

George IV, while Prince of Wales, had laid siege to the twice-widowed Maria Fitzherbert.

Unfortunately, the lady was virtuous as well as beautiful. She seems to have loved him, but the role of mistress did not attract her.

In desperation he staged an attempted suicide, ostentatiously stabbing himself, but carefully avoiding any vital spot. Four of his associates were then despatched to Mrs Fitzherbert.

They assured her that the Prince lay hovering between life and death and that only her presence could pull him through.

Love could not resist such a summons, but discretion insisted on a chaperone. The Duchess of Devonshire accompanied her.

The Prince, when they arrived, spoke of marriage. Maria knew that, under the Royal Marriage Act, this was impossible. They might, indeed, take the marriage vows in the presence of a priest, but the union would be invalid under the laws of England.

George, however, was wounded – he had tried to kill himself for love of her. She allowed him to slip a ring upon her finger.

In the end they were married secretly. No court would have recognised the ceremony, but that was just as well. Maria was a Roman Catholic, and a Prince of the Blood who married a Catholic was barred from succession to the Throne.

For a time they were happy. But George was in debt. His bill for clothes averaged £10,000 a year – and that, naturally, was but one item among many. And his father was living too long. There came a day when no one would lend to the Prince of Wales.

Even when he offered for every £5,000 paid him now £10,000 and an Irish peerage after the King's death there were no takers. His bond, it was known, was as bad as his word.

In the end he had to appeal to his father, then suffering one of those recurrent attacks of sanity, during which he was aware of the misconduct of his sons.

George III agreed to pay his debts – but only if the Prince married Caroline of Brunswick.

To his lasting sorrow and discredit the Prince agreed to his father's terms. But he agreed unwillingly. At his first meeting with his bride he called for brandy because the touch of her lips had made him sick.

On their wedding day he came drunk to the altar, scarce able to hiccough the vows he never meant to keep. They were, indeed, a mockery after those he had exchanged with Mrs Fitzherbert.

For a year they maintained some pretence of marriage. Then they separated. There was one child of the union – a girl destined to die in childbed, victim of the fashionable fallacies of the Royal physicians.

Caroline's life after the parting was packed with indiscretions, committed, for the most part, abroad, but she denied that she had ever been guilty of adultery, save with Mrs Fitzherbert's husband.

There was, however, evidence of a sort against her. There were grounds, not unreasonable, for a presumption of guilt.

And George IV's first acts on succeeding to the Throne were to order that her name be omitted from the Prayer Book and to demand that his Ministers free him from her.

The Ministers did their best. They introduced a Bill to dissolve the marriage on the ground of the Queen's adultery with the Italian Bergami, and proceeded to force it through Parliament with the aid of a dragooned majority.

Caroline returned to England, protested her innocence. Lord Brougham brought his powerful eloquence to her aid. The nation was split into two camps, the larger of which was for the Queen.

There were ominous mutterings, riots, indeed. Even the most complacent of political 'yes-men' took fright; the Ministry was in danger. The Throne itself seemed to be threatened. The Bill was abandoned.

But George was resolved that there should be no crowning for the Queen. Strict orders were given that on no account was she to be admitted to the Abbey on Coronation Day.

In spite of this she presented herself, attended by Lord Hood and her ladies, at the Abbey shortly after six in the morning. A doorkeeper demanded to see their tickets.

'I present you your Queen,' protested Hood. 'She is entitled to admission without such a form.'

'My orders are specific, and I feel myself bound to obey them,' was the answer.

'Then you refuse the Queen admission?'

The doorkeeper hesitated, but a higher official came forward. Hood asked him if any preparations had been made for Her Majesty. The reply was 'No.'

The party withdrew, but drove to another door. The result was the same. From door to door went the carriage. At each in turn Caroline presented herself. At each she was turned away.

Her progress was watched by a great crowd of spectators and punctuated with cheers and hisses.

'Off! off!' cried many. There were voices that shouted: 'Go away to

Bergami!' 'Be off to Como!' In the end the cheers were overwhelmed by the insults.

The King was unpopular – as Prince Regent he had been stoned when he drove to the State opening of Parliament – but the Queen's honour was doubtful. And this day, the people seemed to feel, belonged to the King and to the Crown, and so to them all.

They resented Caroline's appearance because of the scandal to the Monarchy.

At last the Queen recognised that the case was hopeless and drove off. Soon afterwards she died. George lingered on, a gross, debauched corpulence no longer to be kept in by stays, for a few more years.

It is not the least notable tribute to the qualities and character of King George V that he redeemed the name which his great-grand uncle had brought into such disrepute and unpopularity.

The multitudes who now see and hear a Coronation have brought home to them, in words of power and beauty, a sense of the continuity of the Crown.

When, for instance, the Sceptre is given into the Sovereign's hand, the Archbishop of Canterbury says:

'Receive the Rod of Equity and Mercy. . . . Be so merciful that you be not too remiss; so execute Justice that you forget not Mercy. Punish the wicked, protect and cherish the just, and lead your people in the way wherein they should go.'

The exhortation is the same, not only in substance but in form as was spoken at the 'hallowing' of the Saxon Kings.

Some of the ancient words, indeed, have a deeper content today than when they were first uttered. Such is the Archbishop's charge, when the Sovereign is girt with the Sword of State, that the Sovereign should 'help and defend widows and orphans.'

The ceremony of the Homage, which follows the Crowning, Benediction, and Inthronisation, has also an abiding significance.

First, the Archbishop of Canterbury, then the Prince of Wales or senior Prince of the Blood, then the first of each order of the peerage, performs the act of homage.

All the arrangements for the Coronation are in the hands of the Earl Marshal, an office which, since the reign of Charles II, has always been held by the Head of the House of Howard.

The late Duke took the keenest personal interest in everything that pertained to his ancient office, and was a keen student of the public ceremonials of his own and earlier times.

As a result he restored to the Coronation Service a number of historic rites which had fallen into desuetude.

The Duke of Norfolk is not only a great hereditary Officer of State but a symbol of the loyalty which Catholics, as well as Protestants, bear to the Crown.

The old unhappy quarrels are ended, and though the Sovereign still swears to maintain in the United Kingdom, to the utmost of his power, 'the Protestant Reformed Religion established by law,' the last possible vestige of offence to the Roman Catholic community has been removed from the Oath.

And the present Earl Marshal, like his ancestors, is a Catholic. In spite of that, he bears his part – and a leading part – in this, the greatest of the Anglican rites.

Always on Coronation Day the thoughts of English people and their friends and well-wishers – not a few – wherever they may be are in the Abbey.

There was a time when the word 'Dominion' was greatly esteemed. But now, almost instinctively and certainly spontaneously, the many States, nations and races included in the British Commonwealth have found in the word 'Realm' the expression of their sense of unity, combined in most cases with a positive allegiance to the Crown or a proud and respectful association with it.

No absolute rules can be laid down about the Crown, but on the whole it is wise in human affairs and in the government of men, to separate the Crown from politics. While the ordinary struggles, turmoils, and inevitable errors of healthy democratic government proceed, there is established upon an unchallenged pedestal the title deeds and the achievements of all the realms, and every generation can make its contribution to the enduring treasure of our race and fame.

Queen Elizabeth II came to the Throne at a time when a tormented mankind stood uncertainly poised between world catastrophe and a golden age. She was well aware that wearing a crown can never be an easy task. The constitutional kingship of today is the hardest task of all. The function of the monarchy is very real – indeed, it is of paramount importance. The throne is the final guarantee of freedom. It is also the last, but enduring link of the Commonwealth.

It is our surest shield and safeguard against those violent cataclysms which have convulsed and plunged ancient civilisations into the night of despotism.

It requires of its occupant special qualities. It makes the most exacting demands.

Queen Elizabeth possesses these qualities. She has been trained to meet these demands. The lofty traditions established by a century of constitutional monarchy in the best and widest sense are ingrained in her. They are part of her very nature. And, with her husband, in the more intimate domestic sphere, she carries on the traditions and example of her parents. That also has its place – one we can hardly over-value in the relationship of Sovereign and peoples. The warmth of its fireside glow travels far, and private happiness combines with unwearying service to the State to provide a light and an example to us all.

It is reassuring to notice that the monarchy is stronger than ever, and that year by year the widening circle of reading, thinking, and acting men and women, not only in this island, but throughout the Commonwealth, look with an increasing sense of loyalty and possession towards our ancient Throne.

There is no difficulty in vindicating the principle of hereditary monarchy. The experience of every country and of all ages, the practical reasonings of common sense, arguments of the highest theory, arguments of most commonplace convenience, all unite to show the wisdom which places the supreme leadership of the State beyond the reach of private ambition and above the shocks and changes of party strife. Further, let it not be forgotten that our monarchy is a limited and a constitutional monarchy. Our monarchy has no interests divergent from those of the people. It enshrines only those ideas and causes upon which the people are united. It is based on the abiding and prevailing interests of the nation, and thus, through all the changes of the years, through all the wide developments of the democratic State, our monarchy has become the most secure, as it is the most ancient and glorious, monarchy in the whole of Christendom.

How proud we may be to have preserved the symbols and traditions of our glorious past, enshrined and perpetuated in an hereditary monarchy, and to have reconciled these treasures with a religious, civic, and political freedom unexampled in any quarter of the globe.

The Greatest Half Hour
In Our History

THE RIGHTS AND liberties of Englishmen are older and more sacred than Parliament itself.

Runnymede is indeed worthy of the celebrations, in the form of a National Pageant, held there in its memory. We need to be reminded how much Englishmen have to lose, how long and bitterly our ancestors have had to fight for our freedom, and how much we owe to the Barons of England who assembled upon the banks of the Thames in the early summer of 1215.

The charter they won – the famous Magna Carta – laid down the root principles of English citizenship fifty years before the first beginnings of the English Parliament; and nearly six hundred years before the French Revolution opened the road to modern democracy.

King John was the kind of tyrant most obnoxious to England. He was a legal expert. Everyone recognised the extraordinary cleverness of his oppression. His dictatorship was buttressed by every sharp catch and gadget of the law. By subtle means he undermined and largely broke down local government. He hired foreign soldiers. He swayed the courts to such an extent that justice was denied both in the King's courts and in the Church courts, and even independent tribunals maintained by great nobles in the country were subject to an increasing interference. The sheriffs, as officers of the King in each county, ground down the poor, and harshly used the forms of justice to carry on every sort of legal knavery. Everywhere the claims of the Crown were pushed too far by agents of great ability with a fair-seeming show of law and precedent.

King John even attempted to make himself master of the Church in England, and when that failed he did not scruple to combine with an ambitious Pope, Innocent III, in order to exploit England for their common benefit.

At last this cleverness struck the hard rock of the English character. The country had no organisation to resist. The revolt of the Barons had no great leader; but there was such a universal stir and movement that the moment came when the King saw all of a sudden that he was in the midst of a measureless crisis where all his legal defences would be swept away together with his throne and his life.

This scene at Runnymede is still wonderfully vivid for us. John was caught by surprise. He knew of course that certain Barons were preparing against him; but for this his measures had been taken. He had money. Mercenary soldiers were collected. At first he was not really anxious. For fifteen years he had been a chief figure in European affairs. He felt confident in his ability to deal with any little provincial disturbance to be expected in his English dominions.

But a revelation awaited him. He was totally unprepared to find the whole country turn stubbornly to fight for liberty. His confidence melted beneath his feet like a quicksand. He found even his own feudal tenants unwilling to support him. His personal favourites felt the pressure of incalculable forces. His local agents, the sheriffs and the captains of castles, began to think of their own safety.

In a first effort to stem the tide he took the Cross. He became a Crusader whose person and property were sacred till he had finished the crusade. From this sanctuary he negotiated with the Church to have the rebel Barons excommunicated. But once again he had underestimated the sturdy foundations of England. The English Church stood firm with the English Barons, and the Archbishop, Stephen Langton, refused to pronounce the ban. Then at last was King John forced to come to terms with the Barons.

Let us imagine this meeting, on a Monday morning, in June, between Staines and Windsor. As the Barons and Churchmen began to collect on the great meadow an uneasy hush fell on them from time to time. Many had failed to keep their tryst; and the bold few who had come knew the King would never forgive this humiliation. He would hunt them down when he could, and the laymen at least were staking their lives in the cause of liberty. They had arranged a little throne for the King and a tent. They had drawn up, it seems, a short parchment. The handful of resolute men, their retainers, and the groups and squadrons of horsemen in sullen steel kept at some distance and well in the background. For was not armed rebellion against the Crown the supreme feudal crime?

Then events followed with great rapidity. A small cavalcade appeared from the direction of Windsor. Gradually men made out the faces of the King, the Papal Legate, the Archbishop of Canterbury, and several bishops. They dismounted without ceremony. Someone, probably the Archbishop, stated briefly the terms that were suggested. The King declared at once that he agreed. He said the details should be arranged immediately in his chancery. A short parchment may have been sealed; if so it is now lost. Then the King returned to Windsor. Everything must have been over in half an hour.

How then has this quiet, short scene become the most famous in our history? The Great Charter, drawn up during the next few days, laid the foundations of English freedom. It was an elaborate statement of liberties, and dwelt particularly on those rights which John had infringed.

Again and again during the century it was confirmed. Even in those high feudal times some mention crept in – almost by accident – of the English freeman and his rights, of the very ploughmen, the villeins and the trifles to which even they were entitled. Magna Carta showed that in the last resort every Englishman possesses a freedom which the authority of Government itself must respect.

There was established then what we trust and pray we shall never lose, that in this island the people own the Government and not the Government the people.

It is not only our Empire and our place in the world that we owe to our ancestors. There is our Freedom.

CHAPTER 7

Freedom

WHAT IS FREEDOM? There are one or two quite simple, practical tests by which it can be known in the modern world in peace conditions, namely:

Is there the right to free expression of opinion and of opposition and criticism of the Government of the day?

Have the people the right to turn out a Government of which they disapprove, and are constitutional means provided by which they can make their will apparent?

Are their courts of justice free from violence by the Executive and from threats of mob violence, and free of all association with particular political parties?

Will these courts administer open and well-established laws which are associated in the human mind with the broad principles of decency and justice?

Will there be fair play for poor as well as for rich, for private persons as well as Government officials?

Will the rights of the individual, subject to his duties to the State, be maintained and asserted and exalted?

Is the ordinary peasant or workman who is earning a living by daily toil and striving to bring up a family free from the fear that some grim police organisation under the control of a single party, will tap him on the shoulder and pack him off without fair or open trial to bondage or ill-treatment? These are the title-deeds of freedom which should lie in every home.

It must be the first concern of the citizens of a free country to preserve and maintain the independence of the courts of justice, however
inconvenient that independence may be on occasion, to the Government of the day.

Only so can we have, in those famous lines of Tennyson:

> A land of settled government,
> A land of just and old renown,
> Where freedom broadens slowly down
> From precedent to precedent.

And also:

> Some reverence for the laws ourselves have made.
> Some patient force to change them when we will.

'The masses,' said Napoleon in one of his most pessimistic announce-
ments, 'care little for liberty, but much for equality.' But well over a
hundred years have passed since then, and the world has moved on.
Today, individual freedom, especially when combined with a higher
standard of living makes a potent appeal to the men and women of
every country and every system.

Why should not an ordinary toiler have the chance to keep a home
together and rear a family, without being vilely trodden upon by well-
paid uniformed officials and professional party agents? Why should the
police harry ordinary households in so many lands? Why should the
ordinary wage-earner not be allowed to express his opinion about the
government of his country, and say whether he thinks it is being
wisely and honestly conducted?

Why should men's opinions be condemned as crimes, and buzzing
functionaries conduct an inquisition into the political or party views of
law-abiding folk? Why should religion be the subject of oppression?
Why should racial persecution endure?

Was it not Frederick the Great who said, 'Every man must get to
Heaven in his own way'? Can anyone help being born with red hair?

How is it we have developed our own way of life; our own tolerant
civilisation? I recall the lines:

> Time and the Ocean and some Guiding Star
> In high cabal, have made us what we are.

Our inheritance of well-founded slowly conceived codes of honour,
morals and manners, the passionate convictions which so many

hundreds of millions share together of the principles of freedom and justice, are far more precious to us than anything which scientific discoveries could bestow.

You have no doubt noticed in your reading of history – and I hope you will take pains to read it – that we have had to hold out from time to time all alone, or to be the mainspring of coalitions against a Continental tyrant or dictator, and we have had to hold out for quite a long time: against the Spanish Armada, against the might of Louis XIV, when we led Europe for nearly twenty-five years under William III and Marlborough, and when Nelson, Pitt and Wellington broke Napoleon, not without assistance from the heroic Russians of 1812. In all these world wars our island kept the head of Europe or else held out alone. And if you hold out alone long enough, there always comes a time when your opponent makes some ghastly mistake which alters the whole balance of the struggle.

We have our mistakes, our weaknesses and failings, but the cause of freedom has in it a recuperative power and virtue which can draw from misfortune new hope and new strength. There is little use in abstract assertions of freedom unless there is an understanding of the use that is to be made of it.

The more a man's choice is free, the more it is likely to be wise and fruitful, not only to the chooser but to the community in which he dwells. We hold that planning, with all the resources of science at its disposal, should aim at giving individual citizens as many choices as possible of what to do in the ups and downs of daily life. Now there is an important distinction between the quality and kind of planning. This kind of planning differs fundamentally from the collectivist theme of grinding them all up in a vast State mill which must certainly destroy in the process the freedom and independence which are the foundation of our way of life.

We have taught our principles of government, representative institutions, impartial courts of justice, freedom of thought, conscience, speech, and writing to a large proportion of the population of the globe. We have these priceless treasures to preserve, and we are capable of preserving them.

There are numerous masses who ardently long for the conditions of ordinary free life and citizenship such as are enjoyed by the parliamentary countries. Surely it is plain that our ceaseless endeavour should be to cultivate the closest relation with nations friendly to peace and freedom wherever they may lie in any part of the world. We ought to recognise more clearly every day the enormous body of common principles which unite us, and also the deep cleavages of moral and mental outlook which separate us from Dictator States.

There is a deep gulf of principle between freedom-loving nations and other states. They put their faith in the organisation. We put ours in individual men and women. They believe in the maximum control of daily life. We believe in the maximum choice.

The very essence of what they believe was expressed in an observation by a Minister who said: 'The men in government really know better what is good for the people than the people know themselves,' and this unwarrantable assumption lies at the root of all their thinking and policy-making. It takes too poor a view of the common sense and ingenuity of ordinary men and women in living their daily lives. It assumes a degree of what they call 'supra' – wisdom in rulers which is in bitter contrast with their proved incompetence. Freedom involves the essential quality of self-respect on which our way of life has been built up. This can be the only foundation for a healthy, buoyant and progressive society.

The word 'civilisation' means that officials and authorities whether uniformed or not, whether armed or not, are made to realise that they are servants and not masters.

Civilisation means that the civilians and ordinary folk have rights and liberties which they can effectively enforce against hierarchies and bureaucracies. Without this there can be no assured happiness or dignity to the individual citizen, and in my view no exceptional abundance of material things.

Moreover, any man or woman head of a household requires for happiness and for prosperity some steady continuity of life and conditions. Everyone must feel that he has the right to enforce a contract upon another, and is bound to respect one himself. Without this there can be no great accumulation of wealth.

Rulers and ruling cliques and factions everywhere have at all times great interest in establishing conditions of obedience and loyalty in their realms or jurisdictions in order to enable them to indulge their ambitions and to exalt themselves high above the common run.

I judge any community by tests that are an extension of those I apply to freedom:

What is the degree of freedom possessed by the citizen or subject?

Can he think, speak and act freely under well-established, well-known laws?

Is he furnished with a set of conditions and rules of long trial and experience within which he can push about as he pleases and make the best of himself?

Can he choose his employment or change it if he wishes?

Can he criticise the executive government?

Can he demonstrate, agitate and organise to change a government which he does not like, or of which he has got tired?

Can he sue the State if it has infringed his rights?

Are there also great processes for changing the law to meet new conditions?

Do these processes take full account of those who have made their arrangements and contracts under the old conditions?

There are nations which are governed by dictators, there are the nations governed by the Communists, and there are the nations which govern themselves. We are interested in the nations which govern themselves through Parliaments freely elected under a democratic franchise. We live where thought is free, speech is free, religion is free. In short, we live in a liberal society, the direct product of the great advances in human dignity, stature and well-being. We not only have constitutions which secure our rights, but we have been able to produce a greater material prosperity, more widely diffused among the masses of the people, than any form of despotism has yet been able to show.

Self-governing countries also claim to lead the world alike in accumulated wealth and in compassionate treatment of misfortune. Moreover, and this is what really matters, although we have differences among ourselves and wrangle about our internal affairs, and although we are very much aware of the shortcomings of our civilisation, and the need of continual social betterment, we believe fervently that our institutions are such as to enable us to improve conditions and correct abuses steadily, and to march every year and every decade forward upon a broader front into a better age. We believe that if we are only worthy of the rights, freedom, and opportunities that our forebears won for us, we can combine the glories of the past with the hopes of the future and make the world a better place for all.

We must recognise, therefore, that we have a great treasure to guard. The inheritance in our possession represents the prolonged achievement of the centuries. There is not one of our simple uncounted rights today for which better men than we are have not died on the scaffold or the battlefield. We have not only a great treasure, we have a great cause. Now, this is the question I ask: Are we taking every measure within our power to defend that cause? That is the question we must ask each other and ask ourselves.

I am sure that we would be very miserable if we were suddenly put under tyrannical rule. How could we bear, nursed as we have been in a free atmosphere, to be gagged and muzzled, to have spies, eaves-droppers, and informers at every corner, to have even private conversation caught up and used against us by the secret police and all their agents and creatures, to be arrested and interned without trial, or to be tried by political or party courts for crimes hitherto unknown to civil law?

How could we bear to be treated like schoolboys when we are grown-up men, to be turned out on parade by tens of thousands, to march and cheer for this slogan or for that, to see philosophers, teachers, and authors bullied and toiled to death in concentration camps, to be forced every hour to conceal the natural normal working of the human intellect and the pulsations of the human heart?

I say that rather than submit to such oppression there is no length we would not go to. Our cause is good. Our rights are good. Let us make sure that our conduct is wise. Let us make sure that it is governed by forethought and statesmanship.

The ordinary citizen cannot afford to neglect any precaution or with-hold any labour or sacrifice which is necessary to preserve the health and strength of institutions. We will not surrender the title deeds of individual rights for which uncounted generations of illustrious men and women have fought and conquered to the morbid regimentation of a totalitarian State, whether it be pressed upon us by force from without or by conspiracy from within. Free people are bound by nature and by history to be the foe of aggression and oppression, to the best of their ability and to the limits of their strength. We must take every step of policy, of self-discipline, and of heroic endeavour which circumstances may require to overcome dangers.

Good defences alone would never enable us by themselves to survive in the modern grim gigantic world. There must be added to those de-fences the power of generous motives and of high ideals; in fact, that cause of freedom, moral and intellectual, which I have endeavoured to describe. We must trust something to the power of enlightened ideas. We must trust much to our resolve not to be impatient or quarrelsome or arrogant. We desire faithfully and fairly to bear our part in building up a true collective security which shall not only lighten the burden of the toiling millions but also provide the means by which the grievances of great dissatisfied nations, if well founded, can be peacefully adjusted.

We are invited to believe that our only choice in political philosophy at present is between two violent extremes. We must, it seems, live either at the North Pole or at the Equator. Now I am for the temperate zone. Between the doctrines there ought to be room for you and me, and a few others, to cultivate opinions of our own. But it is the nature of extremists to be violent and furious, whereas the great central mass of temperate, tolerant, good-natured humanity is apt to be feeble in action and leadership.

But if the cause of ordered freedom, of representative government, of the rights of the individual against the State is worth defending it is worth defending efficiently. We are the guardians of causes so precious to the world that we must, as the Bible says, 'lay aside every impedi-ment' and prepare ourselves night and day to be worthy of the faith that is in us. Of this I am sure: If we do our duty fearlessly and tire-lessly in whatever station we stand, we will not easily be trampled down, nor the lights which freedom offers mankind be quenched in barbaric gloom. Liberty leads to licence, restraint to tyranny.

Although we praise and exalt the ideals of freedom, we do not seek to alter the system or government in any country. That is not our business as a nation, still less is it our business as a society. We wish to dwell in peace and good will with all. The liberties we are proud to regard as our birthright, and have been tenacious to defend, did not fall into our laps as a gift from the gods. Such liberties were painfully won over the centuries. Not one of them is enjoyed today by the serf-like citizens of countries under collectivist control. In all the societies around us we can see the difference. We have no affection for systems which concentrate excessive power over the lives and activities of citizens in the hands of a clique of Party doctrinaires who think they are super-men. The ordinary man wants nothing so much as to be left to go his own way, to get on with his job in life, to enjoy himself according to his own lights, to spend his own money as he thinks fit, to give his children a good home and a rather better start in life than he had himself, and to do his duty as a citizen to the community. This is the sort of life that our people seek. This is what they mean by freedom. It is common sense, and far removed from regimented Utopias.

I believe that the greatest days of that system of free enterprise which has done so much for the world during the last century lies in the future and not in the past. But the gains of tomorrow can be won only by thought and effort. Work and good will are still the keys that unlock the doors of wealth. The specious promises of the prophets of an un-earned plenty are a mirage which beckons and lures us, not to the millennial city, but into the deserts of disillusion and ruin. And perhaps we shall even lose our freedom on the way.

Looking back over the past we may see the milestones of Freedom: Magna Carta; the Habeas Corpus; the Bill of Rights; the abolition of Catholic and Jewish disabilities; the abolition of slavery and the forcible suppression of the slave-trade. And in our own time we have seen the vote given to everyone, the men and the women too: we have seen the barriers of privilege removed; we have seen liberal and social legislation. All this noble procession of thoughts and deeds has brought us today a fortune, an inheritence, a treasure, a trusteeship, which we must contemplate with awe, but also with pride. These glories con-stitute that good and broad estate which is ours and our children's, which we have not failed to guard.

We have still to guard it. There is our duty. There is the first of our responsibilities. We must not neglect the means to discharge it. We work – we work hard and patiently – to bring about a peaceful, tranquil, untroubled age. That is our wish: that is our intent: that is our policy. The freedom, the rights, the tolerances, the decencies, so slowly and painfully gathered by our forebears, must not lack vigilant and instructed defenders in whose hearts there burn the fires of yore.

We look forward to the day when the authority of all nations will be respected by every State and every Government. That is our aim, and we mean to do our part to bring about that supreme result. Our interests are in harmony with the general interest of many peoples. In all the coalitions or alliances or leagues of nations we have led in successive centuries against tyranny or military overlordship, we have always hitherto succeeded because our cause was inseparable from the cause of freedom and progress. Whenever we have strayed from this path, we have suffered. Not with our own strength, or for our own sake alone, shall we be able to guard our treasure or give forth our message. We can only march, with the larger hopes of mankind.

The Union Jack of Freedom will for ever fly from the white cliffs of Dover.

CHAPTER 8

Of The People, By The People, For The People

NOTHING IS MORE true than the saying: 'Every nation gets the Government it deserves'.

But whereas it takes many centuries to build up a good form of government resting on and expressing a decent human society, both may be thrown into confusion in a few disastrous months.

Our life and traditions have created parliamentary institutions which have spread in varying forms all over the world, and are still considered the best defence for the ordinary citizens and the best hope for social stability and economic well-being.

But shallow chatterboxes are ready to talk with fearsome levity about sweeping away the old-fashioned parliaments and erecting in their place some great, fine, vague new Thing or 'New Order' which will make everybody better off, and make all the work do itself.

Nations have been found ready to demolish the entire political structure of government under which they have dwelt, and to adópt entirely new methods, without the slightest attempt either to appraise the value of what they are throwing aside or to measure the future.

Many people, even in England, will speak of getting a different system of government with no more seriousness than they would bestow on choosing a new suit of clothes. 'We have had enough of the House of Commons and all that; let's try something else. So-and-So seems a good man: tell him to run the country and make it powerful and rich.'

For forms of government let fools contest,
Whate'er is best administered is best.

Yet these same forms of government have, from the dawn of civilisation, engaged at frequent intervals the thoughts and the passions of the leading races of mankind.

Despotisms, wise or wicked; monarchies, hereditary or elective republics and oligarchies of every character, together with interludes of democracy or mob rule, have filled the histories of every progressive people.

Always the constitutional instrument has been judged of supreme importance, and attempts to change it suddenly or drastically have usually been accompanied by the shedding of much blood.

Certainly, one would not feel that any nation would go far, or survive long, if it were careless or ignorant about the relation of its individual citizens to the State.

The first question which we must ask ourselves is: What kind of a life do we wish to lead in our brief span?

When we have made up our minds about this it will be much easier to judge the merits of various systems of government.

It should be noticed that up till this chaotic twentieth century the chief desire of all the noblest and most successful races has been to secure and preserve the rights and status of the individual citizen, and to protect him from the ambition, greed, malice, or caprice of rulers.

The original conception of these privileges, or some of them, was born in ancient Greece. They were practised in the classic days of Rome. They were trampled underfoot in the Dark Ages of brutish barbarism.

For more than a thousand years the whole world grovelled under dictatorships and tyrannies of absolute kings, soldiers, and priests.

But the inspiration lived while it slumbered. It revived again in this small island shrouded in the Northern mists.

Leaders arose who struggled and suffered. The rights and freedom of citizens or subjects were asserted, albeit in a primitive form, against arbitrary power. Parliament came into effective being. Wars were fought; battles were gained. Tyrants, or those who represented tyranny, were decapitated.

Very slowly, inch by inch, year by year, generation by generation, the rulers were taught that a new force had established itself.

Champions reached the summit of England – Oliver Cromwell,

William III, John, Duke of Marlborough – who by their swords made the system of free government resound with ringing blows upon the pates of the dictatorships of Europe, with their ground-down, miserable populations.

Fortune, or perhaps it was Almighty God, rewarded the prescient island.

For a long space the treasures of the New World, and of the future, were poured into its lap. Dazzling Empire came, and wealth and greatness to the land which was governed by law, and by debate in which many, and, indeed, ever-increasing numbers, took part.

The small country of four or five millions of people, which had repulsed the servitude to which the might of Spain would have condemned them, which broke the military and religious tyranny of Louis XIV, which – grown larger – faced, fought, and overcame the formidable splendour of Napoleon, emerged triumphant into the sun-lit glories of the Victorian era.

All this was gained because of a vigorous, active, law-making citizenship expressing itself through Parliament, and especially through to House of Commons, and by the fact that English people loathed and abominated one-man rule and tyrannies of every kind.

In the twentieth century came the great extensions of the franchise. We were told to entrust our liberties to democracy.

If every man and every woman had a vote there would be more freedom; there would be better government. Education – universal, compulsory, secular, free – would afford these vast masses the means of judging the problems of government.

It was a great hope. We must not lightly let it die. We must take effective means to realise it. But how melancholy it would be if, when everybody had the vote in England, all they did with it was to throw away the rights and liberties so painfully and nobly gained in three or four hundred years.

Surely these are matters worthy of the attention of young men and women of education and courage, determined to keep their country great?

But are Parliaments obsolete? Are they losing power, or is the public opinion which it expresses exerting itself in a different way?

The object of a Parliament is to substitute argument for fisticuffs, for Parliament is not only a machine for legislation; perhaps it is not even mainly a machine for legislation, it is a great forum of Debate. If it is not able to discuss matters which the country is discussing, which fills the newspapers, which everyone is anxious and pre-occupied about, it loses its contact; it is no longer marching step by step with all the thought that is in progress in the country.

It is remarkable that in recent years Governments have been changed in moments of crisis, not by a vote of the House of Commons, but by the working of vehement forces in the background.

Our institutions, threatened, on trial, and to some extent in eclipse in this harsh authoritarian world, depend for their life and vigour mainly upon good feeling and decent behaviour. This enables Parliament to rise to great occasions with a measure of unanimity, or at least of unity, which astonishes beholders.

The only foundations for good government and happy results to the people is a high standard of comradeship and fellowship between those who are called upon to handle their affairs.

When I think of all the ways there are in which men may be tampered with, it is reassuring to feel that Members of the House of Commons, to say nothing of Ministers of the Crown, stand high above all imputations upon their personal integrity. Here and there a case occurs, but is never concealed, and always hunted down. No one who understands what is going on and who has lived the life of the House of Commons will have any doubt that personal and sordid interests play no part either in its decisions or in its hesitancies. We may muddle, but we do not cheat.

Every Parliament is entirely free to behave like a gentleman or like a cad; every Parliament is entirely free to behave honestly or like a crook. Such are the sovereign rights of this august assembly. Nothing can bind it, and once a hue and cry is raised, once motives are impugned, once lists of names are circulated by rumour, and suspicion spreads on all sides, thoroughly legitimate actions or connections may be profoundly dangerous to a public man.

But there is always one sure defence for confident integrity: a modest, austere mode of living, domestic accounts which can be laid before the whole world, a proud readiness to account for every source of income.

When the pestilence of suspicion taints with its infecting breath on every side reputations are broken or assailed, and each falling man strives to drag down others. In the delirium of such days, the slightest contact with the guilty is held to compromise a public man.

Dark days, indeed, and leering triumphs of once-trampled foes!

As one who has spent the longest time in the cradle of Parliamentary

Government, I believe it to be the enduring guarantee of British liberties and democratic practices. The vitality and the authority of the House of Commons, and its hold upon an electorate based upon universal suffrage, depend to no small extent upon its episodes and great moments, even upon its scenes and rows. Destroy that hold which Parliament has upon the public mind and has preserved through all these changing turbulent times, and the living organism of the House of Commons would be greatly impaired. You may have a machine, but the House of Commons is much more than a machine; it has earned and captured and held through long generations the imagination and respect of the nation. It is not free from short-comings; they mark all human institutions. Nevertheless, I submit that it has proved itself capable of adapting itself to every change which the swift pace of modern life brought upon us. It has a collective personality which enjoys the regard of the public, and which imposes itself upon the conduct not only of the individual Members but of parties. It has a code of its own which everybody knows, and it has means of its own of enforcing those manners and habits which have grown up and have been found to be an essential part of our Parliamentary life. It is truly government of the people, by the people, for the people.

The House of Commons has lifted our affairs above the mechanical sphere into the human sphere. It thrives on criticism, it is perfectly impervious to newspaper abuse or taunts from any quarter, and it is capable of digesting almost anything or almost any body of gentlemen, whatever be the views with which they arrive. There is no situation to which it cannot address itself with vigour and ingenuity. It is the citadel of liberty; it is the foundation of our laws; its traditions and its privileges are as lively today as when it broke the arbitrary power of the Crown and substituted that constitutional monarchy under which we have enjoyed so many blessings. It has shown itself able to face the possibility of national destruction with classical composure. It can change Governments, and has changed them by heat of passion. It can sustain Governments in long, adverse, disappointing struggles through many dark, grey months and even years until the sun comes out again.

The twentieth century has been very hard towards Parliaments. Democracy seems inclined to maul and disdain the institutions to which its rights and liberties are due. I am deeply anxious that the walls shall not be undermined by slow decay or overthrown by violent battering-rams.

I believe in Parliamentary institutions as, upon the whole, the most tolerable form of Government for men and women, but I cannot be blind to the fact that Parliament has steadily declined in public repute. The tendency of political parties to discourage individual thought and independent views may suggest one reason for this; another may be found in the extension of the franchise to the utmost limits of adult suffrage.

When the vote was given to a few, all coveted it; when it was given to many, some coveted it. Now it is given to all, you cannot get them all to go to the poll. In every class in every rank and walk of life, in both sexes, there are large numbers of persons thoroughly capable of discharging electoral functions. But at the same time there are in every class large numbers who do not concern themselves with politics at all, and who are solely absorbed in the serious business of their own private lives and in the trifles which amuse their leisure. In consequence, the sustained discussion of great public questions of vital concern to our national fame and security does not proceed as it used to do.

The main issues of politics are not fought out inch by inch, and step by step, with the thoroughness and tenacity which characterised the controversies of our fathers or of our grandfathers or of our forebears running back into the past. A sort of universal mush and sloppiness has descended upon us, and issues are not brought to the clear-cut cleavages of former times.

In fact, we feel we are drifting and, in a sense, dissolving as we drift. The time has come when we should take more grip and when we should consider our institutions with a view to tightening and vitalising and bracing them. The time has come when we should endeavour to put some bone and structure in our political organism, and to make it more truly responsive to the national need.

So here you have what is called complete democracy and an assembly supposed to embody all the fruits of its wisdom and no opportunity, or very defective opportunities, for presenting issues to its judgment. That is very serious. It requires the deep attention of all those men and women who have what is called 'a sense of the State'.

But it will be said there remains the process of M.P.s and candidates and their backers boldly mounting the platform to harangue the crowd. In this way the public discussion of national issues will be maintained.

When I first went into politics there were 10,000 or 12,000 electors in a constituency. You could gather a very large proportion of them in a big hall. They could see you and you could see them. In an electoral campaign a member could easily address every person who meant to vote and wished to hear him. But that is a thing of the past. The number of voters in the modern constituency has extended far beyond the capacity either of the halls or of the speakers.

So there is no longer any real forum for the severe thrashing out of national affairs. At the same time, these national affairs, far from diminishing in importance, have greatly increased both in magnitude and in complexity.

If ever people ought to be thinking hard about their collective life future, it is in this present age. We are elevated on a high platform with enormous advantages, with a far-ranging vision, and, if we chose to use them, many hopeful opportunities for the future. But there we are, perched aloft, and the structure itself degenerating, loosening, crumbling. What are we going to do about it?

Should we not build watertight compartments in our ship of state which would increase its ability to resist storms and injury? Should we not draw to these new centres fresh streams of public and political capacity to enrich and nourish our parliamentary personnel?

What is the use of sending men and women to Parliament who just say popular things of the moment, and merely endeavour to give satisfaction by cheering loudly every platitude, and by walking through the lobbies oblivious to the criticisms they hear?

People talk about our Parliamentary institutions and Parliamentary democracy; but if these are to survive, it will not be because the constituencies return tame, docile, subservient members and try to stamp out every form of independent judgment.

What is the use of Parliament if it is not the place where true statements can be brought before the people? Woe betide those public men who seek to slide into power down the slippery slope of vain and profligate undertakings.

Here in this country, the forerunner of all the democratic and parliamentary conceptions of modern times, we in this country, who are very old at the game of party politics hard fought out, have learned how to carry through and debate great fiercely contested political issues, in spite of the fact that we do so knowing there is no gratitude in politics. But why should there be? No one who looks for gratitude deserves it. The reward is to be looked for not in people voting majorities to particular statesmen or parties, but in the general outlook and condition of the race.

Politics and party strife can be very exciting. Millions of people in the country follow it. All the 'stars' are known; their values and performances appraised from week to week. Politicians rise by toil and struggles. They expect to fall; they hope to rise again, and the struggles of politics are hard fought and sometimes bitter. Often their tumult echoes down the years. Death cannot still them, and a century or more after the actors in a great event have passed away, the pen of the historian may be steeped in gall of the partisan. It is therefore all the more remarkable that some of the fiercest political controversies of our time were so swiftly resolved. Party politics are necessary if a focused opinion is to be brought on public life. Party has a place in a nation, but people must see to it that the nation is not subordinated to the Party.

Supreme affairs should be, in Mr Gladstone's words, 'high and dry above the ebb and flow of party politics.'

I have always held the view that each of the great Parties has much to give to the service of the State, and that their conflict and alternations in power are necessary, except in times of great crisis, to the healthy working of our democratic parliamentary system.

The Party system is the dominant fact in our experience. Parties are associations of men, gathered to pursue common objects and principles and to defend common interests, and Party government is an outstanding feature of all branches of the English-speaking race all over the world. I know of no equal force which assures the stability of democratic institutions. I know of no other method by which enfranchised millions can be continuously attracted to practical things. I know of no other method by which small intrigues, small combinations, and petty personal rivalries can be prevented from swaying unevenly the course of public affairs.

As the oldest child of the House of Commons, I take the view that 'It is a fine thing to be Member of the House of Commons,' as John Morley said to me one day in the autumn of 1904. 'Look at this House,' he said, 'all the clever, ambitious fellows in the country trying to get into it, and everybody having a chance.'

I must say that in those days it seemed a thrilling thing to belong to this historic Assembly, which has shaped the development of all our free and friendly life, and has evolved constitutional ideas and gained great battles for principles which have spread all over the world and thrive among all English-speaking peoples.

I well remember the sense of mingled pride and awe with which I entered the House for the first time.

The tasks were inspiring and risks were small. In

> A land ...
> Where Freedom broadened slowly down
> From precedent to precedent,

there was an appointed place for the active Radical reformer. He did not fear the repression of autocratic power, nor the violence of revolutionary success. The world it seemed, had escaped from barbarism, superstition, aristocratic tyrannies, and dynastic wars.

There were plenty of topics to quarrel about, but none that need affect the life or foundations of the State. A varied but select society, observing in outward forms a strict, conventional morality, advanced its own culture and was anxious to spread its amenities ever more widely through the nation. The leadership of the privileged passed away.

The function of Parliament is not only to pass good laws, but to stop bad laws, and its duty is to sustain the Government or to change the Government. If it cannot change it, it should sustain it.

In the act of Parliament of 1919 where responsible government is mentioned in the preamble, there is a special clause, Clause 41, which makes it plain that all progress towards responsible government must only be at the discretion of Parliament, and that Parliament can, if it chooses, stop the progress, or slow it down, or turn it into another channel, or even retrace its path if that were necessary. Until another Act of Parliament, there is no ground whatever on which we are committed to any particular step at any particular time.

How do people feel about this? I am sometimes told that they do not care. If this is so, it would mean the great liner is sinking in a calm sea. One bulkhead after another gives way; one compartment after another is bilged; the list increases; she is sinking; but the captain and the officers and the crew are all in the saloon dancing to the band. But wait till the passengers find out what is their position.

Parliament can compel people to obey or to submit, but it cannot compel them to agree. If a Government is hampered by a small majority, it may be necessary to appeal to the electorate, but in general principle, I am not in favour of affairs being conducted with an eye to immediate electorial gain. Elections were made for Parliaments, not Parliaments for elections. It is not a good thing for any nation to be always living on the verge of a General Election. The weapon of a General Election is a process which should only be used sparingly. It is an intense political convulsion. It disturbs business; it frustrates economy; it poisons administration. Governments and administrations are always at their worst when they are standing on a trap door.

Despite its faults, Parliament is a living deathless entity which survived unflinchingly tests and hazards in a manner which has given us a sense of stability not only in this island, but as an example to the nations in many lands.

So is Parliament obsolete?

The question is asked so frequently in so many different quarters and in so many different countries that it deserves attentive consideration and careful answer.

We may ask, first of all, What are the alternatives? For more than three hundred years we have lived upon the basis of a representative House of Commons capable on the one hand of controlling, and if necessary changing, the Executive Government, and on the other hand of commanding the acceptance of its decrees by the nation as a whole.

Most people in our country, except extremists, have been for generations accustomed to bow to Parliamentary authority, whether it manifested itself in the shape of new laws or in the lawful administrative actions of the Executive; and thus Parliament has been and is still today the great sanction which associates the whole nation with the conduct of the State and binds every individual as a partner and a comrade, not as a servant or merely as a subject, to obey it and to sustain it.

It is obvious that the disappearance or obsolescence of an instrument so vital, which has played and is playing this supreme part, would oblige us immediately, unless we wished to degenerate into pure anarchy, to adopt some other alternative.

What then are the alternatives? There is really only one, although it may be clothed in many forms and many disguises, may use the most diverse extremes of language, may be erected on the most opposed views, namely, a Dictatorship. The reign of an absolute monarch ruling by right divine; the rule of a priest-craft entrenched in superstition, laying its fingers not only on the bodies but on the minds of its servants; the rule of a military caste with blaring bands and drill sergeants, and at its head some War Lord duly crowned; the rule of a caucus consisting of political sectaries banded together in the close confederacy of a common doctrine held and propagated with bigoted conviction – all these – and there are many others – are but variants of one and the same thing, a Dictatorship or Tyranny.

There are, of course, enlightened and scientific tyrannies capable of producing opulent results in the material sphere and of nourishing a very high degree of specialised culture. Such a tyranny led the German people along that path of ambition which shattered them and which came near to shattering civilisation. We were confronted with the monstrosity of the totalitarian State, All to think alike. No one to disagree. To point out an obvious mistake or miscalculation was to be convicted of heresy and treason. Every link with the past, even with the most glorious traditions was shivered. A despotism was erected.

Religion had to be read from the drill-book. Jews were baited for being born Jews. Little children insulted by regulation and routine on particular days of the week or of the month, appointed in the curriculum of the schools, to make these children feel the ignominy of the state of life to which the Creator has called them.

Christ, it appears, was born in Potsdam.

Venerable pastors; upright magistrates; world-famous scientists and philosophers; capable statesmen; independent-minded, manly citizens; frail, poor old women of unfashionable opinions, were invaded, bullied and brutalised by gangs of armed hooligans against whom mere resistance is a capital offence.

To be thought disloyal or even unenthusiastic to the regime, warranted indefinite bondage in an internment camp under persecutions which, though they may crush the victim, abase also the dignity of man.

Was there anything in all this which should lead us to repudiate the famous chain of events which made us what we are – to cast away Parliament, Habeas Corpus, rights, freedoms, tolerances, decencies?

There are crazy tyrannies producing nothing but cruelty and squalor and collapsing in the passage of time through their inherent vices in vermin, pestilence and famine.

And between these extremes are many intermediate forms; but, numerous as these forms may be, all proceed upon a common basis of thought, namely, that the Government owns the people, and may use them for their good or for their ill according to its liking; and all proceed on the same basis of action, namely, force and terrorism, open or veiled. As with the mental eye we survey them – majestic or sombre, scientific or frenzied – we can trace their common parentage from their lineaments under skins of every hue and in garbs of every age and land. Against this row of monsters there rose up more than three hundred years ago, an entirely different conception of the government of men which evolved itself painfully and perilously in the council chamber and on the battlefield. It liberated the consciences of men; it freed their speech; it freed their action; it freed their trade; it freed their Press. Reaching hands all over the world, it freed the slave. In successive centuries it was the main instrument which freed Europe. Though not always with the same success or in the same degree, it was imitated in every civilised land. Leaping across the Atlantic Ocean, it found a mighty ally in the new world. Up to the present it has proved unconquerable. Every antagonist has gone down before it. The mordant words of Pym – 'None have gone about to break up Parliaments but that Parliaments have broken them' – have stood against the storms and tumults and hazards of three centuries.

It must occur to everyone who reflects upon the prodigious events of modern history to ask himself: 'What is there in this Parliamentary instrument which has given it irresistible driving force to win such astounding victories and yet at the same time to afford a practical and even a prosaic means of dealing with so many changing situations?'

After all, the plan is a very simple one. Parliamentary government is government by discussion between duly and freely chosen representatives. One would hardly have thought that so innocent a process could have been strong enough to work the undoing of so many powerful foes and the overthrow of so many base systems. Yet there are the facts.

We see Charles the First, the most virtuous of tyrants, at the scaffold in Whitehall; and Napoleon, the most splendid, on the rock of St Helena; and Kaiser William, the most theatrical, cowering in his Dutch retreat. Then Hitler and Mussolini, and now, because of the despotic power in Moscow, vain doubting voices put the question:

'Are Parliaments played out?' It would be an ill day if they were.

We must buttress and fortify our ancient Constitution and make sure that it is not ignorantly or lightly deranged. What a lamentable result it would be if we squandered in a few short years, or even between some night and morning, all the long-stored, hard-won treasures of our civilisation. It must not be.

The contrast between freedom and Dictatorships of all kinds presents itself vividly to our eyes. We uphold the idea: 'Live and let live'. We show respect for Constitutional authority and for old customs. We hate regimentation. We believe in the advantages of variety, which alone can give scope to the measureless fertility of human contrivance.

Our system is the guarantee for all this. But we must not put too much strain on Constitutional institutions; that would be like putting too strong an electric current upon a cable. All that happens is that the cable fuses and the lights go out.

Parliament means a place where things are talked over. It presupposes a certain broad measure of agreement on fundamentals. It can deal only with things that are capable of being talked over. It would be impossible, for instance, to have a free and fair debate about whether one set of Members should kill the other set; about whether the Government should proscribe or imprison the Opposition, or vice versa. These matters do not lend themselves to speech: they belong to the sphere of violence.

If Parliamentary Government is to justify its name, it must be capable of preserving – if necessary by force – order within the agreed limits of the Constitution. A weak Parliament totters along until all the pillars of the State and of society have been undermined. It does not follow, however, that Parliaments cannot make great changes. They make them gradually, like Nature, which changes everything by steps which are barely perceptible to those who are being changed.

In the years in which I sat in Parliament I have seen a revolution as complete as any which the nineteenth century witnessed abroad. Everything changed except the benches.

We are told how the human body renews itself in the course of every seven years. Every scrap of the old fabric is worn out and replaced, and yet the living being goes on preserving his life upon new tissues and is unconscious that he has lost the old.

We have never been in the position of those trampled-down peoples of the Continent to whom Lenin said: 'You have nothing to lose but your chains.' Our democracy – old, instructed, fundamentally goodhearted – does not feel weighted down by chains, and treasures its rights and liberties. It does not require to be taught a lesson in self-government by people who have, until the nineteenth century, been serfs, and have done their best to make themselves serfs again.

The question which must present itself to every man and woman is how to vivify and sustain from generation to generation that system upon which freedom depends. For this purpose it is imperative that we should recognise and understand the dangers or causes of decay which threaten it. This is a period of men of action rather than of Parliamentarians. The swift rush of great and formidable events has absorbed the attention of the nation and the energies of its servants. No one can pretend that there has not been a decline in the personal distinction of the leading Parliamentary figures. The general average of ability and political knowledge is far higher probably than in the classic times of Pitt and Fox or the palmy days of Peel and Gladstone and Disraeli. But we cannot claim to have been able to fill what Lord Morley has called 'the vacant thrones' with House of Commons figures of the same commanding eminence. Still less can we rival their eloquence, their learning, or their mental force. Least of all can our debates compare with the earnestness and intensity of those famous discussions which riveted the attention of the Assembly through successions of grand continuous arguments lasting from dusk to dawn.

The vital strength of Parliaments depend upon their power to renew from generation to generation their hold upon the public mind by drawing to themselves a stream of men who, by their gifts, by their force, and by their virtues, are the true leaders.

But to say that Parliament needs strengthening is not necessarily to imply any censure upon its members. It is merely a recognition of the dangers in which our Parliamentary institutions stand and of the need for those who care about them, and about the life we have hitherto led in this country, to take effective steps in their defence.

Unless the reform and strengthening of Parliamentary institution is actively undertaken, we shall see ourselves involved in a succession of disastrous fluctuations attended by continual constitutional decay, and that the regeneration of the country and the establishment of sincere and vigorous government will be achieved through agencies very different from those which have hitherto been the peculiar glory and achievement of our island. The attitude of caution may bring about the very evils it was designed to avoid.

There are some who think that a system of proportional representation, securing as it probably would to eminent men a lifelong political association with great cities and centres of national thought, might invigorate and enrich the character of the House of Commons. There are some who think that a reconstituted and reformed Second Chamber would add elements of reinforcing strength. And certainly every political party which wishes to survive and aspires to guide the national fortunes should scour the land in search of earnest, brilliant youth to carry on the torch.

The hackneyed phrase, 'Measures not men', should not mislead us. Great measures require great men. The genius of the British people has always prompted them to trust and follow men, and to count more on leaders than on programmes.

With the enormous electorates of the present day, gathering their education and ideas from so wide an area and in such crude forms, we need the effective, faithful and united efforts of all true servants of the country to carry us safely along in the periods of rapid transition through which we are passing.

The fearful sacrifices of war, the stupendous victory, the triumph of institutions and ideals, have opened to us several generations of august responsibility and splendid hope. We shall need the united action of all healthy institutions if we are worthily to use the opportunity now in our hands.

There is another danger still more formidable and harder to remedy. Earnestly and patiently used, Parliamentary institutions are capable of presiding over and ushering in changes of an absolutely fundamental character, either in the political or the economic sphere, if such changes represent the settled wish of the nation. They are, however, only capable of accomplishing these great changes by an evolutionary process requiring time and growth, and paralysed by shock or over- turn. There comes a point in the disputes and agitations of men and classes in which argument breaks down and the resort to force super- venes.

There are grave dangers to a Parliamentary system through alter- nation between a party based on a Capitalistic Monarchy and one aim- ing at a Socialist Republic. We shall not evade such an issue by foment- ing unreal divisions between those who agree on fundamentals. On the contrary, we must look to their continued union for a means of pre- venting such a collision until the issue itself is softened by the general progress of our broadening civilisation.

We must not allow this issue to fall unmitigated upon Parliament. It must be fought in the first instance by argument, education and propa- ganda in every constituency, in every village, in every street. Thus Parliament must be shielded from a strain which, if brought too suddenly to bear upon it, might rupture fatally its power to guide events.

The amazing quality of Parliament is its power to digest, assimilate, conciliate, and tame all kinds of new elements. The Mother of Parlia- ments combines the fecundity of the rabbit with the digestion of the ostrich. But most of her progeny die of the diet, and already hardly any of the poor foreign sprigs survive.

In truth this method of governing by debate – i.e., by talking – can only continue where there is a balanced society and a basic acceptance of fundamentals. In theory the Socialist Party would repudiate both these factors. In practice and in a minority they have hitherto shown themselves strongly impressed by them.

The essence of the ancient procedure of Parliament was that it could always discuss whatever was troubling the nation. Countings of votes were few and far between, and always taken upon large points of principle. There was no idea of preventing the majority from legislating or from carrying through all their necessary financial business by setting in their path an endless series of minor obstacles. The ordinary routine business was disposed of with great rapidity, and Parliament devoted itself to its true function – namely, the discussion of all the burning questions which disturb the public mind. On any day upon the presentation of a petition the House could, if it chose, discuss the question of the hour. Meanwhile, it was understood that the Government, if not defeated on a question of principle, would have their Supply and all their necessary business.

Superior persons dwell upon the well-known weaknesses of democracy. Dictators never cease to deride free institutions, and no doubt democracy working upon a broad franchise is oppressed by many difficulties and risks. But is it not true, as was said in the past generation: 'The worst Chamber is better than the best ante-chamber'?

The House of Commons has recognised, to a large extent, its own limitations. It is a college in which Ministers are trained, and from which they are selected. It survives and flourishes at the head of all the parliamentary institutions of the world because, in interpreting the mandate it receives from the electors, it practises unfailing self-restraint.

How important this is to us all and to the age we live in ought to be widely realised. Parliament does not presume to govern the country. His Majesty's Ministers govern the country. The function of Parliament is to supervise, criticise, correct, sustain, or change the Government, and to lead the thoughts of the nation upon the politics of the day.

There is no greater guarantee of our liberties than the House of Commons. Go at Question Time and listen to all the highest Ministers of State being questioned and cross-questioned on every conceivable subject, and entering into the whole process with respect and with good will. Where else in the world can you see the representatives of democracy able to address the leading personages of a powerful Government with this freedom?

How foreigners gape at this performance when they visit the Gallery! In the vitality of the House of Commons, in its scenes, in its sensations, in its turbulences, in its generosity, and above all, in its native tolerance and decency, it is the august symbol and instrument of all that liberates and dignifies us. Ah! But guard these treasured privileges which are the envy of men of thought and culture in every quarter of the globe.

High-brow critics confronted with these facts say: 'Only the British people could make it work.'

If that be true, it is their trouble and not ours. I am full of confidence in the inherent health and vitality of our ancient institutions. What always strikes one in reading histories of the past is the failure of the sober, moderate, virtuous forces to act with vigour and, if need be, with violence against aggression. Repeatedly we see them talking while others are acting: in agreeable disorder while others are in grim array.

We hear the specious appeals and sometimes, even, clamours for the calm, strong man, and for autocracy in all its never-ending forms. But the lessons of Wars were that Parliamentary governments, if boldly led, can beat despots. It can be done. There is no need to alter our system of government. The flexible character of our Constitution enables necessary adjustments to be made from one generation to another in accordance with the needs and dangers of the times.

It would be possible to improve the system of electing Parliament so as to preserve and increase its hold upon national esteem without in the slightest degree endangering the foundations of our rights and liberties. But it is not only upon formal political safeguards that we should rely.

So long as reasonable time for consideration is assured, the genius and character of people will assert itself, and, provided fair and full opportunity of reflection and discussion is afforded them, we may trust in their judgment.

There was a time in bygone days when the growth of our fortunes depended upon mariners who scoured the seas, or upon adventurous commanders who gained great battles and territories. Those days are done. We seek no wars and no conquests. The only conquest we have to make is over ourselves. And shame it would be upon us if by mere vacuity of mind or discursiveness of purpose, or neglect of the instruments of government, we suffer their victories to be cast away.

CHAPTER 9

I'd Sooner Be Right
Than Consistent

IT IS BETTER to be both right and consistent. But if you have to choose – you must choose to be right.

I would sooner be right than consistent.

In the course of my life I often had to eat my words, and I must confess that I always found it a wholesome diet.

In the days of my youth I was much reproached with inconsistency and being changeable. Many many years later I was scolded for adhering to the same views I had in early life and even for repeating passages from speeches which I made long before most of you were born. Of course the world moves on and we dwell in a constantly changing climate of opinion. But the broad principles and truths of wise and sane political actions do not necessarily alter with the changing moods. What one man calls progress another will call reaction. If you have been rapidly descending the road to ruin and you suddenly check yourself, stop, turn back and retrace your steps, that is reaction, and no doubt your former guide will have every reason to reproach you with inconsistency.

Human judgment may fail you. You may act very wisely, you think, but it may turn out a great failure. On the other hand, one may do a foolish thing which may turn out well. I have seen many things happen, but the fact remains that human life is presented to us as a simple choice between right and wrong. If you obey that law you will find that that way is far safer in the long run than all the calculations which can ever be made.

In critical and baffling situations it is always best to recur to first principles and simple action. It is vain to imagine that the mere perception or declaration of right principles, will be of any value unless they are supported by those qualities of civic virtue and manly courage, and by those instruments and agencies of force and science which in the last resort must be the defence of right and reason.

When we reflect upon the magnitude of modern events compared with the men who have to try to control or cope with them, and upon the frightful consequences of these events on hundreds of millions, the importance of not making avoidable mistakes grows impressively upon the mind. Men may make mistakes, and learn from their mistakes. Men may have bad luck, and their luck may change.

I do not think it is a good thing to change one's party label, even when agreed on the merits, for the sake of getting a seat or office.

If a number of people are agreed upon some great issue, they can always work together sincerely and honestly, and due respect must be shown for the position of anyone who may be asked to be their representative.

People often mocked at me for having changed parties and labels. They said with truth that I had been Tory, Liberal, Coalitionist, Constitutionalist, and finally Tory again. But anyone who has read my account of my life with good will and fairness will see how natural, and, indeed, inevitable, every step had been. My views were a harmonious process which kept them in relation to the current movement of events.

My own feeling is that I was more truly constant than almost any other well-known public man, although I saw political parties change their positions on the greatest questions with bewildering rapidity.

We often see how quickly Fortune's wheel may turn this way or that without much relation to what one does oneself or to what people expect.

In this world of human error and constant variations, usually of an unexpected character, I had no need to recur for safety or vindication to that well-known maxim, or dictum, that 'Consistency is the last resort of feeble and narrow minds.'

No one has written more boldly on the subject of consistency than Emerson.

'A foolish consistency is the hobgoblin of little minds, adored by little statesmen and philosophers and divines . . .

'Speak what you think now in hard words and tomorrow speak

what tomorrow thinks in hard words again, though it contradict everything you said today.'

These are considerable assertions, and they may well stimulate thought upon this topic.

A distinction should be drawn between two classes of political inconsistency. First a statesman in contact with moving current of events and anxious to keep the ship on an even keel and steer a steady course may lean all his weight now on one side and now on the other.

His arguments in each case when contrasted can be shown to be not only very different in character, but contradictory in spirit and opposite in direction: yet his object will throughout have remained the same. His resolves, his wishes, his outlook may have been unchanged, his methods may be verbally irreconcilable.

We cannot call this inconsistency. In fact it may be claimed to be the truest consistency. The only way a man can remain consistent amid changing circumstances is to change with them while preserving the same dominating purpose.

Lord Halifax, on being derided as a trimmer, replied: 'I trim as the temperate zone trims between the climate in which men are roasted and climate in which they are frozen.'

It is inevitable that frequent changes should take place in the region of action. A policy is pursued up to a certain point; it becomes evident at last that it can be carried no further.

New facts arise which clearly render it obsolete; new difficulties, which make it impracticable. A new and possibly opposite solution presents itself with overwhelming force. To abandon the old policy is often necessarily to adopt the new.

It sometimes happens that the same men, the same Government, the same party have to execute this *volte face*. It may be their duty to do so because it is the sole manner of discharging their responsibilities, or because they are the only combination strong enough to do what is needed in the new circumstances.

In such a case the inconsistency is not merely verbal, but actual, and ought to be boldly avowed. In place of arguments for coercion, there must be arguments for conciliation; and these must come from the same lips as the former.

Questions of this kind depend on taking a just view of the actual and governing facts of different periods. Such changes must, however, be considered in each particular case with regard to the personal situation of the individual.

If it can be shown that he swims with the current in both cases, his titles to a true consistency must be more studiously examined than if he swims against it.

In all societies and in all times there is a pressure operative upon individuals to make them conform to the dominant tendencies. Within reasonable limits it is not an unhealthy pressure, but a statesman should always try to do what he believes is best in the long view for his country, and he should not be dissuaded from so acting by having to divorce himself from a great body of doctrine to which he formerly sincerely adhered. Policy proclaimed must, if possible, be carried to success – lasting success, although sometimes things can be done by saying 'Yes', and sometimes things can be done by saying 'No'. Yet there are times when so many things happen, and so quickly, and time seems to pass in such a way that you can neither say it is long or short, that it is easy to forget what you have said three months before. You may fail to connect it with what you are advocating at the particular moment. Throughout a long and variegated life this consideration led me to try and keep a watchful eye on that danger myself. You never can tell, for with opportunities comes responsibility yet how often has golden opportunity been allowed to slip away! How often have rulers and governments been forced to make in foul weather the very journey which they have refused to make prosperously in fair weather!

Of course, the world, nature, human beings do not move like machines. The edges are never clear-cut, but always frayed. The mind must weigh, balance, see both sides, especially all the flaws and faults in a case. I always tried to economise the use of false arguments as much as possible, because a false argument is so often detected, and it always repels any listener who is not already a convinced and enthusiastic partisan.

Consistency, like perseverance, is usually described as a great virtue, but perseverance with an eye on the future, perseverance towards a definite objective, is a great virtue; perseverance with an eye on the past is an equally serious vice.

Distinguished people get into positions which they cannot get out of by themselves. We often help them to get down off awkward perches. Evils can be created much quicker than they can be cured, and there are many who are ready to make great sacrifices for their opinions, yet have no opinions. They are ready to die for the truth, if they only knew what the truth was.

It is almost as if indiscretion were the secret of permanence, and distortion were stronger than truth. But perhaps it is merely that our enemies are more careful to preserve the memory of our mistakes than our friends to recall our wisdom.

We must not examine and weigh the life-impact of a man without comprehending his story. Biographers of eminent persons are prone to ignore or slur over harshly practical considerations. They have their value, however, in the career of any public man.

To the defence of his principles and prejudices, a man must summon every resource of conduct, oratory, and dialect. And he must know when to change, and not only when to change, but how to change in accordance with the irresistible pressures of events. Holding to his own convictions, steering always by the same stars, diverging only so far as inevitable under the thrust of adverse winds to move with the times.

Parties are subject to changes and inconsistencies not less obvious than those of individuals. How should it be otherwise in the fierce swirl of political and Electoral fortune? A sincere conviction, in harmony with the needs of the time and upon a great issue, will be found to override all other factors; and it is right and in the public interest that it should do so.

Nothing is more obvious in our public life than the failure of pretence, so it is very often unfair to accuse men of being 'Turncoats' when they change their minds, risk political friendships and position for their convictions, and cross from one side of the House of Commons to the other. The act of 'crossing the floor', as it is called, requires serious consideration. I am well informed on the matter, for I accomplished that difficult process not only once, but twice. I felt it my duty to cross this dreaded gulf of the 'floor' and to re-cross it when it seemed to me that it was right to do so.

But at all times, according to my lights and through the changing scenes through which we are all hurried, I always faithfully served two public causes which, I think, stand supreme – the maintenance of the enduring greatness of my country, and the historic continuity of our life.

Changes may be capable of reasonable and honourable explanation. Statesmen may say bluntly: 'We have failed to coerce; we have now to conciliate,' or alternatively: 'We have failed to conciliate; we have now to coerce.'

Ireland has been responsible for many changes of this kind in politics. In 1886, after five years of coercion and the fiercest denunciation of Irish Nationalists, Mr Gladstone turned in a month to those policies of reconciliation to which the rest of his life was devoted.

In his majestic and saintly manner, he gave many comforting and convincing reasons for his change, and there is no doubt that his whole nature was uplifted and inspired by his new departure. But behind all the eloquence and high-sounding declamation there was a very practical reason for the change which, in private at any rate, he did not conceal.

He held office with the support of the Irish vote, and so felt it impossible to march further along the path of coercion.

Through his miscalculation he gave to his opponents what was virtually a twenty years' reign of power. Nevertheless, the judgment of history will probably declare that he was right both in his resistance to a certain point, and then in his espousal thereafter of what he had previously opposed.

Few men avoid such changes in their lives, and few public men have been able to conceal them. The normal progression is from Left to Right, and often from extreme Left to extreme Right. Mr Gladstone's progress was a striking exception in the opposite direction. In the immense period covered by his life, he moved steadily from being 'the rising hope of stern, unbending Tories' to become the greatest Liberal statesman of the nineteenth century.

Enormous was the change of mood which this august transition represented. From the young Member of Parliament whose speech against the abolition of slavery attracted the attention of Parliament in 1833; from the famous Minister who supported the Confederate States against the North, to the fiery orator who pleaded the cause of independence and whose matchless strength was freely offered to the cause of Irish self-government. It was a transit almost astronomical in its scale.

It is a thankless theme to examine how far ambition to lead played its unconscious but unceasing part in such an evolution. Ideas acquire a momentum of their own. The stimulus of a vast concentration of public support is almost irresistible in its potency. The resentments engendered by the warfare of opponents, the practical responsibilities of a party leader – all play their part. And in the main, great numbers are at least an explanation for great changes.

It is evident that a political leader responsible for the direction of affairs must, even if unchanging in heart or objective, give his counsel now on one side and now on the other of many public issues. Take, for instance, the strength and expense of the armed forces of a country in any particular period. This depends on no absolute natural law. It relates simply to the circumstances of the time and to the view that a man may hold of the probability of dangers, actual or potential, which threaten his country.

Would there, for instance, be any inconsistency in a Minister urging the most extreme and rapid naval preparations in the years preceding the outbreak of a war, and advocating a modest establishment and strict retrenchment in the years following the destruction of the enemy's naval power?

He might think that the danger had passed away and had carried with it the need for intense preparation. He might believe that a long period of peace would follow the exhaustion of war, and that financial and economic recovery were more necessary to the country than continuous armed strength. He might be right and truly consistent both in the former and latter advocacy. But it would be easy to show a wide discrepancy between the series of argument he had used in the one period and the series on which he relied in the second.

A more searching scrutiny should also be applied to changes of view in relation not to events, but to systems of thought and doctrine.

We live in such a febrile and sensational age, that even a month or two is enough to make people not merely change their views, but to forget the views and feeling they entertained before. A Statesman should always try to do what he believes is best in the long view for his country, and he should not be dissuaded from so acting by having to divorce himself from a great body of doctrine to which he formerly sincerely adhered. Those, however, who are forced to these somewhat gloomy choices must regard their situation in this respect as unlucky.

A change of party is usually considered a much more serious breach of consistency than a change of view. In fact, as long as a man works with a party he will rarely find himself accused of inconsistency, no matter how widely his opinions at one time on any subject can be shown to have altered. Change with a party, however inconsistent, is at least defended by the power of numbers. And to remain constant when a party changes is to excite invidious challenge. Moreover, a separation from party affects all manner of personal relations and sunders old partisanship.

Politics is, upon the whole, a generous profession. The motives and characters of public men, though constantly criticised, are in the end broadly and fairly judged, but we should not shrink from fair criticism, for that is the most dangerous of all. Criticism in the body politic is like pain in the human body. It is not pleasant, but where would the body be without it? No health or sensibility would be possible without continued correctives and warnings of pain.

We are not judged by the criticisms of our opponents but by the consequences of our acts. I have been a critic myself. But there is a kind of criticism which is a little irritating. It is like a bystander who, when he sees a team of horses dragging a heavy waggon up a painful hill, cuts a switch from a fence and belabours them lustily. He may well be animated by a benevolent purpose, and who shall say the horses may not benefit from his efforts, and the waggon get quicker to the top of the hill?

I have derived continued benefit from criticism at all periods of my life, and I do not remember any time when I was ever short of it, although there sometimes steals across the mind a feeling of impatience at the airy and jaunty detachment of some of those critics who feel so confident of their knowledge and feel so sure of their ability to put things right. It is a fine thing to be honest, but it is also very important to be right.

Some kinds of criticism remind me of the simple tale about the sailor who jumped into a dock to rescue a small boy from drowning. About a week later this sailor was accosted by a woman who asked, 'Are you the man who picked my son out of the dock the other night?' The sailor replied modestly, 'That is true, Ma'am.' 'Ah,' said the woman, 'you are the man I am looking for. Where is his cap?'

CHAPTER 10

Words

WORDS ARE THE only things that last forever.

The most tremendous monuments or prodigies of engineering crumble under the hand of Time.

The Pyramids moulder, the bridges rust, the canals fill up, grass covers the railway track; but words spoken two or three thousand years ago remain with us now, not as mere relics of the past, but with all their pristine vital force. Leaping across the gulf of Time, they light the world for us today.

All the great things are simple, and many can be expressed in a single word: Freedom; justice; honour; duty; mercy; hope.

It is this power of words – words written in the past; words spoken at this moment; words printed in the newspapers; words sent speeding through the ether in a broadcast; the flashing interchange of thought – that is our principal agency of union. Its work must continue indefinitely – will continue, indeed, on an ever larger scale.

With every new school that is opened, with every book printed, with every improvement in travel, with every film, with every record, identity of language gathers greater power and applies its processes more often to people. Books in all their variety are often the means by which civilisation may be carried triumphantly forward, so one should enter the tabernacles of literature under a double dose of humility and awe which are proper. But it is not only the written word that counts. One of the most important things in the life of a great country is that no important transaction or episode of personal conduct should be left without the recording of a clear and measured judgment upon it, and nothing is more incalculable than the survival of the spoken word.

The history of every country abounds with brilliant and ready writers who have quailed and faltered when called upon to compose in public; or who have shrunk altogether from the ordeal. But the spoken word, uttered from the summit of power, should hold no terrors.

I always took immense trouble to prepare a speech, and by many repetitions, so engraved it upon my memory that I could reduce my notes to a very few cryptic signs and jottings.

There are three ways of making a speech. The first, and incomparably the best – indeed, one may say, the only one in which real quality resides – is to speak spontaneously. But the gift of composition, swift, easy, spontaneous, is the rarest and most valuable of all.

As the thought of the orator clothes itself with words and phrases, he seems to be conducting his audience upon a fascinating journey to some wonderful palace or castle, opening or half opening one door after another and closing them again, after displaying the treasures which the building contains; pointing here and there to the dungeons with their atmosphere of haunting tragedy, and finally bringing all who have followed him out of the front door with a sense of having spent a delightful hour.

The second method which I recommend to the average speaker is to have meditated long and carefully upon the structure of argument, and to have this argument with its heads and subheads carefully written down, and then to trust to the words as they come at the moment to carry one through. This is a fairly safe method; it does not often rise very high, but, on the other hand, one has not far to fall.

The third method is to have a full note of what you mean to say in the most attractive form which thought and preparation can give to it, and then be so familiar with the text that at times it seems to be coming out quite naturally. However, there are great dangers in this method, as I found once to my cost when I adopted it.

I was making a speech in favour of the rights of trade unions, and all was going very well and I had got to the end. I had not written out the closing sentence except for the words: 'It rests with those who . . .'

I thought I knew it so well that this clue would be sufficient, but, alas, at this culminating moment my memory failed me. I saw nothing but a blank beyond 'It rests with those who . . .'

Who 'they' were, and what 'they' were to do was completely lost.

Moreover, as it was the end of the speech one could not slur over this and get on to a new point. So after several prolonged pauses and repeated encouragements from the good nature of my audience, I had to sit down with the sentence unfinished.

Naturally all my political enemies said: 'There you are! He is breaking up already,' and some charitably suggested drink and others drugs, whereas the explanation was far less exciting.

I drew from this the moral never to make memorised speeches without a full note. If the memory fails, it is often impossible to start up the ordinary process of spontaneous composition.

It was my ambition all my life to be master of the spoken word. Of course you learn a lot when you have spoken publicly for as many years as I have, and as a result of my great experience, I was no longer afraid of saying something in the House of Commons which would get me into a hole. In my youth I was always fearing that.

The emergency and compulsion of public speech forces on you at high rate of speed, the exposition of thought. Short words are best, and the old words when short are best of all.

There are orators who, before they get up, do not know what they are going to say; when they are speaking, do not know what they are saying; and when they have sat down, do not know what they have said. They are decided only to be undecided, resolved to be irresolute, adamant for drift, solid for fluidity, all-powerful for impotence.

If it is thought there is nothing behind your words, when you are in fact in a position of greater danger yourself, not much attention is paid to what you say; the march of events takes place regardless of it.

There are also those who have the gift of compressing the largest amount of words into the smallest amount of thought.

One must never be afraid or ashamed of ramming home a point. It is reiteration which is important. One must never be shy of pressing home the great points of public controversy which make their appeal to common sense and conscience.

The greatest tie of all is language. There is nothing like it. Ancient alliances, solemn treaties, faithful services given and repaid, important mutual interests – not all of these taken together are equal, or nearly equal, to the bond of a common tongue.

Words and phrases derive their importance from the atmosphere of opinion in which they are breathed. The finest sentiments expressed in the happiest terms will be inaudible without the sounding board of human consciousness. A broadcast message, however important, however powerfully launched, only agitates the ether idly, unless millions of individual instruments are attuned to receive it. The moments when nations can speak to one another occur only at irregular and infrequent intervals. Such moments are precious, but also fleeting. They must not be wasted. During the last war, a wave of good will, welling from mysterious depths, swept across the continent. A keen, intense, and self-surprising glance of recognition, of kinship, of comradeship, of identification, flashed across the Atlantic to catch or kindle the answering light of other eyes.

What manner of men are we, what language do we speak, what laws do we follow, what books do we read, what tests do we apply to the problems of daily life, what songs do we sing, what jokes do we laugh at, what sports do we pursue? And the answer, at once obvious and wonderful, 'They are the same', grips, be it only with a momentary thrill, the hearts of vast communities. The sharp realisation of all we have in common is the dominant factor, and is only more remarkable and pregnant because it springs from nothing new or previously unknown.

Many events and causes have contributed to produce this situation. First among them all are the associations of the Great War, where, for the first time after so many generations of severance, all the English-speaking peoples found themselves in a common line of battle, and for the first time for a hundred and fifty years the two kindred nations had history to write in common. Apart from association in the field, valuable new ties were established between individuals throughout the wide spheres of munition supply, war finance, and diplomacy.

The gift of a common tongue is a priceless inheritance, and it may well some day become the foundation of a common citizenship. I like to think of British and Americans moving about freely over each other's wide estates with hardly a sense of being foreigners to one another. But I do not see why we should not try to spread our common language even more widely throughout the globe and, without seeking selfish advantage over any, possess ourselves of this invaluable birthright. So it is a relief to contemplate the majestic edifice of Anglo-American friendship. But let us not deceive ourselves. Look more closely. In places the facing stone has been eaten away by acids in the atmosphere. There are cracks in the pillars that support the mighty dome.

Pierce to the foundations. Beneath a crust that sometimes seems all too thin are bitter waters of suspicion, a marsh of misunderstanding. No one is really afraid that the building will collapse. Something stronger than any masonry holds it together – a cement of spirit. But it would be well to strengthen the foundations; to grout and bind and buttress till the great structure is indeed secure.

We can best serve the cause of Anglo-American friendship if we understand clearly the factors that threaten and diminish it. And to do that we must examine the past as well as the present. As a nation we have short memories. We fight and forget. But others remember.

The founders of America fled from Britain to escape persecution. Tyranny – or what can be more disastrous than tyranny, a purblind, pettifogging legalism – pursued them across the Atlantic. Taxed by men they had never seen, sitting in a Parliament in whose deliberations they had no voice, the descendants of the Pilgrim Fathers and the Virginian Cavaliers raised, together, the standard of revolt.

But we forget – and America remembers – that the first shots in the War of Independence were fired by British troops on men who offered no resistance. The long war, in which German mercenaries were lavishly, if unsuccessfully, employed, was ended by a grudging peace. Suspicion and bitterness remained.

France beheaded a King – and crowned an Emperor whose armies trampled the map of Europe. At death-grips with Napoleon, Britain blockaded the coast of the United States, seized American ships, and pressed American sailors into service on her men-o'-war. The resulting war of 1814 to 1815 was to Britain only a vexatious diversion. But it was a life-and-death struggle to the United States, and its incidents left an indelible impress on the American mind.

Indian tribes fighting as allies of England, killed and ravaged. Fort Dearborn, on the site where Chicago now stands, was stormed by painted savages and the entire garrison massacred. Women and children were murdered. A British fleet sailed up the Potomac to Washington, burned the Capitol and the Government offices and the President's house.

It is doubtful if one in ten thousand of our population has ever heard of that raid of reprisals. But we should remember – vividly – for centuries after the event, if London were even for a day, in the hands of an American force that destroyed Buckingham Palace, the Houses of Parliament, Whitehall, and Downing-street.

True, we should also remember the strong ties of blood and race that bound the Americans and ourselves. But might not these make the injury all the worse?

In the American Civil War, again, it seemed to the North that we thought more of cotton than of principles. A majority of Englishmen, including Mr Gladstone, believed that it was impossible to maintain the Union by force of arms, and were prepared – at any rate at one point in the struggle – to recognise the Confederate States.

There was a moment when Britain and America almost blundered into a war which would inevitably have established the independence of the South and perpetuated the shame of slavery.

During the early stages of the first World War, many awkward incidents arose from differing interpretations of neutral rights. But for the U-boat campaign and its atrocities, the blockade of Germany might have led to a grave crisis in Anglo-American relations.

In the long series of quarrels and disputes, Britain was not always in the wrong, nor America always in the right. Usually, at the root of our differences there was the clash of incompatible rights, or sheer misunderstanding. We have done terrible things to each other through misunderstanding. Odious chapters of our common history are stained with blood and the hatreds that are fed by blood.

Wrongs, revenges, insults, calumnies, battles and executions crowd the pages, with noble, suffering, or conquering figures silhouetted against the dull red haze. To us, however, these conflicts have, as a rule, been side issues. That has helped us to forget. And sometimes we have wanted to forget because we were ashamed. But America was concerned more vitally, and some of the most glorious episodes of her history are bound up with these tragic happenings. So Americans have a double reason to remember, and the words of history books help them to remember.

The cheers of vanished armies, the rumbling of long-silenced cannonades, still come down to them today.

Turn from those old unhappy events to our present situation. Although the ideals of the two countries are similar, their interests in some respects diverge. Their industries are competitive in the world market. Every instinct of America is to keep out of European affairs; Britain cannot do so even if she wished.

We must remember that for over a century America has attracted immigrants not only from Britain, but from all Europe. There is a great German population in the Middle West. Swedes and Italians are to be found everywhere. Practically every nation on earth has contributed to this vast melting-pot. These foreign elements learn to speak English, but will they think English thoughts?

Though those of European stock are fused into the nation of their adoption and become 'hundred per cent Americans', it can only be by processes which tend to separate the American mind from ours.

Another factor – though, happily, fading – must be taken into account: the powerful and highly-organised Irish-American community. Many of them have taken with them across the ocean a burning and deep-rooted hatred of the English name. Of great practical force was the removal from American politics of the Irish question. The slow, virulent poison distilled against Great Britain for more than a century suddenly exhausted itself. The great mass of Irishmen in the United States accepted the Irish Treaty as a full and lasting settlement. They gladly absorbed themselves in the general issues of American politics and in an expanding prosperity.

The professional hate-manufacturer was at a loss to find either the patrons or the materials for his wares. The politics of a hundred cities were simultaneously freed from an element of jarring and extraneous bias. A purely American outlook superseded and overrode this dismal particularism. The change was widespread and swift, and its consequences unceasing.

When we talk of collaboration and the bond of words between the two great branches of the English-speaking peoples, and of Anglo-American friendship, these are facts which we must face. Otherwise we shall merely be repeating our wishes in the form of platitudes. Yet, when all has been urged and weighed, it still remains true that the conceptions which unite us are incomparably stronger than those that divide; that they are vital, not morbid; that they embrace the future rather than the past.

The mischances of history have riven and sundered us, but our roots lie deep in the same rich soil. The great Republic of the West, no less than the British and the Commonwealth, sprang from the loins of Shakespeare's England. The beginnings of American history are to be found, not across the Atlantic, but where the Thames flows between green lawns and woodlands down to a grey sea.

Britain and America are joint sharers in a great inheritance of law and letters. Our political institutions, under the mask of outward difference, bear the marks of a common origin and a common aim, and today our countries are among the last great strongholds of Parliamentary government and individual liberty. We keep alight the torch of Freedom. These things, and our words are a powerful incentive to collaboration.

With nations, as with individuals, if you care deeply for the same things, and these things are threatened, it is natural to work together to preserve them. Of course, there is the other side. There is always the other side. A common language may become a vehicle of quarrel.

I remember that sometimes trouble arose in France between British and American soldiers that would not have arisen had one party been French or Belgian. But such troubles blow over. They are, no doubt, to be expected after so many generations of misunderstanding. As British and American troops stood in the line together, shoulder to shoulder in a common cause, the bitterness gradually melted away. So far as these men were concerned the sponge was drawn across the scores of the past.

It is for us to see that this lever of common language is rightly used. We must employ it to explore and, so far as possible, compose the differences between us, and to bring to the surface our underlying identity of outlook and purpose. Above all, we must use it to understand each other.

We, on this side of the Atlantic, know too little of American history. Not only are we ignorant of the full extent of our past quarrels with the United States, but we have only the most superficial comprehension of that great Westward drive which carried civilisation across a Continent. We have heard of Buffalo Bill, and, thanks to films, we have been introduced to Wild Bill Hickock, but we see the story through a reducing-glass. The Odyssey of a people has been an individual adventure; the epic has been dwarfed to the proportions of a fairy-tale.

We talk glibly of the Monroe Doctrine, but how many of us understand its words? How many of us realise that for over a hundred years the United States has been the guarantor of the whole of the Western Hemisphere against aggression from without? Such is the practical effect of the Monroe Doctrine.

I should like to see American history taught in our schools concurrently with our own Island story. Washington, Hamilton, Jefferson, Jackson, Adams, and Marshall – these men, soldiers, statesmen, lawyers, made a nation. They fashioned the instruments of government and established broad lines on which American politics were to develop. But when they leave the stage, the searchlight of history wheels – save for the years of the Civil War – to the struggle to subdue and utilise a Continent. That struggle has necessarily and rightly taken the first place in the life of the American people.

We, in this country, must try to understand all these things, just as we must seek to correct American misconceptions of Britain, and there are many ways in which both countries might, with advantage, learn from each other.

It is encouraging that so many American books are read in England and so many English books in America. The literature of a nation is the best interpreter of its spirit. Reading each other's books, we come to appreciate more clearly our fundamental kinship, and to see our differences in true perspective. The most common form of diversion is reading. In that vast and varied field millions find their mental comfort. Nothing makes a man more reverent than a library. 'A few books,' which was Lord Morley's definition of anything under five thousand, may give a sense of comfort and even of complacency.

But a day in a library, even of modest dimensions, quickly dispels these illusory sensations. As you browse about, taking down book after book from the shelves and contemplating the vast, infinitely-varied store of knowledge and wisdom which the human race has accumulated and preserved, pride, even in its most innocent forms, is chased from the heart by feelings of awe not untinged with sadness.

As one surveys the mighty array of sages, saints, historians, scientists, poets and philosophers whose treasures one will never be able to admire – still less enjoy – the brief tenure of our existence here dominates mind and spirit.

Think of all the wonderful tales that have been told, and well told, which you will never know. Think of all the searching inquiries into matters of great consequence which you will never pursue. Think of all the delighting or disturbing ideas that you will never share. Think of the mighty labours which have been accomplished for your service, but of which you will never reap the harvest.

But from this melancholy there also comes a calm. The bitter sweets of a pious despair melt into an agreeable sense of compulsory resignation from which we turn with renewed zest to the lighter vanities of life.

'What shall I do with all my books?' was the question; and the answer, 'Read them,' sobered the questioner. But if you cannot read them, at any rate handle them and, as it were, fondle them. Peer into them. Let them fall open where they will. Read on from the first sentence that arrests the eye. Then turn to another. Make a voyage of discovery, taking soundings of unchartered seas. Set them back on their shelves with your own hands. Arrange them on your own plan, so that if you do not know what is in them, you at least know where they are. If they cannot be your friends, let them at any rate be your acquaintances. If they cannot enter the circle of your life, do not deny them at least a nod of recognition.

It is a mistake to read too many good books when quite young. A man once told me that he had read all the books that mattered. Cross-questioned, he appeared to have read a great many, but they seemed to have made only a slight impression.

How many had he understood? How many had entered into his mental composition? How many had been hammered on the anvils of his mind and afterwards ranged in an armoury of bright weapons ready to hand?

It is a great pity to read a book too soon in life. The first impression is the one that counts; and if it is a slight one, it may be all that can be hoped for. A later and second perusal may recoil from a surface already hardened by premature contact.

Young people should be careful in their reading, as old people in eating their food. They should not eat too much. They should chew it well.

Since change is an essential element in diversion of all kinds, it is also naturally more restful and refreshing to read in a different language from that in which one's ordinary daily work is done.

To have a second language at your disposal, even if you only know it enough to read it with pleasure, is a sensible advantage.

Our educationalists are too often anxious to teach children so many different languages that they never get far enough in any one to derive any use or enjoyment from their study. The boy learns enough Latin to detest it; enough Greek to pass an examination; enough French to get from Calais to Paris; enough German to exhibit a diploma; enough Spanish or Italian to tell which is which; but not enough of any to secure the enormous boon of access to a second literature.

Choose well, choose wisely, and choose one. Concentrate upon that one. Do not be content until you find yourself reading in it with real enjoyment. The process of reading for pleasure in another language rests the mental muscles; it enlivens the mind by a different sequence and emphasis of ideas. The mere form of speech excites the activity of separate brain-cells, relieving in the most effective manner the fatigue of those in hackneyed use.

One may imagine that a man who blew the trumpet for his living would be glad to play the violin for his amusement. So it is with reading in another language than your own.

For all classes the need of an alternative outlook, of a change of atmosphere, of a diversion of effort, is essential. Indeed, it may well be that those whose work is their pleasure are those who most need the means of banishing it at intervals from their mind.

A man may acquire great knowledge of topics unconnected with his daily work, and yet hardly get any benefit or relief.

It is no use doing what you like; you have got to like what you do.

A man's education should be the guiding line for the reading of his whole life, and I am certain that those who have made good use of their studies will be convinced of the importance of reading the world's great books and the literature of their own land. They will know what to read and how to understand it. He who has received a good education possesses a rich choice. He need never be inactive or bored, there is no reason for him to seek refuge in the clack and clatter of our modern life. He need not be dependent on headlines which give him something new every day. He has the wisdom of all time to drink from, to enjoy so long as he lives.

There is a good saying to the effect that when a new book appears one should read an old one. As an author I would not recommend too strict an adherence to this saying. But I must admit that I have altered my views about the study of classical literature as I have grown older. At school I never liked it. I entirely failed to respond to the many pressing and sometimes painful exhortations which I received to understand the full charm and precision of the classical languages. But it seems to me that should classic studies die out, a unifying influence of importance would disappear.

But reading and book-love are only one aspect of the use and importance of words. The best of British and American films carry this work of mutual illumination a stage further, although direct personal contact is still of the first importance. We cannot dispense with it. Every year thousands of Americans come to this country. As yet, we do not return these visits to a sufficient extent. But increasing numbers of our people are learning the delights of travel, and its field widens every year. Look forward to the day when British holidaymakers who now spend weeks on the Continent, will be able to visit America with equal ease. I can conceive of nothing better calculated to remove prejudices. Ties are formed strong enough to defy time and distance. We cherish pleasant memories of American homes, and they of ours.

Such friendships make a notable contribution to the cause of Anglo-American understanding. It is in the homes, not the hotels, of a nation that we each can learn the truth about our people.

In various ways the two great divisions of the English-speaking race may be drawn close together. Private contacts and friendships between individuals, by increasing the area of understanding and good will, pave the way for a closer understanding between the two nations and their Governments, with all that this would mean to the peace of the world, and there is nothing in such an understanding that need arouse fears elsewhere. Collaboration of the English-speaking peoples threatens no one. It might safeguard all.

In spite of all impediments, Britain and America have never been closer in aim and purpose, or nearer to full mutual understanding. Events and causes worked silently but ceaselessly beneath the uneven and often changing surface of American sentiment. They had the effect of liberating, or rendering more powerful, strong elements traditionally friendly to us. Powerful groups of newspapers which for years indulged merrily and profitably in the pastime of 'twisting the lion's tail', now advocated close co-operation of the English-speaking peoples to promote the peace of the world.

If leaders faithfully try to understand each other's point of view and clearly expose all the facts, set in their proper proportion, to the judgment of their countrymen, then no harm can come to Anglo-American friendship. Let them therefore lay their difficulties soberly and amicably before each other. Let them not hesitate to state the causes of any soreness or complaint which may arise. Let them meet as friends, and not as rivals, to make agreements which shall secure the strength and safety of each and the partnership of both in the maintenance of world peace, for law, language, literature, are considerable factors. Common conceptions of what is right and decent, a marked regard for fair play, especially to the weak and poor, a stern sentiment of impartial justice, and above all the love of personal freedom – these are common conceptions on both sides of the ocean among the English-speaking peoples.

Our ways have diverged in the past. I believe that, increasingly, they will be together in the future. We shall certainly follow the path of our joint destiny more prosperously and far more safely, if we tread it together like good companions, understanding each other's words, and making the best use of our priceless common bond – our language.

CHAPTER II

Peering Through A Glass Darkly

A HOPEFUL DISPOSITION is not the sole qualification to be a prophet.

It is a rash man who tries to prophesy. Although it is always wise to look ahead, it is difficult to look further than you can see.

The human story does not always unfold like an arithmetical calculation on the principle that two and two make four. Sometimes in life they make five or minus three; and sometimes the black-board topples down in the middle of the sum and leaves the class in disorder and the pedagogue with a black eye. The element of the unexpected and the unforeseeable is what gives some of its relish to life and saves us from falling into the mechanical thraldom of the logicians.

While only astrologers and other merchants of superstition declare the future, I believe only one link in the chain of destiny can be handled at a time.

I usually avoided prophesying because it is much better policy to prophesy after the event has already taken place.

It is only by studying the past that we can foresee, however dimly, or partially, the future. It may well be that it is only by respecting the past that we can be worthy of the future, and we cannot say 'the past is the past' without surrendering the future.

'Let the great world spin for ever down the ringing grooves of change,' as Tennyson said many years ago. Let us have no fear of the future. Wherever you go you need have no fear.

When you are doing your duty and you are sure of that, you need not worry too much about the dangers or consequences. We do not need to be deterred from action by pictures which our imagination or careful forethought paint of what the consequences would be.

I know of nothing more remarkable than the willingness to encounter the unknown, and to face and endure whatever might be coming.

It is our duty to peer through the mists of the future, and to try our utmost to be prepared by ceaseless effort and forethought for the kind of situations which are likely to occur.

You cannot tell from appearances how things will go. Sometimes imagination makes things out far worse than they are; yet without imagination not much can be done. People who are imaginative see many more dangers than perhaps exist, certainly many more than will happen; but then they must also pray to be given that extra courage to carry this far-reaching imagination.

The most wonderful of all modern prophecies is found in Tennyson's 'Locksley Hall'.

For I dipt into the future, far as
   human eye could see,
Saw the Vision of the world, and all
   the wonder that would be;

Saw the heavens fill with commerce,
   argosies of magic sails,
Pilots of the purple twilight,
   dropping down with costly bales;

Heard the heavens fill with shouting,
   and there rain'd a ghastly dew
From the nations' airy navies
   grappling in the central blue;

Far along the world-wide whisper
   of the south wind rushing warm,
With the standards of the peoples
   plunging thro' the thunder-storm;

Till the war-drum throbb'd no longer,
   and the battle-flags were furl'd
In the Parliament of man,
   the Federation of the world.

Slowly comes a hungry people,
as a lion creeping nigher,
Glares at one that nods and winks
behind a slowly dying fire.

These six stanzas of prediction, written well over a century ago, have been fulfilled. The conquest of the air for commerce and war, the world struggle of Armageddon, the League of Nations and United Nations, the Bolshevik revolution – all divined by the great Victorian – all now already in the history books and stirring the world around us today! We may search the Scriptures in vain for such precise and swiftly vindicated forecasts of the future. Jeremiah and Isaiah dealt in dark and cryptic parables, pointing to remote events and capable of many varied interpretations from time to time. A Judge, a Prophet, a Redeemer would arise to save his chosen People; and from age to age the Jews asked, disputing 'Art thou he that should come? or look we for another?' But 'Locksley Hall' contains an exact foretelling in their sequence of stupendous events, which many of those who knew the writer lived to see and endure! The dawn of the Victorian era opened the new period of man; and the genius of the poet cast back the curtains which veiled it.

There are two processes which we adopt consciously or unconsciously when we try to prophesy. We can seek a period in the past whose conditions resemble as closely as possible those of our day, and presume that the sequel to that period will, save for some minor alterations, be similar. Secondly, we can survey the general course of development in our immediate past, and endeavour to prolong it into the near future. The first is the method of the historian; the second that of the scientist. Only the second is open to us now, and this only in a partial sphere. By observing all that Science has achieved in modern times, and the knowledge and power now in her possession, we can predict with some assurance the inventions and discoveries which will govern our future. We can but guess, peering through a glass darkly, what reactions these discoveries and their applications will produce upon the habits, the outlook, and spirit of men.

The great mass of human beings absorbed in the toils, cares, and activities of life, are only dimly conscious of the pace at which mankind has begun to travel. We look back a hundred years and see that great changes have taken place. We look back fifty years and see that the speed is constantly quickening. This century has witnessed an enormous revolution in material things, in scientific appliances, in political institutions, in manners and customs.

The greatest change of all is the least perceptible by individuals; it is the far greater numbers which in every civilised country participate in the fuller life of man. 'In those days,' said Disraeli, writing at the beginning of the nineteenth century, 'England was for the few, and for very few.'

'The twice two thousand for whom,' wrote Byron, 'the world is made,' have given place to millions for whom existence has become larger, safer, more varied, more full of hope and choice. In the United States scores of millions have lifted themselves above prime necessities and comforts, and aspire to culture. Europe, though stunned and lacerated by Armageddon, presents a similar advance. We all take the modern conveniences and facilities as they are offered to us, without being grateful or consciously happier. But we simply could not live if they were taken away. We assume that progress will be constant.

'This 'ere progress,' H. G. Wells makes one of his characters remark, 'keeps going on.' It is also very fortunate; for if it stopped, or were reversed, there would be a catastrophe of unimaginable horror.

Mankind has gone too far to go back, and is moving too fast to stop.

There are too many people not merely whose comfort, but whose very existence is maintained by processes unknown a century ago, for us to afford even a temporary check, still less a general setback, without experiencing calamity in its most frightful forms.

When we look back beyond one hundred years over the long trails of history, we see immediately why the age we live in differs from all other ages in human annals. Mankind has sometimes travelled forwards and sometimes backwards, or has stood still for hundreds of years. It remained stationary in India and China for thousands of years. But now it is moving very fast.

What is it that has produced this new prodigious speed of man? Science. Her groping fingers lifted here and there, often trampled underfoot, often frozen in isolation, are now a vast organised, united army marching forward on all fronts towards objectives none may measure or define. It is a proud, ambitious army which cares nothing for all the laws that men have made; nothing for their most time-honoured customs, or most dearly-cherished beliefs, or deepest instincts. It is this power called Science which has laid hold of us, conscripted us into regiments and batteries, set us to work upon its highways and in its arsenals; rewarded us for our services, healed us when we were wounded, trained us when we were young, pensioned us when we were worn out. None of the generations of men before the last two or three were ever gripped for good or ill, and handled like this.

We all speak with great respect of science. Indeed, we have to. One of my great friends, Lord Hugh Cecil, defined science as organised curiosity.

Man in the earliest stages lived alone and avoided his neighbours with as much anxiety and probably as much reason as he avoided the fierce flesh-eating beasts that shared his forests. With the introduction of domestic animals, the advantages of co-operation and division of labour became manifest. In neolithic times, when cereals were produced and agriculture developed, the bleak, hungry period, whilst the seeds were germinating beneath the soil involved some form of capitalism and the recognition of those special rights of landed proprietors, the traces of which are still visible in our legislation. Each stage involved new problems, legal, sociological, and moral. But progress only crawled, and often rested for a thousand years or so.

The two ribbon states in the valleys of the Nile and the Euphrates produced civilisations as full of pomp and circumstance and more stable than any the world has ever known. Their autocracies and hierarchies were founded upon the control and distribution of water. The rulers held the people in an efficiency of despotism never equalled till Soviet Russia was born. They had only to cut off or stint the water in the canals to starve or subjugate rebellious provinces. This gave them powers at once as irresistible and capable of intimate regulation as the control of all food supplies gives to the Bolshevik commissars. Safe from internal trouble, they were vulnerable only to external attack.

But in these states man had not learned to catalyse the forces of Nature. The maximum power available was the sum of the muscular efforts of all the inhabitants. Later empires, scarcely less imposing, but far less stable, rose and fell. In the methods of production and communication, in the modes of getting food and exchanging goods, there was less change between the time of Sargon and the time of Louis XIV, than there was between the accession of Queen Victoria and the early thirties of this century. Darius could probably send a message from Susa to Sardis faster than Philip II could transmit an order from Madrid to Brussels. The bathrooms of the palaces of Minos were superior to those of Versailles. A priest from Thebes would probably have felt more at home at the Council of Trent two thousand years after Thebes had vanished, than Sir Isaac Newton at a modern undergraduate physical society, or George Stephenson in the Institute of Electrical Engineers. The changes have been so sudden and so gigantic, that no period in history can be compared with the past century. The past no longer enables us even dimly to measure the future.

Whereas, formerly, the utmost power that man could guide and control was a team of horses, or a galley full of slaves; or, possibly, if they could be sufficiently drilled and harnessed, a gang of labourers like the Israelites in Egypt, it is today possible to set off with one finger an explosive capable in an instant of destroying the work of thousands of man-years. These changes are due to the substitution of molecular and nuclear energy for muscular energy, and its direction and control by an elaborate beautifully perfected apparatus.

These immense sources of power, and the fact that they can be wielded by a single individual, made possible novel methods of mining and metallurgy, new modes of transport, and undreamed-of machinery. These, in their turn, enabled sources of power to be extended and used more efficiently. They facilitated the improvement of ancient methods. They substituted turbo-generators at Niagara for the mill-wheel of our forefathers. Each invention acted and reacted on other inventions, and with ever-growing rapidity, the vast structure of technical achievement was raised which separates the civilisation of today from all that the past has known.

The long ages of uniformity in technique, production, and commerce accompanied long stationary periods in which social and political institutions were immune from any cataclysmic change.

The accumulation of knowledge proceeds on the principle of compound interest; the more we have, the faster it grows.

Many of the stresses which make the world so anxious today arise from the fact that our system and institutions have not had time to adapt themselves to the vast changes which have actually taken place.

After this backward glimpse, let us scan the future.

In the fires of science, burning with increasing heat every year, all the most dearly loved conventions are being melted down, and this is a process which is going to continually spread.

There is no doubt that this evolution will continue at an increasing rate. We know enough to be sure that the scientific achievements of the next fifty years will be far greater, more rapid, and more surprising than those we have already experienced. The slide-lathe enabled machines of precision to be made, and the power of steam rushed out upon the world. And through the steam clouds flashed the dazzling lightnings of electricity. But this was only a beginning. Nuclear energy is incomparably greater than molecular energy. The coal a man can get in a day can easily do five hundred times as much work as the man himself. Nuclear energy is vastly more powerful, and there is no question that gigantic untapped sources of energy exist. It can scarcely be doubted that a way to induce and control these will be found.

The new fire is laid, but the particular kind of match is missing. But it will be found.

If and when these sources of power become available our whole outlook will be changed. Geography and climate, which have conditioned all human history, will become our servants rather than our masters. The changing of one element into another could transform beyond all description our standards of values. Immensely strong materials will create engines fit to bridle the new forms of power. Communications and transport by land, water, and air, will take unimaginable forms if, as is in principle possible, we make an engine carrying fuel for a thousand hours in a tank the size of a fountain-pen.

The struggle for life is unceasing. There is no easy or pleasant road. It is uphill all the way. But give science its chance! Create conditions of confidence and good will! Without these wealth and well-being will forever elude the clutching hand. With them it will soon be found that there is plenty of room and plenty of food for all mankind.

Science which now offers us a golden age with one hand, offers at the same time with the other the doom of all that we have built up inch by inch since the Stone Age and the dawn of any human annals. My faith is in the high progressive destiny of man. I do not believe we are to be flung back into abysmal darkness by those fiercesome discoveries which human genius has made.

Up till recent times the production of food was the prime struggle of man. That war is won. There is no doubt that civilised races can produce or procure all the food they require. Food is at present obtained almost entirely from the energy of sunlight. The radiation from the sun produces from the carbonic acid in the air more or less complicated carbon compounds which serve us in plants and vegetables. We use the latent chemical energy of these to keep our bodies warm, we convert it into muscular effort. We employ it in the complicated processes of digestion to repair and replace the wasted cells of our bodies. Many people, of course, prefer food in what the vegetarians call 'the second-hand form', i.e., after it has been digested and converted into meat for us by domestic animals kept for this purpose. In all these processes, however, ninety-nine parts of the solar energy is wasted for every part used.

Even without new sources of power great improvements are certain here. New strains of microbes will be developed and made to do a great deal of our chemistry for us. With a greater knowledge of hormones, the chemical messengers, it will be possible to achieve greater control of growth. Nor need the pleasures of the table be banished. That gloomy Utopia of tabloid meals need never be invaded. New synthetic foods can be practically indistinguishable from the natural products, and any changes so gradual as to escape observation. With gigantic sources of power, food can be produced without recourse to sunlight.

It also seems very probable that methods may be discovered to enable one to dispense without strain with sleep for days or weeks on end, and to take it in doses of any convenient length when the time can be spared.

After all, many animals can go into cold storage for the winter, and there seems no reason why it should not be possible to extend this comfortable escape from reality to humanity at large. Indeed, it is conceivable that those who desire it will be able to have themselves put on the shelf for ten or fifteen years to be resuscitated according to instructions, and make a fresh start on some given date without having grown any older in the interval.

Here would be a good way to save money. But alas, what happens if the Communists get hold of it while Rip Van Winkle is asleep?

Many of our problems today are due to the increased span of life to which we can all look forward. This tendency may well increase. We may imagine the difficulties and complications which will arise if it becomes possible for people not only to extend their life to 120 or 150 years, but to take it in instalments so that one person may be sometimes older or sometimes younger than the other in the years they have actually used. The possibility of systematic interference with the human mind is beginning to become apparent in many parts of Europe. But this science is only in its infancy. The influence of great preachers and orators has frequently been somewhat disparagingly attributed to mass suggestion. When all modes of communication are centralised and all information is canalised, no great oratorical power is required to produce the same effect.

The Jesuits said: 'If you give me a child for its first five years, I do not mind who has him afterwards.'

Scientific suggestion in the first few years of an infant's life would probably give a bend to the mind that nothing later could eradicate. In the hands of a ruthless dictatorship these possibilities are exploited. To those of us who believe that progress depends upon individuals rather than that individuals exist for the State, the results will be appalling.

But the arguments are plausible, and in many countries not even arguments are tolerated before new scientific possibilities are put into action.

Awful developments are already just beyond our fingertips in the breeding of human beings, and the shaping of human nature. It used to be said, 'Though you have taught the dog more tricks, you cannot alter the breed of the dog.' But that is no longer true.

There seems little doubt that it will be possible to carry out in artificial surroundings the entire cycle which now leads to the birth of a child. Interference with the mental development of such beings, expert suggestion and treatment in the earlier years, would produce beings specialised to thought or toil.

The production of creatures, for instance, which have admirable physical development, with their mental endowment stunted in particular directions, could result in a being produced capable of tending a machine, but without other ambitions.

Our minds recoil from such fearful eventualities, and the laws of a Christian civilisation will prevent them. But might not lop-sided creatures of this type fit in well with doctrines with aims to produce a race adapted to mechanical tasks and no other ideas but to obey the State?

The present nature of man is tough and resilient. It casts up its sparks of genius in the darkest and most unexpected places. But Robots could be made to fit grisly theories.

I have touched upon this sphere only lightly, but with the purpose of pointing out that in a future which our children may live to see, powers will be in the hands of men altogether different from any by which human nature has been moulded.

Explosive forces, energy, materials, machinery are available upon a scale which can annihilate whole nations. Despotisms and tyrannies can prescribe the lives and even the wishes of their subjects in a manner never known since time began.

If to these tremendous and awful powers is added the pitiless sub-human wickedness which we now see embodied in powerful reigning Governments, who shall say that the world itself will not be wrecked, or, indeed, that it ought not to be wrecked?

There are nightmares of the future from which a fortunate collision with some wandering star, reducing the earth to incandescent gas, might be a merciful deliverance.

It is indeed a descent almost to the ridiculous to contemplate the impact of the tremendous and terrifying discoveries approaching upon the structure of institutions. How can we imagine the whole mass of the people being capable of deciding upon the right course to adopt amid these cataclysmic changes? Too many governments drift along the line of least resistance, taking short views, paying their way with sops and doles, and smoothing their path with pleasant-sounding platitudes, and yet towards them are coming changes which will revolutionise for good or ill not only the whole economic structure of the world, but the social habits and moral outlook of every family. The future of invention is uncommonly difficult to predict. It is like forecasting the winner of the Derby. If one knew what was going to be invented one would patent it and become a millionaire. But perhaps we can draw some conclusions from what has happened in the past.

When we speak of invention we mean generally the application of some well-known scientific principle to produce something which will be of use in everyday life.

Invention is the stage between the discovery of the fundamental scientific principle and the industrial production and distribution of the article in question.

Thus the inventor need not be a great scientist; indeed, he seldom is.

A great scientist is a man who hews new pathways through the jungle of our ignorance; who discovers new phenomena and new theories to interpret them.

The inventor is the man who realises that such pathways lead to delectable places and paves and drains them.

Then comes the producer, who floats a company, puts up a turnstile, runs a tourist service, and makes the profit.

Around the middle of the last century Joule, a great English scientist, discovered the fact that an electric current passing through a wire caused the wire to grow hot.

He measured the amount of heat produced and related it exactly to the resistance of the wire and the voltage of the battery he used.

It was only a generation later that Swan and Edison realised that this fact could be utilised to produce 'electric light'.

A great deal of patient investigation was required before they found methods of producing thin carbon threads and passing the current through them in a vacuum glass bulb, thus preventing the air getting to them and burning them up.

Better substances and better arrangements have since been found.

But the immense electric light industry, producing billions of bulbs every year and employing scores of thousands of men, all dates back, in the first place, to Joule's observation that wire could be made red-hot in this manner; and in the second, to Swan and Edison, who realised that this fact might have an industrial application.

Be it observed that there were many croakers, who pointed out how foolish the latter proposal was. And really their arguments sound conclusive.

This method, they said, first uses heat from coal to work a steam-engine; then it uses the steam-engine to drive a dynamo and make electricity; then, finally, it uses the electricity to heat a wire – what a roundabout performance! Losses are bound to occur at each stage. Surely it must be more economical to use gas, which one gets from the coal directly.

But they had forgotten the convenience factor; the advantage of being able to switch on the light instead of having to light the gas.

The question so familiar to inventors was asked, 'Will the public pay for this convenience?' The public answered, 'Yes, please.' Otherwise we might still be using coal gas.

The best-known example, of course, is the origin of radio.

Some years ago Maxwell predicted, on the basis of the electro-magnetic theory, that waves in the ether, which we now call 'wireless waves' existed.

It is years since the German Jewish physicist Hertz produced them in the laboratory, and sent wireless signals some score of yards from one end of the lecture theatre to the other.

The methods of detecting the incoming signals at that time were crude, though they were shortly afterwards improved by the invention of the coherer by the French professor, Branley.

Still, nobody considered these matters had any practical importance; they were merely interesting ways of demonstrating in a laboratory the truth of Maxwell's theories.

It was, of course, the young Italian, Marconi, who shortly afterwards had the idea that these wireless waves could be put to military and commercial use for sending signals in cases where it was not possible to lay wires or cables.

He was laughed at and discouraged at first, but his enthusiasm prevailed over every obstacle. He was helped by a piece of good fortune.

'Your process,' he was told, 'can never work over great distances, because the earth is not flat. Your waves cannot go through the solid earth. Mountains will get in the way, and, even where there are no mountains, over the sea and the plains the earth's surface bulges out thirty miles between two stations a thousand miles apart.'

This seemed to settle it, but it was here that Marconi's stroke of luck came in. The upper atmosphere reflects these waves.

Just as we could see over a mountain if we could fix a looking-glass in the sky, so, owing to the reflecting nature of the upper air, can wireless signals be transmitted over the Alps, or over the bulging contours of the world.

Fortunately, Marconi, unlike most inventors, was a business man. He was rewarded not only with honours but with cash.

But it is a chastening thought that for every man who has heard of Maxwell or Hertz there must be 10,000 who have heard of Marconi.

Another example which springs to the mind is the genesis of the radio valve.

One or two physicists in their laboratories measured how much electricity leaked away on to a metal plate from a wire heated in a vacuum. A dull and uninteresting investigation it seemed, even to some of their colleagues.

It was only a great many years later that it occurred to some inventors (it is, perhaps, safer to name no names, as there has been much patent litigation on these topics) that one could put a grid between the hot wire and the plate which would let more or less of the electricity from the filament through to the plate according to its own electric charge.

This was a magnificent device. It was like being able to turn a tap on or off.

Quite a small change in the charge on the grid made a tremendous difference in the amount of electricity reaching the plate. This, briefly, is the radio valve.

Then someone realised these valves could be used in series. The plate of one valve could be connected to the grid of a second valve so that the process of amplification could be repeated, not once only, but again and again. The trickle could be converted into a cascade. All our radio, our cinema films, and a great fraction of modern electrical technique depended upon this invention.

The scientist who discovered the phenomenon and established the laws governing it, gained practically nothing from it. The original inventor of the valves, it is to be hoped, did better.

These examples show that the successful inventor is a man who can sense the need which the science of the day is capable of meeting, rather than a man of extraordinary scientific capacity.

For it is one of the features of our time that there is often a great lack of contact between those who know what is wanted and those who could tell them how to do it.

On reading that a certain invention has been made, many scientists can say how it works. They can see at once that it is useful; but it never entered their heads to design that particular thing.

In war, particularly, the fighting men do not know how to specify in simple language what it is they want done for them.

If this were just perceived and stated, it would probably be easy for Science to supply it.

The invention of the tank arose from a correct visualisation of a war need. Until this was understood, the various inventors stood idle.

The difficulty about establishing contact is that those people who realise and ought to tell the inventor what is wanted must have a sufficient smattering of science to be able to see whether it is a reasonable proposal they are making or not. Merely recognising 'a long-felt want' is not enough.

One scientist I know was approached in the first World War and asked to invent a dark ray.

On asking what was meant, he was told that it ought to be possible to make a ray which, when thrown upon an aeroplane, would render it invisible in the same way as a searchlight beam rendered it visible.

No doubt such a ray would be very nice, but anybody with the most superficial knowledge of physics can see at once that it is simply silly to ask for such a thing.

But never mind; always ask. Ask for what you want. Seek and you shall find. If you don't find one thing, sometimes you find another.

It costs little to ask, and very often a terrible price has to be paid for just sitting about gaping.

Another very distinguished physicist was once approached by an individual who asked him for a little scientific help in putting the finishing touches to an invention he had made.

On being asked what it was, he told the scientist, under promise of the deepest secrecy, that it was a machine which would convert the spoken word into the written word, i.e., one dictated into it and it typed one's words upon paper.

On being asked how he proposed to make such a machine, he said that this was precisely the trifling difficulty which he wished the physicist to solve!

It is well to remember the gulf that exists between a man of science and the man in the street.

The man of science can say at once that many suggestions are ridiculous; but how ridiculous the ordinary Victorian would have considered it if he had been told that his son could carry about a little box which would play or sing or repeat the news to him wherever he happened to be!

The only thing to do if we wish to have here and there a glimpse of the future of invention seems to be to take one or two scientific phenomena and principles which have recently emerged and which do not seem to have been applied to anything in particular, and to try to imagine to what possible uses they might be put.

If we knew, of course, we should make the invention and our fortune. We can but guess.

Certain it is that while men are gathering knowledge and power with ever-increasing and measureless speed, their virtues and their wisdom have not shown any notable improvement as the centuries have rolled. The brain of a modern man does not differ in essentials from that of the human beings who fought and loved here millions of years ago. The nature of man has remained hitherto practically unchanged. Under sufficient stress – starvation, terror, warlike passion, or even cold, intellectual frenzy – the modern man we know so well will do the most terrible deeds, and his modern woman will back him up.

At the present moment the civilisations of many different ages coexist together in the world, and their representatives meet and converse. Englishmen, Frenchmen, or Americans with ideas abreast of the twentieth century, do business with Indians or Chinese, whose civilisations were crystallised several thousands of years ago.

We have the spectacle of the powers and weapons of man far outstripping the march in his intelligence; we have the march of his intelligence proceeding far more rapidly than the development of his nobility.

We may well find ourselves in the presence of 'the strength of civilisation without its mercy'.

It is, therefore, above all things, important that the moral philosophy and spiritual conceptions of men and nations should hold their own amid these formidable scientific evolutions. It would be much better to call a halt in material progress and discovery rather than to be mastered by our own apparatus and the forces which it directs.

There are secrets too mysterious for man in his present state to know; secrets which once penetrated may be fatal to human happiness and glory.

But the busy hands of the scientists are already fumbling with the keys of all the chambers hitherto forbidden to mankind.

Without an equal growth of Mercy, Pity, Peace, and Love, Science herself may destroy all that makes human life majestic and tolerable. There never was a time when the hope of immortality and the disdain of earthly power and achievement were more necessary for the safety of the children of men.

After all, this material progress, in itself so splendid, does not meet any of the real needs of the human race. I read a book which traced the history of mankind from the birth of the Solar system to its extinction.

There were fifteen or sixteen races of men, which in succession rose and fell over periods measured by tens of millions of years. In the end a race of beings was evolved which had mastered nature.

A State was created whose citizens lived as long as they chose, enjoyed pleasures and sympathies incomparably wider than our own, navigated the inter-planetary spaces, could recall the panorama of the past and foresee the future.

But what was the good of all that to them? What did they know more than we know about the answers to the simple questions which man has asked since the earliest dawn of reason – 'What is the purpose of life?'

No material progress, even though it takes shapes, we cannot now conceive, or however it may expand the faculties of man, can bring comfort to his soul.

It is this fact, more wonderful than any that science can reveal, which gives the best hope that all will be well.

Projects undreamed of by past generations will absorb our immediate descendants; forces terrific and devastating will be in their hands; comforts, activities, amenities, pleasures will crowd upon them, but their hearts will ache, their lives will be barren, if they have not a vision above material things.

And with the hopes and powers will come dangers out of all proportion to the growth of man's intellect, to the strength of his character or to the efficacy of his institutions.

There is a general opinion, which I have noticed, that it would be a serious disaster if the particular minor planet which we inhabit blew itself to pieces, or if all human life were extinguished upon its surface, apart, that is to say, from fierce beings, armed with obsolescent firearms, dwelling in the caverns of the Stone Age. There is a general feeling that that would be a regrettable event. Perhaps, however, we flatter ourselves. Perhaps we are biased, but everyone realises how far scientific knowledge has outstripped human virtue. We all hope that men are better, wiser, more merciful than they were 10,000 years ago. There is certainly a great atmosphere of comprehension. There is a growing factor which one may call world public opinion, most powerful, most persuasive, most valuable. We understand our unhappy lot, even if we have no power to control it.

On many occasions in the past, we have seen attempts to rule the world by experts of one kind and another. There have been theocratic governments, military governments, and aristocratic governments. It is now suggested that we should have scientistic – not scientific – governments. It is the duty of scientists, like all other people, to serve the State and not to rule it because they are scientists. If they want to rule the State they must get elected and so gain access to administrations formed.

It is arguable whether the human race have been gainers by the march of science beyond the steam engine. Electricity opens a field of infinite conveniences to ever greater numbers, but they may well have to pay dearly for them. But, anyhow, in my thought I stop short of the internal combustion engine which has made the world so much smaller. Still more must we fear the consequences of entrusting to a human race so little different from their predecessors of the so-called barbarous ages, awful agencies as the atomic bomb.

Give me the horse.

The choice is offered between Blessing and Cursing. Never was the answer more hard to foretell.

I am a pessimist about the wisdom with which human affairs are conducted, but an optimist about the ways they work out in the end. Who can tell towards what experiences we are being hurried? Where shall we be this time next year? What Government will be in power? What Prime Minister will tender his counsels to the Crown? Have we any assurance that any forecast, however shrewdly and profoundly judged today, will not be stultified before a year – nay, before six months are past? Even in most precise and definite matters it is found impossible to measure the future with any approach to truth. Things turn out neither so well nor so badly as we expect them. Widely different standards of values govern public opinion as each particular set of circumstances comes into being; and always the finger of Caprice, the nimble workings of Chance, the long arm of Coincidence, the trip of Accident, are busy with the levers of life's machinery.

An American writer on nervous diseases drew a clear and just distinction between what he calls 'Fearthought' and 'Forethought'. Fearthought is a futile worry over what cannot be averted or will probably never happen. Forethought is taking the best means at one's command to ward off perils or surmount them if they come.

What we need is vigilance and preparation without panic, and cool heads with cold hearts or cold feet.

And would we know the future if we could? Could we avert or change our destiny if we knew? Wise was the ancient saying: 'Call no man happy till he is dead.' Suppose we were offered just one single, partial, fleeting peep at the future. Suppose one little fragment of futurity was suddenly placed before us, would it be of any help or guidance? A book lies on my table on whose cover is printed the following words:—'My Memoirs. By ex-Kaiser Wilhelm II.' Suppose the German Emperor, one afternoon in 1913, strolling through the library in one of his palaces, and casually reading the titles of the books which filled the shelves, had happened to cast his eye on the cover of this volume. Suppose by an ancestral manifestation it had been placed there for his warning, would he have bettered his position? We can see him in imagination snatching the book from its place: 'A practical joke! An impudent trick! Lèse majesté. Bring the librarian here. What is this insult? Find me the culprit or your place will answer for it.'

We can see him when the trembling official had withdrawn, scornful, disquieted, none the less curious, opening the offending book –

only to find that its pages were blank and awaiting the labour of their Imperial author. Still, we may suppose it would have stuck like a thorn in his memory. The more the idea was put away, the more it would return to his mind. Suppose even he had accepted the revelation as true, and had believed that his splendid reign of power was fated to end in deposition and exile, would it have made any difference to the course which he pursued in European politics? Would it have led him to avoid the war which was his ruin? It is as likely as not that it would only have fortified at every step the decisions which he actually took.

As the pressure of the Socialist forces in Germany upon the Imperial Government grew steadily stronger, he might have said to himself: 'If this goes on the warning will come true. A war is the remedy for these revolutionary dangers. In the midst of my armies I shall be safe, and victory over the French will secure for the Prussian Monarchy a vast renewal of power.' When the Austrian Archduke was assassinated at Sarajevo he would have said: 'This cannot be tolerated. If potentates are to be murdered or overthrown like this, my turn will come and the warning will come true. The Austrians must make an example of Serbia while time remains.'

When on the very verge of war he learned that England would be among his foes and wished to stop at the eleventh hour, and when the Generals made it plain to him that to impede or dislocate the mobilisation of the German Army would involve the downfall of the Hohenzollerns, he would have said to himself that this was no doubt the moment for which the warning was intended. 'I will be strong and ruthless like Frederick the Great. There is nothing for it but to hack a way through.'

The pressures which are operative on persons in the highest station are so complex, so enveloping and so continuous that their actions are, to a very large extent, extorted from them by the force of events. Even if they knew their fate, they would not know which step to take to escape it. Let us turn the glass the other way round.

A friend of ours, a Mr Timmins, was cast away on a remote uninhabited but fertile atoll in the Pacific in June 1914. He managed to subsist in tolerable health for over ten years. He had no connection with the outside world. One day a bottle was washed up on his island from the ocean, which contained some pages of a newspaper published in Australia a few months before.

Mr Timmins devoured the columns from end to end, advertisements and all. There was a great deal about sport. There was much about the money market. There were reviews of several books and plays. There was a debate in the Commonwealth Parliament, somewhat mutilated. A large portion of the space was occupied by the headlines of an astonishingly brutal murder. There was an extract from an article on the decline of British manhood and physical courage. There was a leader on the quarrels between Ulster and the rest of Ireland about some obscure parishes in Fermanagh and Tyrone. This subject appeared to be causing intense political excitement in the Mother Country. Neither Irish party seemed to be willing to entertain any suggestion of compromise, and all English politicians were accordingly preparing to line up for battle on one side or the other.

Mr Timmins had been a keen politician in England before he started on his ill-fated voyage, so this part of the newspaper therefore excited his interest in a most powerful degree. He made the solitudes about him ring with laughter as he reflected on the extraordinary pertinacity of the Irish character, whether Orange or Green, Protestant or Catholic, which had been able to keep exactly the same controversy at the same pitch of keenness and fury for a period of more than ten years, and keep the great British nation convulsed with it all the time. After spending two days and the greater part of two nights in reading and reflecting on the treasure of knowledge which had come so suddenly into his possession, he formed the conclusion that everything was going on exactly the same in England as when he left it; that no events of any importance had occurred to disturb the ordinary flow of British life; and that the Irish still continued to dominate the situation with their quarrels about the parishes of Fermanagh and Tyrone.

There was only one paragraph in the whole paper which he could not understand. It read as follows: 'Anzac Day. Sir Ian Hamilton, unveiling the Memorial to Australians and New Zealanders who lost their lives at the Dardanelles, said –'. At this point, however, the print was so stained by sea water as to become illegible. Mr Timmins took nearly three weeks to puzzle over this, and at last he formed the following opinion: A cricket or football team from Australasia had gone to England for a season's play, and either on the outward or homeward journey had in some way or other been drowned in the neighbourhood of the Dardanelles.

He rested entirely content with this solution, until a few days later a ship hove in sight and relieved him from his long lonely sojourn. For the first few hours after he was rescued he was so overjoyed that he did not trouble to ask questions about what had happened at home during his exile. It was only the next morning that he said to the captain: 'Do tell me about the Australian cricket team that was drowned at the Dardanelles.' The captain did not understand him, and Mr Timmins showed him the mutilated paragraph which he still had upon him.

'Why,' said the captain, 'don't you know that there has been a great world war; that more than ten million men were killed and twenty millions wounded; that one-third of the whole wealth of the world was spent; that Britain won and Germany was beaten; that Australia sent more than half a million soldiers to fight in Europe; that all the Empire stood together like one man; that at the end America came in and helped too; that the war ended in the greatest victory ever won by arms; that it was a war fought to end wars once and for all, and that the League of Nations has now been established to prevent all quarrels between States, great or small? Didn't you know any of this?' 'Dear me,' said Mr Timmins, 'I never should have thought that anything like this had happened from reading the papers.'

It is very difficult to pierce the veil of the future, but have no fear of it. Go forward into its mysteries; tear aside the veils which hide it from our eyes, and move onward with confidence and courage.

CHAPTER 12

Transatlantic Travels And Thoughts:
My Two Countries

IT IS SURELY an elevated prospect which opens to those who are born into the English-speaking world.

Spread wide around the globe and in possession of many of its fairest regions and main resources, are more than 150 millions of men and women speaking the same language, sprung in an overwhelming degree from a single origin, nursed by the same Common Law, and nourished and inspired by the same literature.

Such a vast community abounding in wealth, power and progress, and enjoying liberal and democratic institutions and representative government, constitutes incomparably the largest and most harmonious grouping of the human race which has appeared since the zenith of the Roman Empire.

Although riven by the mischances of history and sundered into two branches, their joint inheritance of law and letters, the crimson thread of kinship, the similarity of their institutions, far outweigh the discordances and even antagonisms of politics, the rivalry of flags, the variants of climate, interest and environment.

Noble, indeed, is the opportunity of life offered to a citizen of this great common body. He moves with ease and very little sense of alienation across enormous distances, and unpacking his gripsack at a thousand centres of industry and culture, finds himself very speedily almost at home.

In dwelling, therefore, upon the differences which time, events, and climate have wrought in the mentality of the various branches of the

English-speaking world, it is, above all things, important to remember that these divergences are far less in volume and importance than the ties of union of homogeneity.

The social life of the United States is built around business.

In Europe the numerous aristocracies overthrown but still influential, the ancient landed families, the hierarchies of the Army, the Navy, Diplomacy, the Law and the Church, frame and largely fill the old-world picture.

Successful business men in Europe find a Society ready made for them. They are welcomed to circles which, especially in England, existed many years before their fortunes were made or the processes and machinery which they direct were devised.

In the United States, on the other hand, the struggle to subdue and utilise a continent has taken the place of dynastic religious and class controversies. It has absorbed the life of the American people.

Everything else falls into a somewhat remote background; and business, commerce, money-making in all their forms, occupy the centre of the stage.

Business dominates the scene and itself gives the reception to which the leaders and members of the services and the professions are cordially invited.

By 'society' I do not, of course, mean the gay world of fashion and amusement. In America as in other countries that is no more than an adjunct and a diversion.

The society which guides and governs the United States is based not on play, but on an intense work which takes from its votaries a first charge on all their thought and energy.

From the innumerable universities all their young men go into business as a matter of course. Business is to them the means of earning their living, of making money, of making a fortune; but it is much more than that, it is that career of interest, ambition and possibly even glory which in the older world is afforded by the learned professions and State services, military and civilian.

A young American wishing to play a worthy part in the control of affairs directs himself instinctively towards the managing of factories, railroads, stores, banks or any other of the thousand and one varieties of American business life.

Practically all the prizes of American life are to be gained in business. There, too, is the main path of useful service to the nation.

Nearly all that is best and most active in the manhood and ability of the United States goes into business with the same sense of serving the country as a young Prussian before the Great War entered the Army, or as a son of a noble house in England in former times sought to represent a family borough in the House of Commons.

The leading men of every State in America are all in business. Their businesses are interlaced, they compete, they collide, they overlap. A continued struggle proceeds, but under rules which, though unwritten, are getting stronger every year.

American industry is greatly the gainer from its power to attract practically all the vital elements in the nation.

It is the gainer also in an increasing degree from the intimate combination in every stage between business and social life.

For the leaders of business are also the leaders of society. They are gregarious, they band themselves together in groups, in clubs, in organisations. They do not only work together, they play together. They develop a strong corporate life carrying with it a continual rising standard of discipline and behaviour.

In every state and city they and their families are the nucleus of the local life, and in New York, where to a very large extent everything takes place on a super scale, the leading business men are the leading figures of the whole nation.

There has developed a confraternity the members of which help one another and stand together and certainly have a far higher sense of comradeship and association than exists in business circles in England.

Very often it is at the golf club, or the country club, or across a private dinner-table that the foundations of the largest transactions are laid.

It is very important, therefore, in American business circles to be a member of the club or to be a welcome guest at the dinner, to be popular, trusted, and thought a genial companion and a good sportsman.

Of course no convention prevents anyone entering and succeeding in business – if he has the qualities and the luck for making a fortune. It is done every day.

New figures armed with fiercely gathered wealth advance resolutely. They require no aid. Liked or disliked, they can stand on their own feet and make their way. It is a free country, they need not bow the knee to any social clique. 'No, Sir.'

Yet it would be very nice to be elected to the golf club, and to be accepted into the social circles; and it would also be very helpful, and never more helpful than in times of crisis and trouble.

These subtle influences invest the business life of the United States with a quality of strength and order which it formerly lacked. They are healthy and far-reaching. They create a new standard of values among successful men.

It is good to have a great fortune, but there is more distinction in having a fine business and in managing it well.

Wealth ceases to be the aim, it becomes the means, agreeable, indispensable, but yet only the means.

Freedom of action, and a sense of close contact with the practical, the elating force of large propositions – all these are the elements of an interesting life.

These colossal modern businesses offer a man in many ways more scope and power than he could find in a Cabinet office, or at the head of a squadron of the Fleet, or a division of the Army.

The prospect is no less attractive because he may become a millionaire in the process.

America's national psychology is that the bigger the Idea, the more wholeheartedly and obstinately do they throw themselves into making it a success. It is an admirable characteristic provided that the Idea is good.

In all concerned with production the American displays pre-eminent qualities.

Conditions in America have favoured and fostered enterprises upon the largest scale. The American business mind turns naturally, instinctively, to bigness and boldness.

In Europe many of the important manufacturing firms have grown up over generations from small beginnings, and the works as they stand today represent the makeshift contributions of many years.

On the other hand, American development has had a clear field. To 'plan the lay-out' of businesses upon a gigantic scale, to sweep away ruthlessly all encumbrances of the past, and to crush out all rivals or merge with them are accepted as obvious ideals.

The enormous plan to make no compromise with the obsolete or the inefficient in any form. Time – even in this land of hurry – is not grudged in preparation.

A most suggestive and illuminating book *The American Omen* extolled the industrial methods of the United States.

In an amusing passage Tsarist Russian and American methods were contrasted.

A horse dies in Moscow. A single Russian arrives with a high narrow cart and a long pole, and by laying the cart on its side and using the wheel as a kind of windlass and the pole as a lever, single-handed after long toil and with the utmost ingenuity, little by little manoeuvres the carcass into the cart and drives off with it.

An American watching this performance would not, we are told, be at all impressed by this cleverness in overcoming difficulties. He would not accept the difficulties but would seek to remove them in the first instance. He would not combat the fact that it is very hard for one man to move a heavy horse; he would change the fact.

Specifically he thinks of a waggon built for the purpose, low-swung on bent axles with proper tackle attached. Having imagined the special waggon he asks himself if it would pay. Perhaps not, nor would such a waggon be right also for general purposes. Therefore the special waggon called for an organised special activity. With two or three of them one might remove all the dead horses in Moscow. Then it would pay.

This instance is typical and illustrates an admirable mental characteristic.

But what business has gained by this concentration of American ability and quality upon itself has been very largely at the expense of politics, and of the professions and martial services.

Except in times of war the United States military or naval man occupies only a very modest position in the public eye or social world.

Politics are neglected as a life-long vocation by the flower of American manhood.

In England at any rate the man of independent means and ability who devotes his whole life to Parliament and public affairs, forswearing the opportunities of gathering wealth and seeking only by serving the State, to rule events, is still regarded as on a higher plane than the prosperous and successful founder of a great business. In the moral hierarchy of our society he is treated as a superior.

In the United States, politics, dominated by the machine, have produced a caste of professional politicians, beneath whose tough sway few illusions thrive. Aspiring ardent youth is repulsed from political life and the aristocracy of business finds ways of solving its political problems other than by personal participation.

The Constitution grips the American people with a strong unyielding hand. Public opinion, so powerful in England, plays less part in the government of the United States.

Presidents, senates, congresses, state-legislatures, public officers of all kinds, sustained and erected by the party machine and working for fixed terms are not to be influenced by day-to-day emotions.

At election time the strong outbursts of popular feelings are all skilfully canalised and utilised. The forces are enormous; but the men in charge know how to bridle and guide them.

The statute books, both Federal and State, are crowded with laws which have fallen into what is euphemistically called 'innocuous desuetude'.

Politics are accepted like the weather; they go on, one must make the best of them, life has to be lived, work has to be done, and there are so many other more interesting, jolly and profitable affairs to attend to.

The visitor to America feels himself in the presence of a race with a keen zest for life. The American is more highly strung than the northern European; and in most cases this does not seem to lead to pessimism or a morbid condition. No doubt there is a material basis for this. The old orthodox tenet of European civilisation that 'money does not bring happiness' is probably only a modern adaptation of Aesop's Fable of the 'Fox and the Grapes'.

Vast wealth does not bring happiness; but that small margin of spare money, after necessities have been provided for, constitutes in America the structure of what is definitely a larger life.

In the United States this larger life – or rather larger share of life in its natural and rightful balance – is enjoyed by an incomparably greater number than in any other country in the world.

Life there is organised not for the few nor for the millions but for the scores of millions. Culture, amusement and reasonable ambitions are provided wholesale by mass production. Culture, indeed, is a standardised article; and the population is almost conscript for university education.

Here is the great achievement and marvellous phenomenon of the Great Republic – namely, the vast numbers participating in the full life.

Because the overwhelming majority of Americans enjoy conditions which are not only incomparably fortunate according to European standards, opinion is hard upon failure in all its forms.

The mortal sin in the American decalogue is failure; all others are venial.

If a man is a failure, the American presumption is that he has himself to blame. There are no vast submerged classes in whose behalf it can be pleaded that they never have had a chance.

The great majority of the United States citizens feel that those who have not been able to come up to the general standard have faults or weaknesses for which they deserve to suffer.

There is little place for pity in the schemes of the Great Republic for the failures, for the impoverished, or the worn-out. A great chance was offered; it was fair and free; it was offered to all; and if these pitiful ones have not taken it, so much the worse for them.

All this is the philosophy of an expanding prosperity and widely diffused success.

But then, swiftly, suddenly, unexpectedly, though for only a spell, misfortune, contraction, disorganisation, stagnation, unemployment, swept down upon the community, and American optimism and complacency were violently shaken.

In all history no nation ever suffered in time of peace the extremes of fortune which fell upon the United States. Between 1927 and 1937 the American people reached the highest extent of material prosperity and industrial activity ever known in any community, fell into the deepest depths of misfortune. They had to rebuild from the ruins.

About 1927 and 1928 it seemed that the problem which had baffled the world since its foundation was at last on the verge of solution. The people of the United States had nearly bridged the gap between the power to produce and the power to consume.

We saw the breadwinners of 25,000,000 homes engaged in the production either of food or raw material, or of 400 or 500 standardised articles, by the most scientific methods and on a gigantic scale.

We saw these same breadwinners buying these articles with the wages they received for making them, using them to add to the ease and pleasure of life, and investing their surplus in the shares of the various companies for which they worked.

The harmonious circle of human transactions seemed about to be completed.

The interests of capital and labour were almost reconciled. We saw employers eager to maintain a high level of wages so that their workmen could buy the things they made, and to shorten hours of labour so that their workmen should have time to use and enjoy these things.

Labour was itself consciously interested in the efficiency of production from which it felt itself a direct beneficiary.

Everywhere there was a keen zest for life, a sure confidence in the future.

The visitor to America had a vivid impression of abounding and universal happiness.

The people had reason to be happy. Business prospered as never before. And all shared in its prosperity.

In the middle years of the nineteen-twenties the United States could boast of 11,000 millionaires – one for every 10,500 citizens.

The purchasing power of the average wages of an American labourer was at least twice that of his English equal; members of the other income strata were probably superior in the same proportions.

Scores of millions participated in a wide and eventful form of existence.

Here was the unique achievement and marvellous phenomenon of the Great Republic.

No one dreamt that these golden days could end.

'Prosperity is here to stay,' said President Coolidge in December 1927. Public opinion throughout America echoed the optimistic words; nor was optimism unjustified.

The United States had got its elbows on the ledge of the greatest advance ever been made in human economics.

The method seemed clear; mass production on the largest possible scale of standardised articles of necessity or convenience for tens of millions and for scores of millions of consumers!

There lay the secret of the mammoth fortunes, of standards of living, and of practical convenience for millions already beyond all compare.

The life and habits of the American people and the structure of their industries grew side by side, acting and reacting upon each other.

The wants of scores of millions of households were comprehended and foreseen before they were expressed, and the individual purchaser adapted himself to the wholesale facilities offered and regulated his life accordingly.

He clambered up, as it were, upon a scaffolding of standardised necessities, comforts, conveniences, and luxuries, and found, so long as his taste conformed to the rules, an incredibly efficient service.

The connection between speculative finance and industry was omnipresent. The frenzies of speculation began on the bounding, buoyant platform of industry.

All the standardised conveniences which the workshops offered to the American home, all the materials and many of the processes of production, were immediately caught into the quotations of the Stock Exchange and whirled about in furious speculation.

The popular features of American life, the essentials of industrial production, were also the favourite gambling counters of the American people.

'Here is a bed. I sleep in a bed. All my neighbours sleep in beds. This is the best kind of bed for Americans to sleep in. Millions were bought last year; I will buy one for myself. I will buy it on the instalment principle.

'What's more, I will buy shares in the company. I will buy them also on margin. The shares will go up: I shall help to send them up by buying a bed.

'If I make a profit on the shares I shall get the bed for nothing. If I make a loss I will work all the harder and earn more wages.'

The producing, financing and consuming powers were all seen striding forward, recklessly perhaps, but in intimate alliance and turbulent strength.

The United States had largely passed the stage where businesses grow up by degrees, adding a little year by year to humble beginnings.

Gigantic enterprises were planned from the outset, and layout plans, financing, advertising, distribution were brought into being as by the stroke of a wand.

The scale of American business and production in 1927–8 was so large, and the market so sure and fertile, that the chiefs could plan and act with such comprehensive range, freedom, and power as had only been wielded in Europe's industrial field under conditions of war

Vast enterprises, acquiring momentum every day, science and organisation smoothing and lighting the path, the very magnitude of every operation facilitating the next: a continent as raw material in the hands of industry, wealth abounding and wealth diffused, millionaires multiplying, wages high and rising, seven million college students, cars also by millions, food plentiful, clean and cheap, room to live, room to breathe, room to grow, room to kick. Socialism a European delusion, politics an occasional pastime, the Constitution a rock – why should they fear? Forward! Headlong! All would be well.

But what was the foundation upon which all this stood? How had this amazing activity been produced? On what foundation did it stand?

Alas! all was tottering.

Throughout America men and women were buying shares, not for the sake of the income they would bring, but in the hope of a further appreciation in price. So long as every speculator was dreaming the same rosy dream, all was well.

Rich men bought up to the limit of their wealth. Little men risked the savings of years. Then, cash exhausted, they pledged the stock they had already bought to secure the credit for new operations.

The bankers, as optimistic as their clients, lent on the basis of the inflated values of the stocks offered as security. They encouraged the wildest gambling. They profited by it.

Still, no one can say the American public was not warned. Many times did the Federal Reserve authorities denounce speculation, and raise the bank rate to check it.

But all warnings fell on ears deaf to unwelcome tidings.

And then, suddenly, the earth trembled, the chimney-stacks fell crashing into the streets, and many dead and wounded were carried away.

Then, when it was assumed that all was over, came other shocks, heavier and heavier, and the fronts of buildings cracked or fell out, spreading havoc and panic in the crowded streets, thousands of millions of capital value were annihilated in ten days; and all the small stockholders were ruthlessly sold out.

Under my very window a man cast himself down 15 storeys and was dashed to pieces, and many over-balanced in similar accidents.

I walked 'The dark, narrow, crooked lane leading to the river and the graveyard,' to quote the local description of Wall Street, at the worst moment of the 1929 Stock Exchange panic. A perfect stranger who recognised me invited me to enter the gallery of the Stock Exchange. I expected to see pandemonium; but the spectacle that met my eyes was one of surprising calm and orderliness. Members of the New York Stock Exchange precluded by the strictest rules from running or raising their voices unduly, were walking to and fro like a slow-motion picture of a disturbed ant heap, offering each other enormous blocks of securities at a third of their old prices and half their present value, and for many minutes together finding no one strong enough to pick up the sure fortunes they were compelled to offer.

No one who gazed on such scenes could doubt that this financial disaster, huge as it was, cruel as it was to thousands, was only a passing episode in the march of a valiant and serviceable people who by fierce experiment are hewing new paths for man, and showing to all nations much that they should attempt and much that they should avoid.

When business closed on the Stock Exchange and brokers took stock of the position it was discovered that the total loss since the September in share values was five times the amount of Europe's war debts to America.

Over 12,000,000 Americans had been 'playing the market'. The great majority had lost, many heavily. At least 1,000,000 people were utterly ruined.

All over the U.S. banks were suspending payment. Roughly, rather more than one in every seven was forced to close.

And now, also, the wheels of industry were slowing down.

The consuming power ebbed with even greater suddenness. Unemployment, almost unknown in the U.S., became formidable.

From the Atlantic to the Pacific the streets filled with workless men. Throughout the agricultural states farmers faced ruin with bulging granaries.

World stocks of primary products had practically doubled themselves in five years.

There had been a time when President Hoover promised 'two chickens in the pot for every American family.'

But there were now millions of families who not only had no chickens, but who had been forced to sell even their pots in order to buy bread.

It was little comfort to them that Hoover, still optimistic, kept on intoning, with monotonous regularity, that prosperity was 'just around the corner.'

In two years the price of gold rose by nearly 40 per cent. In other words, the value of all other commodities in terms of gold fell by the same amount.

This was the terrible event, this was the hideous process of deflation which wrote down the value of all our possessions and exertions, not only in the countries which lacked gold, but in those which had it in super-abundance.

This was the process which flung millions of men out of employment in every land, stilled the traffic upon the railways, quenched the blast furnaces, dried up the springs of human action, and threatened every country and every institution successively with insolvency.

Depression on the vast scale of the U.S. collapse is epidemic.

Like pestilence, it knows no frontiers. It swept the world.

In all the great industrial countries millions of men found themselves workless. Famine and fear stalked the earth.

Both in America and in Europe we were told that the disease we were suffering from was over-production. We were reduced to poverty because we had become too clever in making all the things we wanted. So much wheat had been grown that many people were nearly starving. We were stripped bare by the curse of plenty.

That was the strange diagnosis of the world's condition and the remedy proposed was even more remarkable than the disease.

The disease was over-production, and the remedy was to be further reduction of consuming power through everyone drawing in his horns and spending as little as possible.

Thus one catastrophe led to another.

The importance of the Wall Street crash of October 1929 as a factor in world depression was psychological. It caused a sense of deep impoverishment throughout America.

The elaborate structure of the social services in Britain had hitherto filled Americans with amazed contempt. To them, such things as unemployment insurance and pay were marks of degeneracy.

But now, with their own unemployed running into many millions, American optimism and complacency were violently shaken.

There were bread queues; there were riots; there were even 'Socialists' – a terrible symptom!

Men and women, weakened by privation, unable to obtain suitable clothing, collapsed and died of exposure.

There were too many persons affected by this wave of depression for them to be written down as weaklings incapable of turning to account the grand opportunities offered them.

A system of unemployment insurance, such as had been established in Britain, would have saved many lives and immeasurable suffering.

And a new disaster came on them. Over thousands of square miles the very soil by which they lived began to be blown away.

The foundation of all wealth is the land.

The giant aggregations of factories and workshops of modern industry, the great cities with their shops and offices, their teeming millions of highly specialised workers, all the elaborate structure of finance, the intricate network of commerce and communications draw their strength and sustenance from the fields.

Agriculture is the parent and the prop of all other human activities. And over eleven States of the American Union fields lay desolate and the soil turned to dust. Other States were affected, but not so severely.

The drought of 1935, which brought about this appalling result, was the third since 1930.

It finally convinced America that the character of a large part of the country was changing, and that, unless drastic steps were taken, millions of acres of farm lands would become permanent desert.

What the drought had spared great hordes of grasshoppers devoured. Dust-storms swirled and eddied across the prairie day after day, week after week, month after month.

About one-half of the total American corn crop was destroyed; in one month alone roughly 800,000,000 bushels were lost. Over a million families were reduced to penury.

Here was one of the greatest and most urgent problems facing America. It was a sharp reminder that, in spite of all talk of over-production and the need for crop restriction and limitation, mankind's tenure of the means of life is still precarious, and can only be assured by good husbandry, by a careful conservation of natural resources, by forward-looking policies.

The warning was heeded. Ruined farmers were put to work on soil and water-saving schemes in the drought area. Trees were planted.

The high level of American prosperity before the disaster of 1929 was no accident. It was destroyed – but it was destroyed by circumstances which lay outside the structure and the internal relationships of industry.

The example of what was accomplished remains. The way to prosperity, to a high and an increasing standard of life was shown.

Many a brave ship tried in vain to cross the Atlantic Ocean before Cabot and Columbus discovered the New World that was waiting all the time to reward success.

I am an optimist – it does not seem to be much use being anything else – and I cannot believe that the human race will not find its way through problems that confront it.

Next to happiness a marked heartiness characterises the American people.

This word when used in its English meaning is almost a term of opprobrium; but in America it means a genuine flow of friendly feeling.

The traveller is welcomed with gusts of friendliness, expansive gestures, and every appearance of joy. Hospitality and every form of kindness is thrust upon him.

To this the average British visitor makes but an inadequate return.

He behaves with traditional reserve and frigidity and too often seems to lack the technique for reciprocating the welcome he receives.

There is no doubt that the English people are chary of allowing the feeling of friendliness to take root quickly, and diffident in its outward expression. They embody a complicated mass of sensitiveness and susceptibilities acquired or inherited which are due to a long succession of troubles and frustration.

They are the children of a race for whom life has for many generations been less easy than the life of the last few generations in America.

Since individual frustration and failure have been more common in his experience, the Englishman carries about scars and wounds which are liable to injury at the hands of another.

In consequence he is unwilling to come close to others in terms of friendliness until he has tried and tested them by various means, proved that they are unlikely to give offence in a thousand possible ways, and are capable of the many forms of give and take, self-restraint and understanding which friendship between such sensitive people must involve.

American susceptibilities are of a more childlike and superficial character.

The American is more confident and free from the scars of many battles. He is less afraid of the stranger and is capable of an immediate sensation of genuine friendliness.

Affability and amiability come easier to all classes of Americans than to their corresponding type in England. Another characteristic of the American is his earnestness. He dwells in an atmosphere of intense earnestness and seriousness about all matters of practical concern or general interest.

The American prides himself on his sense of humour, but to a transatlantic visitor his earnestness is the predominating feature.

We, with our experience that the goal, whatever it be, can only be attained by wary, roundabout and imperfect methods, are reluctant to indulge in hopes of quick success. With us the cautious and plodding attitude is appropriate. A super-intense or earnest Englishman always seems to have a flavour of hysteria or the ridiculous about him.

Jests and irony run through our serious discussions, and even the gravest situation in England breeds its joke.

Cynicism and ridicule have their part to play in the gamut of the human mind. Few are the public men in England who do not from time to time indulge such moods.

These attitudes do not represent an ultimate cynicism. They arise from a more just appreciation of the degree of enthusiasm which the situation allows.

Since failure is more common in the Old World, its inhabitants have come to relish painful and cynical observations upon the difference between the ideal and the actual or about the failure of our neighbours or ourselves to live up to our own standards.

Such an attitude is shocking to the average American!

Any flavour of levity applied to the grave affairs of life is obnoxious to his mind. He feels it to be decadent and dangerous.

He regards it in his visitor (although too polite to say so) as a sign of the corruption of the Old World.

These earnest enthusiasms and aspirations lead very readily to a habit of platitudinising. A friend of mine who made prolonged travel with a learned delegation through the United States, far from the fashionable circles of New York, says:

'They never seem to tire of enunciating the simplest truth with all the solemnity at their command.

'This may partly have been due to the belief that the platitudes were good for us, and to their habit of acting quickly on what they believe to be sound.

'Perceiving that we, in many of the matters which were discussed, had failed to give effect to the elementary principles of the subject, they assumed it was because we were ignorant of these principles.

'It was really because we knew that circumstances did not indeed allow the ideal solution, and that therefore old sentiments, prejudices, and tradition favouring less sound principles must not be too hastily discarded for the sake of unattainable ideals.

'Such an attitude was distressing to our American friends. Once they have decided upon the best way of doing something, they proceed to try to do it. They could not conceive that any failure to act on the best principles was due to anything except ignorance of those principles – or worse. Hence the well-meaning platitudes.'

There is no doubt that the American love of platitude has a deeper root than this. It arises from their national situation. They have had great good fortune and success. They have a tremendous and obvious task to perform. Their mixture of many races has to be assimilated.

The 100 per cent. Americans have before them a serious problem of welding the nation together. For this the platitude is a powerful instrument. Everyone must be made to think the same things in certain important matters. Everyone must sing the chorus. Everyone must learn the slogans. Everyone must know the Drill Book by heart. United sentiment must overcome diversity of racial origin. About certain important matters all must be taught to say the same thing, and to repeat it until it becomes tradition itself.

The Americans in their millions are a frailer race with a lighter structure than their British compeers. They are less indurated by disappointment; they have more hopes and more illusions; they swing more rapidly between the poles of joy and sorrow; and the poles are wider apart. They suffer more acutely both physical and moral pain. The texture of their national life is newly wrought; they have all the advantages and defects of newness and modernity.

Even if the first prizes of the future should fall to the United States, he will still remain a vast enduring force for virility, sanity and good will.

But it is in the combination across the Atlantic of these diversified minds, and in the union of these complementary virtues and resources, that the brightest promise of the future dwells.

I feel shy about expressing my opinion about American food. I was everywhere received with such charming hospitality that to give any verdict of a critical character might seem churlish; however, as eating and drinking are matters in which the good taste of different people and different countries naturally and legitimately varies so widely, there may be no harm in my setting down a few general impressions.

Then there is the danger that one may be thought greedy and reproached for setting too much store by creature comfort and of dwelling unduly upon trivialities. But here I fortify myself by Dr Johnson's celebrated dictum: 'I look upon it, that he who does not mind his belly, will hardly mind anything else.'

So I will start out boldly with the assertion that Americans of every class live on lighter foods than their analogues in England.

Fruit, vegetables and cereals play a much larger part in their bills of fare than with us, and they eat chicken much more often than meat – by which, of course, I mean beef and mutton.

All this is, no doubt, very healthful, but personally I am a beefeater.

Moreover, the American chicken is a very small bird compared with the standard English fowl. Attractively served with rice and ancillaries of all kinds, he makes an excellent dish. Still, I am on the side of the big chicken as regularly as Providence is on that of the big battalions.

A dangerous yet almost universal habit of the American people is the drinking of immense quantities of iced water. This has become a ritual.

If you go into a cafeteria or drug-store and order a cup of coffee, a tumbler of iced water is immediately set before you. This bleak beverage is provided on every possible occasion; whatever you order, the man behind the counter will supply this apparently indispensable concomitant.

American meals nearly always start with a large slice of melon or grapefruit accompanied by iced water. This is surely a somewhat austere welcome for a hungry man at the midday or evening meal.

Dessert, in my view, should be eaten at the end of the meal, not at the beginning.

The coffee in the United States is admirable and a welcome contrast to the anaemic or sticky liquid which so many judicious Americans rightly resent in English provincial towns.

The American Blue-point oyster falls into the opposite error to the American chicken. The oyster is too large.

Those we eat in England are small enough to slide with ease down the smallest gullet; the Blue-point is a serious undertaking.

On the other hand, the American lobster is unrivalled anywhere in the world.

A very general custom in American society is to have a little preliminary repast before the company sits down at table.

The guests arrive any time within half an hour of the nominal dinner-hour and stand about conversing, smoking cigarettes and drinking cocktails.

This custom is nothing more or less than the old custom of Imperial Russia called 'The Zakouski'.

I remember, as a child, being taken by my mother on a visit to a duke who had married a Russian princess.

There I saw exactly the same ritual, with kummel and vodka instead of the cocktails, and the same attractive eatable kickshaws to keep them company.

It was only after this was over that the regular dinner began.

There is much to be said for this arrangement. No doubt it encourages unpunctuality, but, on the other hand, it protects those who have already arrived from starving helplessly till the late-comers make their appearance.

The vast size of the United States and the imperative need of moving about has given the American an altogether different standard of distances from that which prevails in our small island.

Whenever I came to an American city I always made haste to climb the tallest building in it, and examine the whole scene from this eagle's nest.

They are wonderful, these bird's-eye views; each one gives an impression of its own which lies in the memory like a well-known picture.

I have heard the opinion expressed that all American cities are alike. I do not agree with this short-sighted view. The hotels are the same in their excellence and comfort, in their routine and service; but anyone who will not only perch himself on a pinnacle, but thread and circumnavigate the streets in a motor-car, will soon perceive that each city has a panorama and a personality all its own.

Nothing, of course, can equal the world-famous silhouette of New York from the sea. It is a spectacle the magnificence of which is perhaps unsurpassed in the whole world; and though each building, taken separately, may have its failings, the entire mass of these vast structures is potent with grandeur and beauty.

From West to South! What lovely country surrounds the city of Atlanta! Its rich red soil, the cotton-quilted hills and uplands, the rushing, turgid rivers are all instinct with tragic memories of the Civil War.

And who would miss Chatanooga, lying in its cup between the Blue Ridge and Look-out Mountain?

The scenery itself is exhilarating, but to it all is added the intense significance of history.

All these rugged heights and peaks have their meaning in military topography; a short drive to the battlefield of Chikamauga, kept like a beautiful park, with many of the field batteries standing in the very positions where they fought, is enough to reward the visitor.

In Minneapolis, amid its rolling plains, my small party had its most affectionate welcome.

Cincinnati I thought was the most beautiful of the inland cities of the Union. From the tower of its unsurpassed hotel the city spreads far and wide its pageant of crimson, purple, and gold laced by silver streams that are great rivers.

There is a splendour in Chicago and a life-thrust that is all its own.

We read of its crimes and vices – largely the result of foolish laws – but to the outward eye all is fair to see, and the immense façade of buildings rises abruptly from the cold, clear, greenish wavelets of fresh-water sea.

Detroit and Toledo are dominated by industry, and nowadays industry brings with it the spectre of social distress which, in the setting of an icy winter, seem gaunt and grim.

To me Rochester makes a personal appeal. Here, in my mother's birth city, I hold a latch-key to American hearts. Here it was that my grandfather and his brother, having married two sisters, built two small, old fashioned houses in what was then the best quarter of the town, and linked them by a bridge. Here they founded the newspaper which is still the leading daily. Here my mother was born. From Rochester come the Kodaks which have amused the world.

It would be easy to illustrate this theme further and recall the kind impressions of Boston, Cleveland, Pittsburgh, Philadelphia, and a dozen other cities; of so many great States, awe-inspiring, as breath-taking as Texas, Louisiana, or Florida, but the examples I have given suffice to convey the sense of variety and character which the great cities and States of America, strung like jewels upon their network of railways, present to a sympathetic and inquiring eye. This was the America I love.

My lecture tours in the United States afforded me many opportunities to learn more of the people and the nation.

For more than 30 years I had been accustomed to address the largest public audiences on all sorts of topics, mainly controversial, under varying conditions.

A lecture tour as such, therefore, had no serious terrors for me.

Still, to a stranger in a foreign land, it must always be something of an ordeal to come into the close, direct relationship of speaker and listener night after night, with thousands of men and women whose outlook and traditions are sundered from his own.

But American audiences yield to none in the interest, attention and good-nature with which they follow a lengthy considered statement. They are most indulgent to the visitor from across the ocean, and eagerly encourage him to speak with candour.

I was not conscious of any difficulty in getting into touch with them. All my quips and turns of phrase went down as well as ever they did at home. I could always feel quite sure where I would get my laughter or my cheers.

A due appreciation of the other man's point of view is the surest foundation for expounding your own.

Of course, one must always be careful, in commenting in another country upon its affairs, not to expose oneself to the retort, albeit unspoken, 'Mind your own business'; and it was only by feeling my way, and getting bolder as I advanced, that I came to the point of openly deriding some things, such as, for example, the Prohibition Law.

These large assemblies always seemed to take particular pleasure in asking questions after my address was over.

At every place I encouraged this, and sheaves of written questions were speedily composed and handed up, covering a discursive range of topics.

The audience appeared delighted when some sort of an answer was given immediately to each. Many searching inquiries were made, but never one that was discourteous or ill-intentioned to the visitor.

Any fair retort, however controversial, was received with the greatest good humour.

I remember, for instance, that I was asked: 'What do you think of the Dole?' I affected to misunderstand the question, and replied: 'I presume you are referring to the "Veterans' Bonus."' This gained an immediate success.

It is easy to set forth the enormous differences of history and environment which separate the two great branches of the English-speaking race, but no one who, like me, can judge from these personal contacts will do anything but marvel how much they are alike.

The most critical of my audiences was, of course, at Washington.

Here one met the leading men of the Union, and the keen society of the political capital, with all its currents of organised, responsible opinion.

But the most interesting, and in some ways the most testing, of all my experiences was not on the public platform.

A Washington hostess, in the centre of the political world, invited the British Ambassador and myself to a dinner of some forty or fifty persons. There were gathered many of the most important men and some of the most influential women in the United States.

After the dinner was over, the whole company formed a half-circle around me, and then began one of the frankest and most direct political interrogations to which I have ever been subjected.

The unspoken but perfectly well comprehended condition was that any question, however awkward, might be asked, and that any answer, however pointed, would be taken in good part.

For two hours we wrestled strenuously, unsparingly, but in the best of tempers with one another, and when I was tired of defending Great Britain on all her misdeeds, I counter-attacked with a series of pretty direct questions of my own.

Nothing was shirked on either side – debts, disarmament, naval parity, liquor legislation, the gold standard, the dole, were all tackled on the dead level.

I had my back to the wall, and when I was hard-pressed the Ambassador came to the rescue. Nowhere else in the world, only between our two peoples, could such a discussion have proceeded.

The priceless gift of a common language and the pervading atmosphere of good sense and fellow-feeling enabled us to rap all the most delicate topics without the slightest offence given or received.

It was to me a memorable evening, unique in my experience, and it left in my mind enormous hopes of what will some day happen in the world when, no doubt, after most of us are dead and gone, the English-speaking peoples will really understand one another.

CHAPTER 13

America! America!

MY MOTHER WAS American and my ancestors were officers in Washington's army, so I am myself an English-speaking union.

In this well-known and long-known island we have succeeded for nearly a thousand years in preventing any invader from coming in, and we have never prevented anyone from going out. Not even in the Mayflower.

When I first went to the United States in 1895, I was a subaltern of cavalry. I was met on the quay by Mr Bourke Cockran, a great friend of my American relations. I must record the strong impression which this remarkable man made upon my untutored mind. I have never seen his like, or in some respects his equal. His conversation, in point, in pith, in rotundity, in antitheses, and in comprehension, exceeded anything I have ever heard.

Originally a Democrat and Tammany Tiger, he took sides against his party and delivered from Republican platforms a memorable series of speeches. Later on, he rejoined his friends. This double transference of party loyalties naturally exposed him to much abuse. I must affirm that never during our acquaintance of twenty years did I detect any inconsistency in the general body of doctrine upon which his views were founded. All his convictions were one piece.

In England the political opinion of men and parties grows like a tree shading its trunk with its branches, shaped or twisted by the winds, rooted according to its strains, stunted by drought or maimed by storm. In America opinions are taken from the standard text-books and platforms are made by machinery according to exigencies of party without concern for individuals. We produce few of their clear-cut political types or clear-cut party programmes. In our affairs as in those of Nature there are always frayed edges, borderlands, compromises, anomalies. Across the ocean it is all crisp and sharp. Cockran evolved a complete scheme of political thought which enabled him to present a sincere and effective front in every direction according to changing circumstances. He was a pacifist, individualist, democrat, capitalist, and a 'Gold-bug'. Above all he was a Free-Trader, and repeatedly declared that this was the underlying doctrine by which all the others were united. Thus he was equally opposed to socialists, inflationists, and protectionists, and he resisted them on all occasions. In consequence there was in his life no lack of fighting.

I learned a lot from Mr Cockran. I also learned that the American Constitution with its checks and counter-checks, combined with its frequent appeals to the people, embodied much of the ancient wisdom of our island.

America, may be larger, and we may be the older. They may be the stronger, but sometimes we may be the wiser.

I must be very careful – all the more because of my American forebears – in what I say about the American Constitution. I will therefore content myself with the observation that no Constitution was ever written in better English. But we have much more than that in common with the great Republic. The key thought alike of the British Constitutional Monarchy and the Republic of the United States of America is a hatred of dictatorship. Both here and across the ocean over the generations and centuries, the idea of the division of power has lain deep at the root of our development. We do not want to live under a system dominated either by one man or one theme. Like nature, we follow in freedom the paths of variety and change. Bismarck once said that the supreme fact of the nineteenth century was that Britain and the United States spoke the same language.

My two countries, parted long ago by war, were brought together again by war in a unity and understanding such as we had never known. Through long years of endeavour and endurance we shared all things, and though we lost so much, we found a lasting friendship.

Our alliance is far closer than many which exist in writing. It is a treaty with more enduring elements than clauses and protocols. We have history, law, philosophy, and literature; we have sentiment and common interest. We are often in agreement on current events, and we stand on the same foundation of the supreme realities of the world.

In the main, law and equity stand in the forefront of the moral forces which our two countries have in common and rank with our common language in that store of bonds of unity on which I firmly believe we depend. Together there is no doubt that we represent a factor in the development of the whole world which no one will have cause to regret. The alliances of former days were framed on physical strength, but the English-speaking unity can find its lasting coherence above all in those higher ties of intellect and spirit of which the law and language are a supreme expression.

The fourth and fifth Amendments of the American Constitution are an echo of the Magna Carta. Governments may obtain sweeping emergency powers for the sake of protecting the community in times of war or other perils, and these will temporarily curtail or suspend the freedom of ordinary men and women, but special powers must be granted by the elected representatives of those same people by Congress or by Parliament as the case may be. They do not belong to the State or Government as a right. Their exercise needs vigilant scrutiny and their grant may be swiftly withdrawn.

It is remarkable that I, a former Prime Minister of a great sovereign State, should have been received as an honorary citizen of another. I am, as you know, half American by blood. In this century of storm and tragedy I contemplate with high satisfaction the constant factor of the interwoven and upward progress of our peoples. Our comradeship and our brotherhood have been unexampled. We stood together, and because of that fact the free world now stands.

And, as I am half American, I feel I am specially qualified to discuss America. I have visited my second home many times; for many different reasons. I have looked down from a window high in a titanic building at the Hudson and the North Rivers, dotted with numerous tugs and shipping of all kinds, and traversed by ocean vessels from all over the world. Beyond lay all the cities and workshops of the New Jersey shore. Around towered the mighty buildings of New York, with here and there glimpses far below of streets swarming with human life.

I have seen much of America and its people. I followed from north to south the great road which runs the entire length of California. The Redwood Highway undulates and serpentines ceaselessly. In the heart of the redwoods the road is an aisle of cathedral trees. Enormous pillars of timber towering up 200 feet. The earthquake-defying City of San Francisco stretches up to the heavens and gazes on the Pacific. Pebble Beach, Santa Barbara, and then Los Angeles. Nothing could be more different from San Francisco than Los Angeles, the one towering up under its cloud canopy, its buildings crowded together on the narrow promontory; the other spreading its garden villas over an enormous expanse, a system of rural townships basking in the sunlight.

Satiating myself with the wonders of the Yosemite Valley, or the Grand Canyon, or the roar of Niagara, or the clack and clatter of the Chicago stockyards was like marching and camping in wartime in enormous lands.

Back in the East, going from Washington to Richmond, we breathe a different air. It is another country. The scenes of bustling progress, of thriving and profuse prosperity, the echoes of the last word in modernity, have been left behind. We have crossed the mysterious boundary which separates the present from the past. More than that, we have crossed the frontiers which divide victory from defeat. We are in the rebel capital.

A mellow and yet a naughty light plays around long-beleaguered, valiantly defended, world-famous Virginia. The hum of Chicago, the rattle of Wall Street, the roar of New York, even the tranquil prosperity of California, all are absent. We have entered the domain of history.

We march with Lee and Jackson, with Stuart, with Longstreet, and with Early through autumn woodlands, lonely in their leafy splendours of old gold and fading crimson. It is still a broken land.

'Lucifer, son of the morning, how art thou fallen!' Virginia, the proud Founder State of the American Union, the birthplace and home of its most renowned citizens, from Washington to Wilson, beaten down, trampled upon, disinherited, impoverished, riven asunder and flung aside while Northern wealth and power and progress strode on to Empire! And yet it had to be. Hardly even would the adherents of the lost cause wish it otherwise.

We chase McClellan through the battle of the Seven Days. We begin with A. P. Hill in the two days' struggle at Beaver Dam Creek and Gaine's Mill, while Jackson's marching columns, brought so swiftly and secretly from the Valley, cannot cope with the difficulties of the ground. It is not until late on the second day that the general attack of Lee's 45,000 Confederates can be launched against the Union right – 25,000 men isolated on the northern bank of the Chickahominy. Then a fierce struggle in the summer evening until darkness falls, and the Union troops magnificently resisting retreat by their five bridges across the river, sullenly covered by their heavy guns. And now a fatal day of uncertainty and delay. The fog of war! The silent woods! Where has McClellan gone? Will he hurl himself upon the denuded lines which cover Richmond, or will he recoil upon his base at White House? Either move loaded with desperate peril for both armies; a day of cruel suspense for Lee!

It is not until after dark on the third day that we know which course McClellan has taken. He has taken neither. With amazing decision and celerity he has thrown away his communications; he has severed himself from his base. He has established a new base on salt water; has ordered his fleet and store ships to meet him there, and is marching down the peninsula with his whole army in a long flank march across the front of the Richmond lines. Lee has not comprehended the meaning of sea-power.

Swift, then, to strike him as he moves, we hurry back with Lee almost into Richmond, and leaving Jackson to follow the Federal tracks, pour down the roads which radiate from the capital, towards Savage Station, and White Oak Swamp. Now to cut the Union army in half as it toils along a single road! But our columns lag, the detour has been too much, the staff work is imperfect, the manoeuvre is too elaborate; we have not got the trained personnel to handle such complex affairs.

McClellan's flank guard holds firm, long enough to let the thirty-mile blue serpent – 80,000 men, with all their wagons and artillery, marching in one column – slip past the hoped-for point of interception. We make another detour, and strike again furiously at Malvern Hill. But here he has entrenched again in full force, and a tremendous position. His left is impregnable, and before we have found out that his right can be turned, our own centre has attacked spontaneously – at half-cock as it were – and we are committed to general battle.

Again a bloody struggle; again late at night the Union positions are stormed; again McClellan retreats under the cover of darkness; and this time brings his whole army intact and in perfect order safely into his new base at Harrisons' Landing on the James River, under the all-powerful guns of his fleet. We thought we had him to cut to pieces, and rounded up; but he had marched through the jaws of death. Never mind, we have driven him twenty miles further from Richmond, and we have gathered 35,000 good rifles from the battlefield. Important, this, because it is so difficult to fight without good rifles. Even the best generals and the bravest troops find it hard.

It was with deep interest that I followed these memorable operations. No one can understand what happened merely through reading books and studying maps. You must see the ground; you must cover the distances in person; you must measure the rivers, and see what the swamps were really like. It is difficult for the modern eye, accustomed to judge military positions in miles, to adjust itself to these battlefields, where the troops faced each other erect in solid lines at a few hundred yards range. And the Chickahominy River! What a surprise! It is little more than a woodland stream; and White Oak Swamp! a thicket with some puddles. These were the days when the greatest dramas were still played on miniature stages.

I was astonished also by the numerous traces which remain. If you could read men's hearts, you would find that they, too, bear the marks.

We stay where Jefferson Davis ruled, and see the Parliament Buildings where Lee received his commission and where Secession was declared. I motor along the famous turnpike to Fredericksburg. Here, again, the battlefields tell their own story. Admirable descriptive iron plates, erected at the cost of Virginia, and inscribed by deeply instructed hands, fix almost every historical point. The stone wall and sunken road at Fredericksburg; the cemeteries of Union and Confederate soldiers; the trench lines trailing away through the deserted forest, revive the past with strange potency.

Here, south of the Rappahannock, is another wide area of battlefields, on which, perhaps, more soldiers have perished in an equal space than anywhere, excepting round Ypres and Verdun. Here the campaigns lie one upon the other; and Fredericksburg and Chancellorsville are overlaid by the Wilderness and Spottsylvania.

We see the celebrated 'Bloody Angle' in the salient of the Spottsylvania lines. The car stops. We alight and walk through sunlit glades of small oak, beech, and maple. 'Here is the Angle,' says our guide. 'Here is where the dead lay thickest.' Yes! in this trench they were piled in heaps, both sides together, blue and grey. Destiny pivoting here stamped the ground with a ruthless heel; the path of the world took a different turn henceforward. Not in vain these deeds were done. . . .

I experienced America's Prohibition experiment and found the effects upon my constitution very much less disturbing than I had expected.

The attempt of the Legislature to prevent by a stroke of the pen 120,000,000 persons from drinking spirits, wines, or even beer was the most amazing exhibition alike of the arrogance and of the impotence of a majority that the history of representative institutions can show.

The extreme self-assertion which leads an individual to impose his likes and dislikes upon others, the spasmodic workings of the electoral machine, and the rigidity of the American Constitution combined to produce on a gigantic scale a spectacle at once comic and pathetic.

The desire of Anna Goodchild to play school-marm to the other little children, to stand Susan in the corner and put a dunce's cap on Johnny's head, was here presented upon the stage of a continent by a mighty community to an astonished world. But the children, especially the younger ones, soon got tired of playing 'school' with Anna Goodchild, and by their forward and rampageous conduct converted it into the vastest game of 'hunt the slipper' that was ever known.

Up and down, to and fro, from ocean to ocean, from Canada to Mexico, by land, by sea, by air, the slipper was hunted by poor Anna. 'See! there it is! Johnny is holding it up.' 'No! Susan is sitting on it.' 'There! Charles has made one all himself!' 'But look! Willie is bringing in a whole basketful!' and Anna, rushing to seize them, is tripped up by the little boy she had picked out specially to help her, and falls head over heels on the ground, breaking the school furniture, and spilling the inkpot all over the carpet. Truly a wonderful game: far more exciting to the players, and entertaining to the spectators, than what Anna had originally conceived.

Obviously there are limitations upon the power of legislative majorities. It is easy to pass a law. All you do is to organise the people who are keen upon it in every electoral area, and set to work to badger the local candidates and the local caucus till they make it a plank in their platform. Out of all these local platforms a high national structure is built up by the same methods, on the top of which is poised a statue of Uncle Sam, winking quizzically, above the inscription, 'This is the Will of the Nation, and this is the Law of the Land'. And all the people who have been walking about below, busy with their daily life, and making the country rich and strong, look up at the new monument and exclaim. 'Fancy that; how funny!'

No folly is more costly than the folly of intolerant idealism. Follies which tend towards vice encounter at every stage in free and healthy communities enormous checks and correctives from the inherent goodness and sanity of human nature; but follies sustained by lofty ideals go far, and set up strange and sinister reactions. When standards of conduct or morals which are beyond the normal public sentiment of a great community are professed and enforced, the results are invariably evasion, subterfuge, and hypocrisy. In the end a lower standard is reached in practice than would have followed from a common-sense procedure.

The melancholy era which followed the victory of the North in the American Civil War affords a glaring example. Inspired by the noblest of ideals – the abolition of slavery – animated by fierce war, hatred and partly lust, the conquerors decreed that black and white should vote on equal terms throughout the Union, and the famous Fifteenth Amendment was added to the Constitution of the United States. Overwhelming force was at their disposal, with every disposition to use it against the prostrate and disarmed Confederacy. The North were no more inconvenienced by the voting of a few handfuls of negroes scattered among their large population, and being outvoted on all occasions, than a teetotaller by Prohibition.

But the South had different feelings. After years of waste, friction, and actual suffering the Fifteenth Amendment was reduced by the persistent will power of the minority and through many forms of artifice and violence to a dead letter. The Southern negroes have the equal political rights it was the boast of the Constitution to accord them; but for two generations it has been well understood that they are not to use them in any State or District where they would make any difference.

As with the Fifteenth, so it had to be with the Eighteenth Amendment. A Chinese dignitary studying American life and law asked blandly, when Prohibition was explained to him, 'When does it begin?' A more serious judgment was expressed to me by one well qualified to form an opinion, 'There is less drinking, but there is worse drinking.'

Ultimate decision upon the abstract rights and wrongs of Prohibition depended upon the view which held of the relation of the individual to the State. Is the State, based upon majorities elected somehow, entitled to enforce its will upon all its individual members in every direction without limit; or is the State entitled to use its delegated powers only within such limits and for such purposes as have led individuals to band themselves together and submit themselves to its organisation?

Has a majority – perhaps in fact a minority – a right to do anything which it can get voted by the legislature, or do its powers when extended beyond a certain point degenerate into tyranny? Was it necessary for the purposes of 'life, liberty, and the pursuit of happiness' that vast sums of money should be spent, and hordes of officials employed against sober and responsible citizens who wished to do no more than drink wine or beer as they would in any other country in the civilised world? Was not the State, on this question, exceeding its duties? Was it not needlessly and wrongfully interfering with the individual and with that very liberty which it was called into existence to guard?

On the abstract merits there were, of course, two opinions, but on the practical results only one. A law which does not carry with it the assent of public opinion or command the convictions of the leading elements in a community may endure, but cannot succeed; and under modern conditions in a democratic country it must, in the process of failure, breed many curious and dangerous evils.

To abstain from wine because one does not like it or need it is good; to abstain in order to set an example is better; to compel others to abstain because one has abstained oneself is, to say the least, bad manners; to indulge oneself while compelling others to abstain is contemptible. Yet this last became one of the commonest features of American life. Millions of people of every class who voted dry, and thereby assumed moral responsibility for all that the attempted enforcement of Prohibition involved, did not hesitate to procure and consume alcoholic beverages whenever they required them. Such a divorce between the civic act and private conduct would have only been possible in a sphere where the vote of the legislative institution did not correspond to the moral convictions and deep-seated habits of the nation.

Was the progress of the United States, in combating the evils of drunkenness under Prohibition comparable with that, for instance, of Britain under a regulated freedom tempered by taxation? I was proud to tell Americans how our convictions for drunkenness had declined to a third of what they were before the war, and how each year, as Chancellor of the Exchequer, I had had to write the Budget down by three or four million pounds on account of the increasingly temperate habits of the public, and how vast was the revenue still gathered to our national coffers, which in the United States flowed to the bootlegger or was squandered in a nightmare warfare to suppress him.

Thoughtful Americans wondered how to escape from the rigid grip of their own political institutions. They were shocked at the growth of drunkenness and of the crimes and diseases of drunkenness in their midst, but resented the constant interference of State with the private life of its citizens, and blushed at the choice between irrational public duty and normal personal habits. Every avenue seemed barred except the one by which the mighty bootlegging interest advanced with the tacit approval of public opinion, and in many cases with the corrupt connivance of the agents of Prohibition.

Yet the remedy was easy. Recognise the imperfections which vitiate even the best representative institutions; recognise that all citizens, majority or minority alike, have inherent rights; recognise that in the sphere of manners and morals the law must carry with it the real consent of the governed. Recur to those fundamental principles of personal liberty which Constitutions and States are created to defend, and strip from drunkenness and bootlegging the shelter of official interference with habits and customs as old as the world.

If the people of the United States had continued in a mediocre station, struggling with the wilderness, absorbed in their own affairs, and a factor of no consequence in the movement of the world, they might have remained forgotten and undisturbed beyond their own protecting oceans, but one cannot rise to be in many ways the leading community in the civilised world without being involved in its problems, without being convulsed by its agonies and inspired by its causes.

If this has been proved in the past, as it has been, it will become indisputable in the future. The people of the United States cannot escape world responsibility, and we may be quite sure that this process will be intensified with every forward step the United States make in wealth and in power.

The life and well-being of every country are influenced by the economic and financial policy of the United States. From the cotton spinners of Lancashire to the people of India; from the peasantry of China to the pawnbrokers of Amsterdam; from the millionaire financier watching the ticker tape to the sturdy blacksmith swinging his hammer in the forge; from the monetary philosopher or student to the hard-headed business man or sentimental social reformer – all are consciously or unconsciously affected.

In the thirties, President Roosevelt's economic adventure claimed sympathy and admiration from all who were convinced that the fixing of a universal measure of value not based upon the rarity or abundance of any commodity, but conforming to the advancing powers of mankind, was the supreme achievement which at that time lay before the intellect of man.

In truth, Roosevelt was an explorer who embarked on a voyage as uncertain as that of Columbus, and upon a quest conceivably as important as the discovery of the New World.

In those old days it was the gulf of oceans with their unknown perils and vicissitudes. In the modern world, just as mysterious and forbidding as the stormy waters of the Atlantic, was the gulf between the producer with the limitless powers of science at his command, and the consumer with legitimate appetites which need never be satiated. Plenty had become a curse.

People asked: 'Why should these things be? Why should not the new powers man has wrested from nature open the portals of a broader life to men and women all over the world?'

And with increasing vehemence they demanded that the thinkers and pioneers of humanity should answer the riddle and open these new possibilities to their enjoyment.

A single man, whom accident, destiny, or Providence placed at the head of one hundred and twenty millions of active, educated, excitable and harassed people, set out upon this momentous expedition. Many doubted he would succeed. Some hoped he would fail. But Roosevelt pulled his wires, played his cards; great things were done, and greater attempted. He brought about a renaissance of creative effort with which the name of Roosevelt will always be associated. He also reduced unemployment by shortening the hours of labour of those employed and spreading labour more evenly through the wage-earning masses.

This twentieth century has exposed both our communities to grim experiences, and both have emerged comforted, restored, and guarded.

Twice in my lifetime the long arm of destiny searched across the oceans and involved the entire life and manhood of the United States in a deadly struggle. There was no use in saying 'We don't want it; we won't have it; our forebears left Europe to avoid these quarrels; we have founded a new world which has no contact with the old.' There was no use in that. The long arm reaches out remorselessly, and everyone's existence, environment, and outlook undergo a swift irresistible change. What is the explanation of these strange facts, and what are the deep laws to which they respond? I will offer you one explanation – there are others, but one will suffice. The price of greatness is responsibility.

I understand and have never underrated the weight of arguments of former days in favour of American isolationism. If my father had been an American citizen instead of my mother, I should have hesitated a long time before I got mixed up with Europe and Asia and that sort of thing.

Why, I should have asked myself, should my forebears have gone across the Atlantic Ocean in little ships with all the perils of wind and weather to make a new home in a vast, unexplored Continent? Why should they have left class and feudal systems of society, or actual tyrannies which denied them religious freedom, to encounter the unknown?

Why should they have struggled on through hard bleak generations cutting down the forests, cultivating the land, fighting the Red Indians, climbing over the mountains, wending across the prairies, driving their covered wagons and presently their railways, to the misty and mysterious Pacific, in order to find, create and consolidate 'the land of the free and the home of the brave' – Why all this, if it was not to find self-expression in isolation?

Why, then, I should have asked myself, have I got to go back to Europe and to Asia, just because they showed me maps of these continents when I was at school? Are not the oceans broad and have we not got one on each side of us? It would have taken me a lot to get over this.

However, there has been a lot, and it is needful to look around upon it all. The United States has become the most powerful force in the world. The fundamental principles which have governed the growth of American democracy are challenged, not only in Europe and Asia, but in every country throughout the world. The doctrine that all men are created free and equal, and are entitled to life, liberty and the pursuit of happiness, is confronted bluntly and menacingly with the totalitarian conception that the State is all and the individual is a slave or a pawn.

The remaining free, democratic countries are preyed upon from within by a sect which has no national loyalties and obeys blindly the orders which it receives from the Supreme Communist oligarchy in the Kremlin. This also raises new and far-reaching issues.

It would seem to force thoughtful and patriotic Americans to ask themselves why should millions of Americans be taken from their homes and farms and businesses, from which they get their living and rear their families, to go across the ocean every twenty-five years in wars, in the making of which they have had no say, in the preventing of which they have so far been no use. Why should the American people pour out its life and treasure generation after generation to try to put things right across the oceans after they have watched them all go wrong?

These are only the questions which I would have pondered over, and perhaps said something about, if I had been born a citizen of the United States.

But I should also have memories and comprehension of what has happened and I should see Europe as a source of great danger to me in my home State – for which I might have been elected (you never know).

When I reflected on the strength of the United States, its freedoms and its many virtues, all the toils, sacrifices, costs and burdens cast upon it, I might well have come to the conclusion that the United States has no choice but to lead or fall.

It is certainly not strange that American opinion should probably be greatly influenced by champions of peace and progress in trying to nip evil in the bud, quench fire at its outbreak, and stop pestilence by timely inoculation.

And then there are other facts. There is this awful thing they call science. It never will leave America alone – not even after conquering the Redskins and the forests and prairies.

Facts, obnoxious and persistent, come reaching out their claws, upsetting the lives of the dwellings or the apartment homes, from Boston to San Francisco, from Chicago to New Orleans. Detestable facts arising from muddle and disaster thousands of miles away, or from terrible discoveries and inventions, but facts none the less, that all can see and have lately felt. These are facts that must be mastered and controlled.

And not only are there these ugly facts, there are the calls of duty inseparable from world-power and its responsibilities.

I am not surprised that many Americans ask whether it would not be worthwhile, would not it indeed be a measure of ordinary prudence, would it not also indeed be a high moral duty, to take a little interest between whiles in matters which make so great a difference to the ordinary life and welfare of the American Common Man?

It must be the interest as well as honour, for every man, in every free country, to see whether these unrelenting, recurring dangers cannot be so governed by a world organisation as to make things better for all humanity.

I have now something to say about my own country. It would be erroneous for Americans to suppose that Great Britain has ceased to be a State and nation of high and enduring power in the world, or that its people have no longer within them the slowly-maturing qualities which have made their history famous, and reached their finest expression in 1940.

British democracy, working under free institutions, and fortuitous elections, appears superficially changeable. Who could compare the Britain of Munich with the Britain of Dunkirk? A casual observer from outside would find it hard to believe that we were the same race of people.

Britain has of course been grievously weakened by the effort she made in the two victorious world wars fought against German aggression. This is especially true of the last, in which we made intense exertions from start to finish. The zeal and energy with which we fought that struggle brought us to a point of exhaustion, psychological, physical, financial, economic, usually seen only in defeated countries, and not always in them.

But this phase will pass. The British nation will rise again, if not to its former pre-eminence, at least in solid and lasting strength.

As I said at Fulton: 'Half a century from now, there will be at least 80,000,000 of Britons spread about the globe, united in defence of our traditions, our way of life, and of the world theme, to which we and the United States have long been faithful.'

Americans should not fear to march forward unswervingly upon the path to which Destiny has called them, guided by the principles of the Declaration of Independence, all written out so carefully and so pregnantly, in the balanced, well-shaped language of the eighteenth century, by the founders of the greatest State in the world. All is there, nothing can be abandoned; nothing need be added, nothing should be denied.

Britain and America both desire peace. God knows we have had enough of war! We have all we want in territory. We seek no aggrandisement; we have no old scores to wipe out. We know we have more to lose by war than any two human organisations that have ever existed.

We have learned that our security and honour are most surely to be found in reconciling and identifying our several national interests with the general interests of the world. We believe that the prosperity of others makes for our prosperity; that their peace is our safety; that their progress smooths our path.

Ought we not then, to take counsel with one another? Ought we not, when necessary, to be prepared to act together?

One great stumbling-block is the determination of the American people to keep clear of European entanglements and to many Americans, Britain is primarily a European Power. We cannot, indeed, cut ourselves adrift from Europe. But it is difficult, if not impossible, for America to maintain a rigidly isolationist attitude. All that is necessary is a willingness to consult together, an understanding that Britain and America shall pursue, side by side, their mutual good and the good of the whole world. We and the civilised world owe many blessings to the United States, but have also, in later generations, made our contribution to their security and splendour. If we are together nothing is impossible, and if we are divided all will fail. In the increasing unity of our thoughts and actions resides the main foundation of freedom. One thing is certain: with the world divided as it is, freedom and the association of free men, can only be formed upon strength, and strength can only be maintained by unity.

Although Britain no longer plays so dominating a role in the modern world as it used to, we are, nevertheless, at certain periods, a people whose opinion is very widely respected. We are felt to deserve attention from enlightened men and women of varied outlook in many lands.

In our active political life we have undoubtedly a great measure of that bi-partisanship, as it is called, which plays such a large part in the United States and is going, I think to play a greater part. This seeks to lift a lot of important things above ordinary electioneering, without in any way preventing free speech or a healthy measure of invective or even abuse. All this is to the good.

The British race have always abhorred arbitrary and absolute government in every form. The great men who founded the American Constitution expressed this same separation of authority in the strongest and most durable form. Not only did they divide the executive, legislative and judicial functions, but also by instituting a federal system they preserved immense and sovereign rights to local communities and by all these means they have maintained – often at some inconvenience – a system of law and liberty under which they thrived and reached the physical and moral leadership of the world.

The two world wars of the terrible twentieth century turned the economic balance of power from the Old World to the New. It is certain that Europe could not have survived without the moral and material help which flowed across the ocean from Canada and the United States.

The experience of a long life and the promptings of my blood have wrought in me the conviction that there is nothing more important for the future of the world than the fraternal association of our two peoples in righteous work. The happiness of future generations depends upon it.

The supreme duty of all of us – British and Americans alike, is to preserve the good will that now exists throughout the English-speaking world. Even if things are said by one country or the other which are untrue, which are provocative, which are clumsy, which are indiscreet, or even malicious, there should be no angry rejoinder. If facts have to be stated, let them be stated without heat or bitterness.

When great and buoyant communities enjoy free speech in the same language, it is not surprising that they often say different things about the confused and tangled age in which we dwell. But nothing must divide us as we march together along the path of destiny. If the world is to be split in twain we know which side we are on.

Republicans and Democrats are the same to us. Our sympathies are with the American nation and with those whom it chooses by the process of democratic election to guide its vast affairs.

We are living in an age, of which it will always be said that Britain and the United States had cast upon them burdens and problems without compare in the history of the world. Under the severest stresses, and under the most hard and searching trials, they have shown themselves not unequal to these problems. On the contrary, they have triumphed over them and thus cleared the way to the broad advance of mankind to levels they have never yet attained, and to securities of which they will never be deprived.

The United States has set an example to the world of how democratic institutions can be worked with the utmost vigour and freedom without injury to the permanent interests of the State.

We know that we have in the United States vast numbers of friends and well-wishers, and that the upholding of Anglo-American relations is cherished by millions over there.

On every ground, national, European, and international, we should allow no matters – even if we feel keenly about them – to stand in the way of our fullest, closest, intimacy, accord and association.

I always tried, agreeably with my own national duty, to move in understanding harmony with American thought. This was proved several times in great moments by supreme events. But I never accepted a position of subservience to the United States. They welcomed me as the champion of the British point of view. They are a fair-minded people. They know a friend when they see one, and they never resented the very blunt and plain things I found it necessary to say to them from time to time. No people respond more spontaneously to fair play. If you treat Americans well, they always want to treat you better.

Our two great English-speaking democracies will have to be somewhat mixed up together in some of their affairs for mutual and general advantage. But I do not view the process with any misgiving. I could not stop it if I wished – no one can stop it. Like the Mississippi, it just keeps rolling along. Let it roll! Let it roll on in full flood, inexorable, irresistible, benignant, to broader lands and better days.

CHAPTER 14

What Good's A Constitution?

NO ONE CAN think clearly or sensibly about the vast and burning topic of the value of a constitution without in the first instance making up his mind upon the fundamental issue. Does he value the State above the citizen, or the citizen above the State? Does a Government exist for the individual, or do individuals exist for the Government?

One must recognise that the world today is deeply divided upon this. Some of the most powerful nations and races have definitely chosen to subordinate the citizen or subject to the life of the State.

All nations agree that in time of war, where the life and independence of the country are at stake, every man and woman must be ready to work and, if need be, die in defence of these supreme objects; and that the government must be empowered to call upon them to any extent.

But what we are now considering is the existence of this principle in times of peace and its erection into a permanent system to which the life of great communities must be made to conform. The argument is used that economic crises are only another form of war, and as they are always with us, or can always be alleged to be with us, it is claimed that we must live our lives in a perpetual state of war,, only without actual shooting, bayoneting or cannonading. This is, of course, the view of those Socialists who present themselves in an international guise as creators of a new world order, with a new human heart to fit these novel conceptions. They could easily be beaten, and have been very effectively beaten both by argument and by nature.

But when new forms of socialism arose which were grafted not upon world ideals but upon the strongest forms of nationalism, their success was remarkable.

In Germany, for instance, the alliance between national patriotism, tradition and pride on the one hand, and discontent about the inequalities of wealth on the other, made the Weimar Constitution 'a scrap of paper'. Either of these two fierce, turbulent torrents separately might have been kept within bounds. Joined together in a fierce confluence, they proved irresistible.

Once the rulers of a country can create a war atmosphere in time of peace, can allege that the State is in danger and appeal to all the noblest national instincts, as well as all the basest, it is only in very solidly established countries that the rights of the citizens can be preserved. In Germany these rights vanished almost overnight. No one could criticise the dictatorship, either in speech or writing. Voters still went to the polls – in fact, were herded to the polls like sheep – but the method of election became a fantastic travesty of popular government. A German could vote for the regime, but not against it. If he attempted to indicate disapproval, his ballot paper was reckoned as 'spoiled'.

The tyranny of the ruling junta extended into every department of life. Friends could not greet each other without invoking the name of Hitler. At least on certain days, the very meals that a family ate in the privacy of its home were regulated by decree. The shadow of an all-powerful State fell between parent and child, husband and wife. Love itself was fettered and confined. No marriage, no love relation of any kind was permitted which offended against a narrow and arbitrary code based upon virulent race prejudice.

Nor was this all. Even in the sphere of religion the State intervened. It came between the priest and his penitent, between the worshipper and the God to whom he prayed. And this last, by one of the curious ironies of history, in the land of Luther.

To rivet this intolerable yoke upon the necks of the German people, all the resources of propaganda were utilised to magnify the sense of a crisis and to exhibit sometimes France, sometimes Poland, sometimes Lithuania, always the Soviets and the Jews as antagonists at whom the patriotic Teuton had to grind his teeth.

Much the same thing happened in Russia. The powerful aid of national sentiment and imperialist aspirations were invoked to buttress a decaying Communism.

In the United States, also, economic crisis led to an extension of the activities of the Executive and to the pillorying, by irresponsible agitators, of certain groups and sections of the population as enemies of the rest. There were efforts to exalt the power of the central government and to limit the rights of individuals. It was sought to mobilise behind this reversal of the American tradition, at once the selfishness of the pensioners, or would-be pensioners, of Washington, and the patriotism of all who wished to see their country prosperous once more.

It is when passions and cupidities are thus unleashed and, at the same time, the sense of public duty rides high in the hearts of all men and women of good will, that the handcuffs can be slipped upon the citizens and they can be brought into entire subjugation to the executive government. Then they are led to believe that, if they will only yield themselves, body, mind and soul, to the State, and obey unquestioningly its injunctions, some dazzling future of riches and power will open to them, either – as in Italy – by the conquest of the territories of others, or – as in America – by a further liberation and exploitation of the national resources.

I take the opposite view. I hold that governments, States, and federations only come into existence and can only be justified by preserving the 'life, liberty and the pursuit of happiness' in the homes, and families of individuals. The true right and power rest in the individual. He gives of his right and power to the State, expecting and requiring thereby in return to receive certain advantages and guarantees. I do not admit that an economic crisis can ever truly be compared with the kind of struggle for existence by races constantly under primordial conditions. I do not think that modern nations in time of peace ought to regard themselves as if they were the inhabitants of besieged cities, liable to be put to the sword or led into slavery if they cannot make good their defence.

One of the greatest reasons for avoiding war is that it is destructive to liberty. But we must not be led into adopting for ourselves the evils of war in time of peace upon any pretext whatever. The word 'civilisation' means not only peace by the non-regimentation of the people such as is required in war. Civilisation means that officials and authorities, whether uniformed or not, whether armed or not, must be made to realise that they are not the masters. Every self-respecting citizen in every country must be on his guard lest rulers demand of him in time of peace sacrifices only tolerable in a period of war for national self-preservation.

Britain and the United States can claim to be in the forefront of civilised communities. But we owe this only in part to the good sense and watchfulness of our citizens. In both our countries the character of the justiciary is a vital factor in the maintenance of the rights of the individual citizen.

Our judges extend impartially to all men protection, not only against wrongs committed by private persons, but also against the arbitrary acts of public authority. The independence of the Courts is, to all of us, the guarantee of the equal rule of law. For the power to sue the State or to defend oneself legally against its exactions is valueless if the judges are servile, or if they are the instruments of the executive government rather than the interpreters of the statute book.

But all this implies an atmosphere of civilisation rather than militarisation or officialisation. It implies a balance and equipoise of society which can only be gradually altered. It is so hard to build the structure of a vast economic community, and so easy to upset it and throw it into confusion. The onus must lie always upon those who propose a change, and the process of change is hardly ever beneficial unless it considers what is due to the past as well as what is claimed for the future.

It is for these reasons, among many others, that the founders of the American Republic in their Declaration of Independence inculcate as a duty binding upon all worthy sons of America 'a frequent recurrence to first principles'. Do not let us too readily brush aside the grand, simple affirmations of the past. All wisdom is not new wisdom. Let us never forget that the glory of the nineteenth century was founded upon what seemed to be the successful putting down of those twin curses, anarchy and tyranny.

The question we are discussing is whether a fixed constitution is a bulwark or a fetter. From what I have written it is plain that I incline to the side of those who would regard it as a bulwark, and that I rank the citizen higher than the State, and regard the State as useful only in so far as it preserves his inherent rights. All forms of tyranny are odious. It makes very little difference to the citizen, father of a family, head of a household, whether tyranny comes from a royal or imperial despot, or from a Pope or Inquisitor, or from a military caste, or from an aristocratic or plutocratic oligarchy, or from a ring of employers, or a trade union, or a party caucus – or worst of all, from a terrified and infuriated mob. 'A man's a man for a' that.' The whole point is, whether he can make head against oppression in any of its Protean shapes, and defend the island of his home, his life and soul. And here is the point at which we may consider and contrast the constitutions of Britain and the United States.

It is very difficult for us to imagine, for instance, a gigantic Bill passed through Parliament and for two or three years in active operation, suddenly being declared illegal by the law lords sitting as a tribunal. Imagine some gigantic measure of insurance as big as our widows' pensions, health and employment insurance rolled together, which had deeply interwoven itself in the whole life of the people, upon which every kind of contract and business arrangement had been based, being declared to have no validity by a court of law. We simply cannot conceive it. Yet something very like that occurred across the Atlantic.

In Britain an act of Parliament which, upon the advice of the ministers responsible for it, has received the royal assent is the law of the land. Its authority cannot be questioned by any court. There is no limit to the powers of Crown and Parliament. Even the gravest changes in our Constitution can in theory be carried out by simple majority votes in both Houses and the consequential assent of the Crown. But we watch a written Constitution enforced by a Supreme Court according to the letter of the law, under which anyone may bring a test case challenging not merely the interpretation of a law, but the law itself, and if the Court decides for the appellant, be he only an owner of a few chickens, the whole action of the Legislature and the Executive becomes to that extent null and void. We know that to modify the Constitution even in the smallest particular requires a two-thirds majority of the sovereign states forming the American Union. And this was achieved, after prodigious struggles, on only a score of occasions during the whole history of the United States.

American citizens or jurists, in their turn, gaze with wonder at our great British democracy expressing itself with plenary powers through a Government and a Parliament controlled only by the fluctuating currents of public opinion.

All classes and all parties have a deep, underlying conviction that Parliament's vast, flexible powers will not be abused, that the spirit of our unwritten Constitution will be respected at every stage. To understand how this faith is justified, how people are able to enjoy a real stability of Government without a written Constitution, it is necessary to consider the beginnings of party politics in Britain. Whigs and Tories were almost equally concerned to assert the authority of Parliament as a check upon the Executive. With the Whigs this was a matter of fundamental principle; with the Tories it was a question of expediency. James II was a Catholic and his efforts to further the cause of his co-religionists alienated the great bulk of the Tory party, who were loyal to the Church of England. Then, from the advent of William of

Orange to the accession of George III with a brief interval in the reign of Queen Anne, the Crown could do nothing without the Whigs and the government of the country was predominantly or exclusively in the hands of that party.

The Tories were thus vitally interested in preserving and extending the rights of the parliamentary opposition. In this way a jealous care for constitutional rights came to mark both the great parties of the State. And as to all men the Constitution represented security and freedom, none would consent willingly to any breach of it, even to gain a temporary advantage.

Modern times offer respect for law and constitutional usage. Nothing contributed so much to the collapse of the general strike in Britain as the declaration by great lawyers that it was illegal. And the right of freedom of speech and publication is extended, under the Constitution, to those who in theory seek to overthrow established institutions by force of arms so long as they do not commit any illegal act.

Another factor making for stability is our permanent civil service. Governments come and go; parliamentary majorities fluctuate; but the civil servants remain. To new and inexperienced ministers they are 'guides, philosophers and friends'. Themselves untouched by the vicissitudes of party fortunes, they impart to the business of administration a real continuity.

On the whole, too, popular opinion acts as a guardian of the unwritten Constitution. Public chastisement would speedily overtake any minister, however powerful, who fell below the accepted standards of fair play or who descended to trickwork or dodgery.

When one considers the immense size of the United States and the extraordinary contrasts of climate and character which differentiate the sovereign states of the American Union, as well as the inevitable conflict of interests between North and South and between East and West, it would seem that the participants of so vast a federation have the right to effectual guarantees upon the fundamental laws, and that these should not be easily changed to suit a particular emergency or fraction of the country.

The founders of the Union, although its corpus was then so much smaller, realised this with profound conviction. They did not think it possible to entrust legislation for so diverse a community and enormous an area to a simple majority. They were as well acquainted with the follies and intolerance of parliaments as with the oppression of princes. 'To control the powers and conduct of the legislature,' said a leading member of the Convention of 1787, 'by an overruling constitution was an improvement in the science and practice of government reserved to the American States.'

All the great names of American history can be invoked behind this principle.

It may well be that this very quality of rigidity has been a prime factor in founding the greatness of the United States. In the shelter of the Constitution nature has been conquered, a mighty continent has been brought under the sway of man, and an economic entity established, unrivalled in the whole history of the globe.

In this small island of Britain we make laws for ourselves. Although we have a free, flexible Constitution at the centre and for the centre of the Commonwealth, nothing is more rigid than the established practice – namely, that we claim no powers to interfere with the affairs of its self-governing component parts. No supreme court is needed to enforce this rule. We have learned the lessons of the past too well.

The so-called 'rigidity' of the American Constitution is in fact the guarantee of freedom to its widespread component parts. That a set of persons, however eminent, carried into office upon some populist heave should have power to make the will of a bare majority effective over the whole of the United States might cause disasters upon the greatest scale from which recovery would not be swift or easy.

I read the novel by Sinclair Lewis – 'It Can't Happen Here'. Such books render a public service to the English-speaking world. When we see what has happened in Germany, Italy and Russia we cannot neglect their warning. This is an age in which the citizen requires more, and not less, legal protection in the exercise of his rights and liberties.

If the Englishman points to the inconvenience of American institutions, the American may well retort by warning him of the precarious fluidity of his own. So far we claim that all has worked out fairly well. But the experiment is one of the most daring ever attempted. I have the greatest possible respect for the House of Commons, but the House of Commons is great because it does not attempt to usurp undue power. It is great because it resigns the larger portion of its powers to a Council of State called the Cabinet, whom it allows to act for it, and to guide it in legislating, while reserving to itself functions of criticism and supervision.

The idea of exalting a single man into a dictatorial position is especially obnoxious, and this profound conception was carried proudly across the Atlantic by the founders of the American Constitution. This is an age in which the citizen requires more, and not less, legal protection in the exercise of his rights and liberties.

The safeguards to our Constitution have been found tolerably effective. You could not have put them down on paper, but we know all about them, and when a Constitution and civilisation reigns in any country, a wider and less harassed life is afforded to the masses of people. The traditions of the past are cherished, and the inheritance bequeathed to us by former wise or valiant men becomes a rich estate to be enjoyed and used by all.

The English wisdom has been never to be troubled by forms. Common sense rather than logic has guided our people, and our Constitution. We have a genius for preserving old traditions and customs and making them work as we want according to the needs of the day.

In theory the British Sovereign possesses an almost unlimited power. We are loyal and devoted subjects. We earnestly await from session to session the gracious speeches which impart to us Royal will.

All authority is derived from the Crown. Every functionary acts in the name of the King. The armed Forces swear allegiance. He is the fountain of honour.

The judges are merely reflection of Royal justice. If a British Sovereign were to commit a crime, no Court could try him. If he entered a Court, even as an accused the judge, according to the Constitution, would vacate his seat and offer it to him. The Royal word would be final in every case, even in his own. An aggrieved subject would have no redress except by persuading Parliament to impeach the Home Secretary for not having advised the King better. But if the King vetoed the impeachment there would be no constitutional remedy open but that of refusing supplies, which in its turn would be found very injurious to the life and safety of the whole nation.

Such are the constitutional doctrines upon which the most ancient and the most progressive of great nations has built its broad practical liberties.

Foreigners all over the world have been amazed and puzzled by the British Constitution. They have never been able to understand how it is that great powers can be possessed and proclaimed and yet lie wholly in abeyance.

They marvel at the spectacle, at which their intellectuals used to scoff, of a King with all the inherent sovereignties of the Plantagenets and Tudors presiding over a vigorous democracy shaping its own future in the van of the modern world. They conclude reluctantly that we must be very muddleheaded in thought, and uncannily sensible in action.

Some people regret that self-governing Dominions had not been willing to accept and enshrine the traditions and anomalies of our ancient Constitution in their most archaic form while putting their own interpretation upon them. But these people do not realise how violent are the jogs and divergencies, economic and political, between societies so widely separated as Britain, Canada, Australia, and New Zealand.

No one of these communities will have its interests decided or, possibly, exploited by one of the others. They do not take orders from anyone. They mean to judge for themselves and join in anything as volunteers and not pressed men.

The British character abhors written constitutions. We have a profound distrust of the legal brain in matters which transcend purely legal processes. What then is the Constitution of the Commonwealth, written and unwritten?

It is that the self-governing countries within the Commonwealth are in every respect partners with Great Britain, and that they have the same direct relation to the Crown as we have. The Queen is several Constitutional Sovereigns rolled into one. The Queen happens to live in Britain; but that does not in any way affect the theory. Complete equality of status has been established.

If the Commonwealth and the Constitution holds together, it is only because it wants to hold together.

Now, at the end of these reflections, I must strike a minor and different note. The rigidity of the Constitution of the United States is the shield of the common man. But that rigidity ought not to be interpreted by pedants. In England we continually give new interpretation to the archaic language of our fundamental institutions, and this is no new thing in the United States. The judiciary have obligations which go beyond expounding the mere letter of the law. The Constitution must be made to work.

A true interpretation, however, of the British or the American Constitution is certainly not a chop-logic or pedantic interpretation. So august a body as the Supreme Court in dealing with law must also deal with the life of the United States, and words, however solemn, are only true when they preserve their vital relationship to facts.

In this wanton, puzzled age, when theories of all kinds are so volatile and words so easily spun and broadcast, it is all the more necessary that there should be firm bulwarks by which every self-respecting man and his family may, as Kipling put it, 'have leave to live by no man's leave underneath the law.'

Let us beware that in trying to rectify the shortcomings of a system we have saved from the rigours and miseries of bygone centuries we do not, by new forms and short cuts and thoughtless adventures, slip back into those very miseries and rigours.

CHAPTER 15

Wise Heads And Young Shoulders

WE HEAR A great deal about 'Safety First'. It is an excellent principle to follow when crossing the road, as I discovered years ago when, owing to a misunderstanding about American traffic customs, I was knocked down by a taxi in New York. It is also extremely useful in politics, where it has elevated many a Member of Parliament to Cabinet rank and kept him there for many years, merely as a guarantee of the respectability of the Government to which he belongs.

But no really worth-while achievement would be possible if everyone adhered to 'Safety First' all the time and in every relation of life. The British Commonwealth exists today because British men and women were willing to take chances.

It is much the same in personal affairs. We recognise it when we talk of 'the game of life'. The finests ports are those into which the element of danger enters. As the great Australian poet, Adam Lindsay Gordon, has written:

> No game was ever yet worth a rap
> For a rational man to play;
> Into which no accident, no mishap
> Could possibly find its way.

Looking back over my youth, I can see few signs of an undue respect for 'Safety First'. I always took chances – and sometimes had reason to regret having done so.

There is no safer thing to do than to run risks in youth. It is very difficult to live your life in the world and not get set in old ways, rather looking back with pleasure to the days of your youth. That is quite right, and tradition is quite right. A love of tradition has never weakened a nation, indeed it has strengthened nations in their hour of peril; but the new view must come, the world must roll forward. I was always ready to learn, although I did not always like being taught.

Usually youth is for freedom and reform, maturity for judicious compromise, and old age for stability and repose. But you have to run risks. There is a precipice on either side of you – a precipice of caution and a precipice of over-daring. Many overcome mountains, yet tremble at molehills.

Safety is not to be found in searching for the line of least resistance. Perhaps it is better to be irresponsible and right than to be responsible and wrong. Pugnacity and will-power cannot be dispensed with.

I commend to all the immortal lines of Kipling:

> If you can dream – and not make dreams your master;
> If you can think – and not make thoughts your aim;
> If you can meet with Triumph and Disaster
> And treat those two imposters just the same –

No boy or girl should ever be disheartened by lack of success in their youth, but should diligently and faithfully continue to persevere and make up for lost time. Would you rise in the world? – You must work while others amuse themselves. There are two kinds of success – initial and ultimate.

I wasted time until I was twenty-two. It was only then I got the desire for learning. My effective education until then was almost entirely technical. Afterwards I wished I had gone to Oxford. But it is no use going to college without a genuine love of learning – wasting time expensively. I tried to make up for lost time when I was twenty-two. I started by reading Gibbon's 'Decline and Fall of the Roman Empire'. I read it through three times. Every young man ought to read it because it gives you the scale and grandeur of human life and tragedy in the finest English.

Education is a task of prime importance. In the keen international race, prizes go to the nation which has the highest skill of brain and hand. Where we are behind, we must catch up; where we lead, we must stay put.

One must not look upon education as something which ends with one's youth. It is the key to many doors, doors both of knowledge and wisdom. While all knowledge continues to expand, the human faculty remains stationary, and that has induced an experimental mood in all studies and sciences, a desire to test matters and not to yield oneself completely to clear-cut and logical definitions.

But expert knowledge, however indispensable, is no substitute for a generous and comprehending outlook upon the human story, with all its sadness and with all its unquenchable hope. The human story does not always unfold like a mathematical calculation on the principle that two and two make four. Sometimes in life they make five or minus three; and sometimes the blackboard topples down in the middle of the sum and leaves the class in disorder and the pedagogue with a black eye.

Youth has to learn that quality and will-power have proved to be decisive factors in the human story. If it were otherwise, how would the race of men have risen above the apes; how otherwise would they have conquered and extirpated dragons and monsters; how would they have ever evolved the moral theme; how would they have marched across the centuries to broad conceptions of compassion, of freedom, and of right? How would they ever have discerned those beacon lights which summon and guide us across the rough dark waters towards better days which lie beyond?

When I was a boy my elders had fixed opinions on all the greatest issues. Though they differed, their minds were made up. They knew what ought to be. They gave definite guidance to youth. Nowadays the young come to the old, and find them equally bewildered and more awestruck than themselves. Everything seems to be in the melting-pot.

Strangely enough, democracy itself has not escaped the universal criticism. Votes, when possessed by all, seem to have lost their savour. But we have a higher comfort amid the uncertainties of our turbulent career. Science, which in Victorian times declared itself the enemy of religion, now, as she strides forward on her remorseless march, admits her limitations – nay, proclaims a new harmony with a Divine Creator.

Thus kindly stars of hope and faith shine in the modern sky to calm and cheer the weary or hurrying wayfarer; and we bravely believe that in the end all will come right.

As I passed through life, I developed a strong feeling that education should not be too practical in its aims. Young people study at schools and universities to achieve knowledge, and not learn a trade. We must all learn how to support ourselves, but we must also learn how to live.

We need a lot of engineers in the modern world, but we do not want a world of modern engineers.

Unless intellect keeps abreast of all material improvements, society is no longer progressing.

It has been said that the dominant lesson of history is that mankind is unteachable. There is a long dismal catalogue of the unteachability of mankind. Want of foresight, unwillingness to act when action would be simple and effective, lack of clear thinking, confusion of counsel until the emergency comes, until self-preservation strikes its jarring gong – these are the features which constitute the endless repetition of history.

It is above all things important that policy and conduct should be upon the highest level, and that honour should be our guide. Consideration for the lives of others and the laws of humanity, even when one is struggling for one's life and in the greatest stress, does not go wholly unrewarded.

Facilities for advanced education must be evened out and multiplied. No one who can take advantage of a higher education should be denied this chance. You cannot conduct a modern community except with an adequate supply of persons upon whose education, whether humane, technical, or scientific, much time and money have been spent. And there is another element which should never be banished from our system of education. We have freedom of thought as well as freedom of conscience. We have been pioneers of religious toleration. But side by side with all this has been the fact that religion has been a rock in the life and character of people upon which they have built their hopes and cast their cares.

Human beings are endowed with infinitely varying qualities and dispositions, and each one is different from the others. We cannot make them all the same. It would be a pretty dull world if we did. It is in our power, however, to secure equal opportunities for all.

There is another angle of this problem – the case of the young man of good education who is unable to find any position in which his training and abilities may be of value. A case in my own constituency was brought to my notice in which a young man had been unable to obtain employment after a brilliant and successful career at one of the oldest and most famous of our universities.

That is not an isolated case. It is typical of many others. Sometimes the young man concerned eats his heart out at home, waiting for the opportunity to make good that never materialises. Sometimes he takes whatever work he can find. I heard of a Scottish graduate who applied for and obtained a job as a labourer. But what a waste of first-class human material!

There is another evil here, the danger that youth, denied legitimate outlets for energy and ambition, may be attracted by the specious promises of political charlatans and rally to the standards of extremism. Communism and Socialism have always had a fascination for reckless and thoughtless youth, and the history of Hitlerism in Germany shows how powerfully another type of mass movement can appeal to the disappointed and the disillusioned of the new generation. Part, at least, of the strength of the Nazis was due to the fact that the educated young men of Germany were unable, under the old regime, to make their talents and training productive. Hence, too, the psychology which is prepared to welcome war because it offers the opportunities that peace has denied.

These are grave considerations which suggest that, apart altogether from any question of individual hardship, some steps should be taken to find useful employment for those young men to whose fate we have often been careless.

A boy must, in the main, choose his own path. As for parents having some say in the matter, it often makes no difference if they try. Modern young people will do as they like. The only time parents really control children is before they are born. After that their nature unfolds remorselessly petal by petal.

The age twenty to twenty-five are the best years. The whole world is then before you, and you soon discover that it is much better to set up an objective, even if it be beyond your reach, than it is to give up the struggle at the onset. Risks and dangers which are warded off and difficulties which are overcome before they reach a crisis are utterly recognised. Eaten bread is soon forgotten.

Life is not so easy, otherwise we should get to the end too quickly. It does not matter so much to old people, who are going soon anyway, but I find it poignant to look at youth in all its activity and ardour, and most of all to watch little children playing their merry games, and I wonder what would lie before them if God wearied of mankind.

To youth I say – It must be world anarchy or world order. Do not let specious plans for a new world divert your energies from saving what is left of the old.

The oldest habit in the world for resisting change is to complain that unless the remedy to the disease can be universally applied it should not be applied at all. But you must begin somewhere. Of course, I do not wonder that youth is in revolt against the morbid doctrine that nothing matters but the equal sharing of miseries; that what used to be called the submerged tenth can only be rescued by bringing the other nine-tenths down to their level; against the folly that it is better that every-one should have half-rations rather than that any by their exertions, or ability, should earn a second helping.

The world was made to be wooed and won by youth. She has lived and thrived only by repeated subjugations. Nevertheless, elderly people and those in authority cannot always be relied upon to take enlightened and comprehending views of what they call the indiscretions of youth, but, for anyone of any age it is always very difficult to know, when you embark on the path of wrong-doing, exactly where to stop, even though it is much easier to stop than to do.

It would be a great reform if wisdom could be made to spread as easily and as rapidly as folly. Logic, like science, must be the servant and not the master of man. Human beings and human societies are not structures that are built or machines that are forged. They are plants that grow, and must be tended as such. Life is a test; this world a place of trial, and in life people have first to be taught 'Concentrate on essentials'. This is, no doubt, the first step out of confusion and fatuity, but it is only the first step. Everything takes time and time must always be used wisely.

Although in the modern world everything moves quickly, and tendencies which 200 or 300 years ago worked out over several generations, may now reach definite decisions in a twelvemonth, im-patient youth must nevertheless learn patience. Nowadays, things happen so quickly and there are such a lot of them going on, that one finds it somewhat difficult to measure evenly the march of time. For myself, I can say some weeks seem to pass in a flash and then again others felt unutterably long and slow. At times it is almost difficult to believe that so much has happened, and at another that so little time has passed.

One does not deny the pleasures of speed, nor the sense of command in being able to reach distant countries in a few hours, but both these will fade very rapidly with usage.

Ideas of speed today are entirely different from when I was a boy. Then the gallop of a horse at 20 miles an hour was wonderful. Hurry, hustle and bustle cast their shadows upon modern life.

I heard a story of an American businessman who received a Chinese visitor in his office in a building towering above Wall Street. When the market closed he took the Celestial back to his home in Fifth Avenue.

They descended at terrific speed 45 storeys in the lift, threaded their way through the swarming crowds on the pavements, clambered up the steps to the elevated railway, nipped into the train and out at an intermediate station where another rush along the crowded pavements brought them to a back street, where a car was waiting clear of the main traffic block.

'This,' said the American host triumphantly, 'saves us over four minutes.'

The Chinese bowed, deeply impressed.

'And what,' he inquired blandly, 'do we do with these four minutes now that we have saved them?'

Time is a tremendous lever and a tremendous weapon either in peace or war. In fact, I think judicious use of time is very often one of the most potent and effective weapons.

Time is a changeable ally. He may be with you in one period and against you in another, and then if you come through that other, he may return again more faithful than before. Repeatedly in life we find there are times when metals are molten and can easily be cast into new shapes.

You must also look at facts because they look at you. A balloon goes up quite easily for a certain distance, but after a certain distance it refuses to go up any farther, because the air is too rarified to float it and sustain it. And, therefore, I would say let us examine concrete facts. We must face facts and draw true conclusions from them.

The butterfly is the Fact – gleaming, fluttering, settling for an instant with wings fully spread to the sun, then vanishing in the shades of the forest. Whether you believe in Free Will or Predestination all depends on the slanting glimpses you had of the colour of his wings.

And there is a fact of modern life which has struck me, and which deserves the attention of the young and the elderly. It is the threatened elimination of the individual. Everywhere, in every country, in every sphere of human activity, as civilisation has spread its multiplying complications, the power of the machine has grown greater, the power of the man grown less; combinations, organisations of all kinds flourish and increase; individuals sink into insignificance.

I do not need to trace the operation of this fact in trade and manufacture. Vast and formidable combinations of labour stand arrayed against even vaster and more formidable combinations of capital; and whether they war with each other or co-operate, the individual is always crushed under.

The independent labourer, the man without an organisation, gets neither help nor pity from anyone. The small trader is crowded out by the multiple shop or the co-operative stores. The independent manufacturer is overwhelmed by the combination, which in its turn is swallowed whole by some mighty trust.

These transactions are the inseparable concomitant of scientific and commercial development. Their result has been to increase the volume of production and improve the economic cultivation of the earth; and however we may lament the transition of stout-hearted independence into disciplined and regulated service we must admit that mankind, better clothed and better shod, is daily being conveyed by swifter, easier roads to a more abundant table.

But the individual must be all the more our care. At either end of the great machine stand the men; the millions who feed it, and the few who control it, and to preserve the rights and personalities of the one class and to curb the unforeseen power of the other must be one of the labours of the State in this twentieth century. Those who think – as opposed to those who follow, shout, or obey – must make it their care, unwearying, bold, intelligent, to assert the individual life of the man who is only a man, as against the man who controls some powerful engine and the men who have become merely some part of its mechanism.

Look into the political world; the same forces are at work. See how the combination grows, and the individual steadily diminishes. Twenty gentlemen formed into a Cabinet draw steadily to themselves the powers of several hundred more or less disorganised or submissive gentlemen, representing the mass of the nation. The private Member of Parliament is, we are frequently told, a public nuisance. He gets in the way of combination. He has got to go under, too. He is the small private trader when the big co-operative store comes along. The independent Member – the Member on whom the Whips cannot quite rely to hold his tongue and vote straight – no words are bad enough for him!

Watch modern political life and see how much less powerful men are than they were a hundred years ago. Perhaps it is because there are not such great men that the organisations have grown stronger; perhaps it is because of the organisations that the men have dwindled. At any rate, there is the fact.

In the old days, when Administrations were formed, all sorts of difficult questions used to arise. Would Lord A accept the seals? Would Mr B? And in that case, what would the Duke of C say? And if these were met, what would be the complexion of the policy on this or that matter?

The Minister whom the King had summoned spent an anxious week trying to make up his Government. No such difficulty confronts him today. Everyone is ready to undertake some great office of power and profit. The only cause for hesitancy is whether some greater might not be obtained by holding out.

My father, the late Lord Randolph Churchill, taught me to regard these matters from a very different angle. His view was that gradually a man came to represent something in the country, a certain association of political ideas, and that he could not surrender his personal freedom of speech and action unless he exerted in return, as a member of a Government, a proportionate influence on public policy.

That was why he refused for three weeks in 1885 to take office until his conditions were complied with. That was why he resigned from the 1886 Government on a matter of principle – a very unpopular matter, economy. Of course, we know now that all that sort of thing is very improper, and misfortunes overtook my father in consequence.

My father felt it was no use trying simply to please everybody or to suppose that well-meaning platitudes and vapid good will can cope with the fierce tides flowing in the world. It is no use presenting a policy which everyone can see follows the line of least resistance. It is ruinous to have a policy which no one can understand.

My father believed that people ask for firm, bold, decided leadership, which, though it may excite antagonism, arouses a counter-enthusiasm and enables every citizen to see where his duty lies.

The true guide of life is to do what is right, and things are not always right because they are hard, but if they are right, one must not mind if they are also hard.

There rises in my mind the vision of the good young man. His manner is polished; his sympathies are controlled; his political views are rigid; his convictions are beyond the reach of argument; he has no doubts or misgivings. He is a model of correctitude. His devotion to his country is second only to his devotion to his party leader. As a back bencher, he will never cause the Whips the least anxiety. As a Minister, he will not be likely to resign.

From the day he honours a constituency by allowing it to return him to the day when a grateful country votes him a statue, he regards the House of Commons, and English political life generally, exactly as if they were a department of the Civil Service in which he will win promotion by being smart and punctual, and giving satisfaction to his superiors.

That is the style that wins, and that is the path to success. But I think some patience should be shown to more intractable people, of whatever party, who insist in their awkward way of thinking things out for themselves, and on examining everything that comes before them with suspicious attention.

The process of self-improvement is, of course, continuous, but every man and woman, in office or out of office, in Government, or in the cities and municipalities – everyone great and small, should try himself by his conscience every day, to make sure he is giving his utmost effort to the common cause.

There is a kind of intolerant spirit now abroad – a spirit which resents individual opinion, which clamours for uniformity.

This spirit should be combated wherever it is manifest. Nothing would be worse than that independent men should be snuffed out, and that there should be only two opinions, the Government opinion and the Opposition opinion. It is only out of the clash and interplay of various and contrary ideas that the truth can be discovered. It is only when we look at questions from many points of view that we begin to understand them. A perpetually unanimous cabinet disquiets me. We do not want 'pliant Ministers'. The Cabinet is enormously powerful, but in spite of this a Minister is relatively a much less important person nowadays.

Why, often when some important Minister resigned in former times, the whole Administration tottered, if it did not fall. But nowadays there are at least a dozen Cabinet Ministers who might resign or be dismissed in couples or in batches without the slightest difficulty being found in replacing them, or the smallest injury resulting to the Government of the day.

We are told at every turn that we must hand matters over to experts of all kinds. It reminds me of the machines in the railway stations and outside post offices. Put a penny in the slot, the machine does the rest. Well, we put our penny in the slot, and nothing happens. And all we can do, so we are told, is to go on putting in pennies and being patient. The machine, again, has the advantage of the man.

Now, a very good rejoinder could be made to this argument. It might be said that the suppression of the individual in politics is only what is happening to the small man in trade, and if in the latter case we get a more efficient service, why not in the former, too?

The cases are widely different. Commerce depends on combination; Parliament depends on personality; trade is based on agreement; politics on discussion. I believe that the influence of individual producers and distributors even in trade is healthy. But the influence of individual thought in politics is indispensable. I was never a rubber stamp M.P.

Truth is incontrovertible. Panic may resent it; ignorance may deride it; malice may distort it; but there it is. Nevertheless, the whole tendency is against the fearless, personal element. Perhaps no man's individuality is strong enough to stand the glare of modern life. Perhaps under our conditions the grand and heroic figures of the past would have withered into mere wire-pullers; or perhaps they were not such great men really in the past, no greater than we have today, and they only seem so because history used rose-coloured spectacles of high magnifying power. But that supposition is too terrible to entertain.

I believe in personality. But the tragedy of the twentieth century is that the development of human beings lags far behind the growth of their undertakings. We live in an age of great events and little men; and if we are not to become the slaves of our own systems or sink oppressed among the mechanism we have ourselves created, it will only be by the bold efforts of originality, by repeated experiment, by free and continual discussion of all things, and by the dispassionate consideration of the results of sustained and unflinching thought. Difficulties mastered are opportunities won, and courage is rightly esteemed the first of human qualities because it is the quality which guarantees all others.

There are many wise heads on young shoulders, and many foolish doctrines preached by grown-up people. Age has little to do with good sense. The new generation receive from the failing but faithful hands of their fathers the faithful inheritance which through the greatest cataclysms of history has been preserved inviolate.

What will they do with it? Will they be worthy of the sacrifices of the past? Will they maintain and earn the fame with which their forebears have endowed them? Will they learn in the years that are coming, and take noble unity into a new, brighter, broader, and, let us pray, tranquil age? Or will they fail? Will they squander in vain chatter and feeble, nerveless irresponsibility the proud possessions and liberties?

Only one thing is certain – the choice is in the hands of youth.

CHAPTER 16

Faith, Hope, And Nationality

PROVIDENCE HAS CONSTANTLY intervened in critical periods of my life and, I believe, protected me in times of danger.

When I was a young man, I passed through a violent and aggressive anti-religious phase which, had it lasted, might easily have made me a nuisance. But my poise was restored by frequent contact with danger. I found that whatever I might think and argue, I did not hesitate to ask for special protection when about to come under the fire of an enemy, nor to feel sincerely grateful when I got home safe to tea.

I saw the protecting presence of God in the fact that I was taken prisoner in the South African War, instead of being shot out of hand, and I am certain that my life was saved many times by Divine protection. Perhaps I was saved for that night in 1940 when at last I had authority to give decisions over the whole scene and felt as if I were walking with destiny, and that all my past life had been but a preparation for this hour and for this trial.

I had the same conviction one night in Scotland, in 1911, when I went to bed and saw a large Bible lying on a table in my bedroom. I opened the Book at random and in the ninth chapter of Deuteronomy I read:

> Hear, O Israel: Thou art to pass over Jordan, this day, to go in to possess nations greater and mightier than thyself, cities great and fenced up to heaven.
>
> A people great and tall, the children of the Anakims, whom thou

knowest, and of whom thou hast heard say: Who can stand before the children of Anak!

Understand therefore this day, that the Lord thy God is He which goeth over before thee; as a consuming fire He shall destroy them, and He shall bring them down before thy face: so shalt thou drive them out, and destroy them quickly, as the Lord hath said unto thee.

Speak not thou in thine heart after that the Lord thy God has cast them out from before thee saying: For my righteousness the Lord hath brought me in to possess this land; but for the wickedness of these nations the Lord doth drive them out from before thee.

Not for thy righteousness, or the uprightness of thine heart, dost thou go to possess their land: but for the wickedness of these nations the Lord thy God doth drive them out from before thee, and that he may perform the word which the Lord sware unto thy fathers, Abraham, Isaac, and Jacob.

This Biblical passage was, at the moment of my appointment as First Lord of the Admiralty, exactly suited to my need. It seemed a message full of reassurance.

God controls our lives, yet they are ours to shape. Cromwell fought his battles confident that God fought with him. On the day after the Battle of Dunbar he wrote to his wife: 'My weak faith hath been upheld. I have been in my inward man marvellously supported.'

Purely rationalistic and scientific explanations only prove the truth of the Bible story. At any rate there is no doubt about one miracle. A wandering tribe, in many respects indistinguishable from numberless nomadic communities, grasped and proclaimed an idea of which all the genius of Greece and all the power of Rome were incapable. There was to be only one God, a universal God, a God of nations, a just God, a God who would punish in another world a wicked man dying rich and prosperous; a God from whose service the good of the humble and of the weak and poor was inseparable.

Books are written in many languages upon the question of how much of this was due to Moses. Devastating, inexorable modern study and criticism have proved that the Pentateuch constitutes a body of narrative and doctrine which came into being over at least the compass of several centuries.

We reject, however, with scorn all those learned and laboured myths that Moses was but a legendary figure upon whom the priesthood and the people hung their essential social, moral, and religious ordinances.

We believe that the most scientific view, the most up to date and rationalistic conception, will find its fullest satisfaction in taking the Bible story literally, and in identifying one of the greatest of human beings with the most decisive leap-forward ever discernible in the human story.

Every prophet has to come from civilisation, but every prophet has to go into the wilderness. He has to have a strong impression of a complex society and all that it has to give, and then he has to serve periods of isolation and meditation. This is the process by which psychic dynamite is made.

Moses received from Jehovah the tables of those fundamental laws which were henceforward followed, with occasional lapses, by the highest form of human society. We may be sure that all these things happened just as they are set out according to Holy Writ. We may believe that they happened to people not so very different from ourselves, and that the impressions those people received were faithfully recorded and have been transmitted across the centuries with far more accuracy than many of the telegraphed accounts we read of the goings-on of today.

Many centuries were to pass before the God that spake in the Burning Bush was to manifest Himself in a new revelation, which nevertheless was the oldest of all the inspirations of the Hebrew people – as the God not only of Israel, but of all mankind who wished to serve Him; a God not only of justice but of mercy; a God not only of self-preservation and survival, but of pity, self-sacrifice, and ineffable love.

The Jews' sacred Scroll of the Law, which contains truths accepted by Jews and Christians alike, is very dear to me. We owe to the Jews in the Christian revelation a system of ethics which, even if it were entirely separated from the supernatural, would be the most precious possession of mankind, worth, in fact, the fruits of all other wisdom and learning together. On that system and by that faith there has been built out of the wreck of the Roman Empire the whole of our existing civilisation.

Some of our Bishops and clergy make heavy water about reconciling the Bible story with modern scientific and historical knowledge. Why do they want to reconcile them? If you are the recipient of a message which cheers your heart and fortifies your soul, which promises you reunion with those you have loved in a world of larger opportunity and wider sympathies, why should you worry about the shape or colour of the travel-stained envelope; whether it is duly stamped, whether the date on the postmark is right or wrong? These matters may be puzzling, but they are certainly not important. What is important is the message and the benefits to you of receiving it.

Let the men of science and of learning expand their knowledge and probe with their researches every detail of the records which have been preserved to us from these dim ages. All they will do is to fortify the grand simplicity and essential accuracy of the recorded truths which have lighted so far the pilgrimage of man.

The light of Christian ethics remains the most precious guide. Their revival and application is a practical need, whether spiritual or secular in nature, whether to those who find comfort and solace in revealed religion or those who have to face the mystery of human destiny alone. And on this foundation alone will come the grace of life and that reconciliation of the right of the individual with the needs of society from which the happiness, the safety, and the glory, of mankind may spring.

If we are to have the higher corporate life we must have the higher corporate incentive, we must have the larger spirit, the larger driving power. I do not think, however, that people can unite in communities unless they possess some guiding principle.

Today, as belief decays, which all Church leaders lament, it is almost impertinent to wonder what a man believes. But although belief may be more out of sight, I do not think it is entirely out of mind, and I think that people realise that without equal growth of mercy, pity, peace and love, mankind and science may destroy all that makes human life majestic and tolerable.

We must also not blind our eyes to religions such as Communism and Fascism and the power they exert in the world. They pervert the good gifts of humanity and science to the most insidious forms of propaganda. They do not lack champions, preachers, devotees, nor even martyrs. They seek to divide the world and to hurl the ancient noble nations of Christendom at one another in ferocious conflict.

When Hitler and Mussolini challenged God, they found the truth of His warning: 'The Kingdom of God shall be taken from you and given to a nation bringing forth the fruits thereof; and whosoever shall fall on this stone shall be broken, but on whomsoever it shall fall it will grind him to powder.'

We have our own world. Let us look after that, always remembering that belief in God; belief in ourselves; belief in nationality and country are essential. Nationalism, for example, is the greatest fact in the world. I remember hearing a Member of Parliament reply to the scornful question, 'What is nationalism?' – 'It is something that men are ready to die for.' That was years ago, and many parts of the world are covered with the graves of millions of men who have testified to this truth.

Many intellectuals believed that after the horrible carnage and desolation of war the thoughts of mankind would turn irresistibly to internationalism. They saw the means by which the World-State would be created. They hoped that Tennyson's prophecy of the 'Parliament of man, the Federation of the world' would be fulfilled with the rest of his memorable predictions. On the contrary, nationalism, the assertion of race, of country or of empire, became more passionate, more striking and more aggressive than ever.

States in every continent are upheld by nationalism. This is their internal strength and the foundation of all their governments; without it they would crumble and fall. Democracy under universal suffrage comprehended nationalism as easily and as light-heartedly as football matches. It is the greatest event in the Olympic games.

The noblest motives of self-sacrifice and duty, of loyalty and comradeship, march side by side with the narrowest prejudices and hungry ambition. Together they constitute an impulse upon human action and destiny incomparably more powerful than any other that can be discerned. Beneath and behind all is the primordial sense of self-preservation, the will to survive, if necessary upon the extinction of others.

The wars of peoples are far more terrible and more ruthless than the wars of kings and nobles. No standards restrain the combatants. The warriors of bygone ages of chivalry would shrink back appalled from the merciless ferocity of the great wars which we lived to endure. There is a callous disregard of life which would have astonished Marlborough, Frederick the Great, or even Napoleon. In the worst of their quarrels some sort of common understanding prevailed even between barbarian opponents. It was reserved for the twentieth century, with its enlightenment, to show wars fought to the last gasp of mighty populations where the wounded were left to die between the lines and no parley, even of the most formal character, regulated the fury or mitigated the course of the conflict.

A far more powerful and pervasive bond between the nations in the past was that of the Catholic Church, a universal church lifted high above the stormy scene. But with the Reformation Christendom was riven in twain and the sense of belonging to a corporate body vanished from the minds of men.

There is not, and there never was on this earth, a work of human policy so well deserving of examination as the Roman Catholic Church. The history of that Church joins together the two great ages of human civilisation. No other institution is left standing which carries the mind back to the times when the smoke of sacrifice rose from the Pantheon, and when the camelopards and tigers bounded in the Flavian amphitheatre.

There remains one other tie which might unite nations – the sense of common citizenship, of the unity of the brotherhood of men 'the wide world o'er', and it is upon this that our hopes for the future must largely be based. But this has been discredited through internationalism, tending into Bolshevism or Communism and revolution. Internationalism has become associated with the idea of destruction of property, of freedom and of civilisation, with mob rule or an ascendancy of blathering, brainless agitators. Indeed, it is this movement, carrying with it the extinction of liberalism, which proved the strongest stimulant of the growth of aggressive nationalism in almost every country in which this fatal illusion made its appearance.

Three main causes, therefore, contribute to the growth of economic nationalism: The desire to 'contract out' of world depression; the determination to maintain national standards of life; and the demands of home defence.

Nationalism is not limited always to the frontiers of races. Herr Emil Ludwig, in his book, 'Leaders of Europe', recalls a conversation with M. Briand, in which the Frenchman criticised President Wilson for placing 'too much importance on the question of ethnographic frontiers. As a matter of fact' he went on, 'each nation is composed of various races held together much more by common historical experiences than by kinship of blood. We and the French are made up of five or six different racial strains; but danger, defence and destiny have firmly welded us into one nation.'

It was in Germany that nationalism presented itself in its most repulsive form. The bitterness of defeat produced a monstrous reaction. A whole people, the most educated, the most scientific and one of the most gifted in the world, cast away every vestige of constitutional law and liberty. It repudiated the whole liberal civilisation of the nineteenth century. It proclaimed in ludicrous defiance of historic fact its possession of a racial purity in the name of which it conceived itself entitled, indeed bound, to drive from its bosom every strain of alien blood. Christianity itself was made to march at the goose-step. The swastika replaced the Cross. The Bible was re-written so that the Jordan became the Rhine, and Jerusalem Berlin – or perhaps Munich. The Eternal Father of mankind and Creator of the universe became a tribal god. This was a terrible reversion. It could be explained only by an inferiority complex which rendered one of the greatest branches of the human family singularly unsure of itself.

The Italian story was different. Here there was no bitterness of defeat. But the result was nationalism so intense as to absorb the whole energies and thoughts of the nation.

'Peoples which are rising, or rising again after a period of deca-dence,' wrote Mussolini, 'are always imperialist; any renunciation is a sign of decay and of death.'

Hitler, on the other hand, stirred his nationalistic brew with a different ladle. He spiced his recipe by plunging Germany back into the Middle Ages with Jew-baiting and official murder as the accepted, nay, the vaunted features of its national life.

This race, across the centuries in so many lands, driven from its own land, and almost throughout the world, has experienced every vicissi-tude, suffering, persecution, martyrdom and oppression in every form, generation after generations, century after century. No past services, no proved patriotism, even wounds sustained in war, could procure immunity for persons whose only crime was that their parents had brought them into the world. Every kind of persecution grave or petty, upon world-famous scientists, writers, and composers at the top to the wretched little Jewish children in the national schools, was practised, was glorified.

The hatred of the Jews led by a logical transition to an attack upon the historic basis of Christianity. Thus the conflict broadened swiftly, and Catholic priests and Protestant pastors fell under the ban of what became the religion of the German peoples, namely the worship of Germany under the symbol of the old gods of Nordic paganism.

None suffered more cruelly than the Jew the unspeakable evils wrought on the bodies and spirits of men by Hitler and his vile regime. In spite of all, Judaism survived and reserved its strength, its destiny, its power for good, its power to develop and to guide and aid by its development the march of the human mind. The passage of several thousand years sees no change in their characteristics and no diminution of their trials or their vitality. They survived in spite of all that the world could do against them, and all they could do against themselves. Their messages in religion, philosophy, and art have been the main guiding lights of modern faith and culture. Centuries of foreign rule and indescribable, endless oppression leave them still living, active communities and forces in the modern world. Their thought, inspiration and culture has been one of the vital dominants in world history. There are none of the arts or sciences which have not been enriched by their achievements. Their survival would never have been achieved or completed but for the main sheet-anchor – their unshakable unswerving adherence to the faith of their fathers. It is a precious thing, a bond of union, an inspiration and a source of great strength.

Some people like Jews and some do not; but no thoughtful man can doubt the fact that they are beyond all question the most formidable and the most remarkable race which has ever appeared in the world.

Disraeli, the Jewish Prime Minister of England, and Leader of the Conservative Party, who was always true to his race and proud of his origin, said on a well-known occasion: 'The Lord deals with the nations as the nations deal with the Jews.' Certainly when we look at countries where Jews were cruelly treated, we must admit that nothing that has since happened in the history of the world has falsified the truth of Disraeli's confident assertion.

The dual nature of mankind is nowhere more strongly exemplified as in the Jewish races, and this same astounding race produced another system of morals and philosophy, as malevolent as Christianity was benevolent.

There can be no greater mistake than to attribute to each individual a recognisable share in the qualities which make up the national character. There are all sorts of men – good, bad and, for the most part, indifferent – in every country, and in every race. Nothing is more wrong than to deny to an individual, on account of race or origin, his right to be judged on his personal merits and conduct. In a people of peculiar genius like the Jews, contrasts are more vivid, the extremes are more widely separated, the resulting consequences are more decisive.

There are three main lines of political conception among the Jews.

First there are the Jews who, dwelling in every country throughout the world, identify themselves with that country, enter into its national life, and, while adhering faithfully to their own religion, regard themselves as citizens in the fullest sense of the State. Such a Jew living in England would say, 'I am an Englishman practising the Jewish faith.'

This is a worthy conception, and useful in the highest degree. We in Great Britain well know that during the great struggles the influence of what may be called the 'National Jews' in many lands was cast preponderatingly on the side of the Allies; and in our own Forces Jews played a most distinguished part, some rising to the command of armies, others winning the Victoria Cross for valour.

The National Russian Jews, in spite of the disabilities under which they suffered, managed to play an honourable and useful part in the national life of Russia. They strenuously promoted the development of Russia's economic resources, and were foremost in the creation of those remarkable organisations, the Russian Co-operative Societies. In politics their support was given, for the most part, to liberal and progressive movements, and they were among the staunchest upholders of friendship with France and Great Britain.

In violent opposition to all this sphere of Jewish effort rose the schemes of men reared up among unhappy populations of countries where Jews were persecuted on account of their race. Most, if not all, of them had forsaken the faith of their forefathers, and divorced from their minds all spiritual hopes of the next world. This movement was not new. From the days of Spartacus-Weishaupt to those of Karl Marx, and down to Trotsky (Russia), Bela Kun (Hungary), Rosa Luxembourg (Germany), and Emma Goldman (United States), this world-wide conspiracy for the overthrow of civilisation and for the reconstitution of society steadily grew. It played a definitely recognisable part in the tragedy of the French Revolution. It was the mainspring of subversive movement during the nineteenth century; and at last this band of extraordinary personalities from the underworld of the great cities of Europe and America gripped the Russian people by the hair of their heads.

The most intense passions of revenge were excited in the breasts of Russian people, and hordes did not hesitate to gratify their lust for blood and revenge at the expense of the innocent Jewish population whenever an opportunity occurred. Brutal massacres, everywhere found among the half-stupefied, half-infuriated population an eager response to anti-Semitism in its worst and foulest forms. This was an injustice on millions of helpless people, most of whom suffered from the revolutionary regime. It became, therefore, specially important to foster and develop any strongly-marked movement which led directly away from these fatal associations. And it is here that Zionism had such a deep significance for the whole world.

Zionism offered the third sphere to the political conceptions of the Jewish race. In violent contrast to international communism, it presented to the Jew a national idea of a commanding character. It fell to the British Government, as the result of the conquest of Palestine, to have the opportunity and the responsibility of securing for the Jewish race all over the world a home and a centre of national life. The statesmanship and historic sense of Mr Balfour were prompt to seize this opportunity. Declarations have been made which irrevocably decided the policy of Great Britain. The fiery energies of Dr Weizmann, the leader, for practical purposes, of the Zionist project, backed by many of the most prominent British Jews, and supported by the full authority of Lord Allenby, all directed to achieving the success of this inspiring movement.

Of course, Palestine was far too small to accommodate more than a fraction of the Jewish race, nor do the majority of national Jews wish to go there. But it was clear that a Jewish State by the banks of the Jordan would from every point of view be beneficial. Zionism became a factor in the political convulsions of Russia, as a powerful competing influence. Nothing could be more significant than the fury with which Trotsky attacked the Zionists generally, and Dr Weizmann in particular. The cruel penetration of Trotsky's mind left him in no doubt that his schemes of a world-wide Communistic State were directly thwarted and hindered by this new ideal, which directed the energies and hopes of Jews in every land towards a simpler, a truer, and a far more attainable goal. The struggle was little less than a struggle for the soul of the Jewish people. The Bolshevik movement was repudiated vehemently by the great mass of the Jewish race. But positive and practicable alternatives are needed in the moral as well as in the social sphere; and in building up with the utmost possible rapidity a Jewish national centre in Palestine which could become not only a refuge to the oppressed from the unhappy lands of Europe, but also a symbol of Jewish unity and the temple of Jewish glory, a task was presented on which many blessings rested.

The exploitation of anti-Semitism as a means by which violent and reactionary forces seize or attempt to seize, despotic power, afflicted the civilised world with a refugee problem similar to that of the Huguenots in the seventeenth century. The brunt of this fell upon the very small country and administration of Palestine. In the years that have passed, many troubles have been overcome there, and great developments have taken place. So may we not hope that Jews and

and Arabs will try to come together to restore the peace and revive the prosperity of their joint estate?

When I look back on the work done in building up a nation, in reclaiming the desert, in receiving refugees from Europe, I feel it is our duty to see fair play. At the same time we earnestly hope that the problem of Arab refugees will receive continuous attention and, particularly, that bickering between Israel and Jordan be brought to an end to mutual advantage to both sides. I had a lot to do with the formation of both these States, and I believe that they have both great services to render each other by living together as good neighbours. Perseverance and good neighbourliness is not a policy with which anyone can find fault. Therefore, I hope and trust that the Arab States will come to peace with Israel, and I earnestly pray that the great conception of a home for this historic people, where they live on the land of their ancestors, may eventually receive its full fruition.

I also have a great liking for the Arabs. I was the man who appointed Abdullah to be King of Transjordan. I acted upon the advice of that great man, Colonel Lawrence, who was at my side in making this arrangement.

Let us be tolerant, and let us be friendly, and let us support Arab rights and help forward legitimate Zionist aspirations. I believe that the building of the Jewish national home will bring blessing to the whole world, as well as to dispersed Jews, to Britain, and to all the inhabitants of Palestine, without distinction or creed.

One thing is clear. Both honour and wisdom demand that the State of Israel should be preserved, and that this brave, dynamic and complex race should be allowed to live in peace with its neighbours. They can bring to the area a valuable contribution of scientific knowledge, industriousness, and productivity. They must be given an opportunity of doing so in the interest of the whole Middle East.

The persecuted Jews of Europe look to the Holy Land to find a national identity, whilst in the Far East, the rivalry of Russia, China, and Japan, and their intensely nationalist policies, are a very real threat. It may seem curious to talk of Communist Russia pursuing nationalist policies. The rulers of that vast country, which sprawls across the maps of Europe and of Asia, are the high priests of internationalism. But though the Bear has been dressed in a red jacket and taught to wave a red flag, it is still the same Bear. Its embrace is just as deadly.

The wheel has turned the circle. The foreign policy of Russia today is not different from the foreign policy of the Czars. The mood of nationalism grows steadily and those who once cried. 'Workers of the world, unite!' now turn their minds to national and imperialistic ambitions. And all over the globe the tide is rising. The problem before us is how nationalism may be diverted into creative, rather than destructive channels, and made to serve the good of the human race. These fierce energies, these unselfish devotions, these ardent loyalties are not evil in themselves, but good. They may be the means of destroying the world. They are also an essential part of its motive power.

Hopes appear to rest mainly on the growth of international feeling and on the United Nations, which represents, even in its present form, a world opinion which no nation can afford to disdain. It is through the United Nations that redress of grievances may gradually be procured and effective power lent to the moral sanctions of mankind. All nations stand upon the portals of supreme catastrophe and of a measure-less reward. My faith is that in God's mercy we shall choose aright. But the path will be long, stony and precarious. All must tread it with patience, but also with vigilant precaution; for many a year has yet to pass before we reach again the proud belief of the Victorian Age that 'all the men in all the lands are necessary to one another', and before states and individuals learn to reconcile duties with the claims of humanity, and find their personal and national well-being only in the general good.

CHAPTER 17

Let's Play Hunt The Millionaire

I PRESENT MYSELF before you as a Seeker after Truth; and if háply in my quest I should discern some glimpses of the more obvious forms of truth, the seeker will not hesitate to become the guide.

I regard parliamentary institutions as precious to us almost beyond compare. They seem to give by far the closest association yet achieved between the life of the people and the action of the State. They possess apparently an unlimited capacity of adaptiveness, and they stand an effective buffer against every form of revolutionary or reactionary violence. It should be the duty of faithful subjects to preserve these institutions in their healthy vigour, to guard them against the encroachment of external forces, and to revivify them from one generation to another from the springs of national talent, interest, and esteem.

We must, however, recognise the great change which has come over our public life. Before, issues fought out in Parliament were political and social. The parties fought one another heartily in a series of well-known stock and conventional quarrels, and the life of the nation proceeded underneath this agitated froth. It is no longer a case of one party fighting another, nor of one set of politicians scoring off another set. It is the case of successive governments facing economic problems, and being judged by their success or failure in the duel. The nation is not interested in politics, it is interested in economics. It has in the main got the political system it wants; what it now asks for is more money, better times, regular employment, expanding comfort, and material prosperity. It turns to Parliament asking for guidance, and never was a body more capable of dealing with political issues. Its structure has stood the strain of the most violent contentions. Its long tradition, its collective personality, its flexible procedure, its social life, its unwritten inviolable conventions have made an organism more effective for the purpose of assimilation than any of which there is record.

The constitutional boa-constrictor which has already devoured and absorbed the donkeys of so many generations only requires reasonable time to convert to its own nourishment and advantage almost any number of rabbits. And similarly the House of Commons tames, calms, instructs, reconciles, and rallies to the fundamental institutions of the State all sorts and conditions of men and women.

Members elected as the result of the antagonisms and partisanship of class and party may find in Parliament the means of adjusting their differences and providing a continual process by which the necessary changes in national life can be made. Political questions can be settled to a very large extent by counting noses, and by the recognised rough-and-tumble of electioneering. One feels grave doubt whether our economic problems will be solved by such methods. One may even be pardoned for doubting whether institutions based on adult suffrage could possibly arrive at the right decisions upon the intricate propositions of modern business and finance.

In the economic world, there have been earthquakes and repeated tremors. Many tall buildings have fallen down. Others are dangerously cracked. Even some of those which were most securely founded are out of the true.

Everyone has quitted the top storeys. We are all dwelling much nearer the ground. The world is at a lower level. It is not so far to the pavement. But people's nerves are strained. They do not know how many more seismic disturbances are coming. They even begin to wonder whether our city of civilisation will not become uninhabitable. Timorous persons are already preparing to take to the woods. They are packing up their belongings, keeping a store of ready money, living with staff in hand and loins girded ready to depart.

But, after all, when we look around, we see that no fatal damage has been done to the strength and structure of world economic life. All its machinery is working regularly; indeed, it is working more perfectly every day. The mills, the trains, the Tubes, the water supply, all the processes by which food and materials are transported to and fro across the globe, are running more smoothly, more easily, than they ever ran before.

Science has marched forward unceasingly. Organisation in every form has improved. The earth has yielded superabundant supplies of all the most necessary and desirable commodities. We have better engines, easier transport, cheaper living, more reasonable and comprehending populations than at any time in recorded history. Still there is this fear.

It persists. It grows. Many important but fitful efforts are made to allay it. None of these efforts has as yet stemmed the tide.

In every highly developed country a profound perplexity exists about what to do. Everywhere the statesmen or rulers have resorted to the experts of economics and finance. Everywhere these experts have given contradictory opinions. Some of them say: 'Save, and all will be well,' Others say: 'Spend, and you will recover.'

In each case, these opposing experts have endless arguments, all extremely logical and refined, in following which ordinary people very quickly lose their way. The Saving School cry: 'Cut your coat according to your cloth. The lesser the cloth the smaller the coat. And so on, ad infinitum.' The Spending School rejoin: 'Set your idle factories at work to make all the cloth you may dream of and make your coat as big as you please, and so expand steadily and without limit.' And the statesmen return to their Cabinets more puzzled than ever about what they ought to do.

Then upon the rostrum arrive the Quacks. Each is sure that his remedy is sovereign; each stultifies his rival and not unfrequently himself. 'The Capitalist system has broken down,' cry the Socialists. 'Only put our crowd in office, let our Trade Union and Labour leaders manage the productive industries, the distribution of goods, their exchange, and, above all, the banks, and in a very short time, with reduced hours, relaxed exertion, and higher rewards, Nature will discharge her inexhaustible cornucopia upon mankind'. So say the Socialists.

But then we look where they have tried all this, and killed, starved, or subjugated everyone who disagreed with or even doubted their policy, and we find much worse conditions in 'the proletariat', the great masses of the people, than prevail in the Capitalist countries.

The advocates of currency reform have much more to say for themselves. They, too, have made some ugly experiments. In Germany they let the mark go to the moon, and built up again from the bottom without finding anything else at the end of their excursions but unemployment, discontent, incipient revolution, and continual financial disorders.

A great danger also seems to arise from the mood to hunt down rich men as if they were noxious beasts. Hunt the millionaire is a very attractive sport, and once it gets started quite a lot of people everywhere are found ready to join in the chase. Moreover, the quarry is at once swift and crafty, and, therefore, elusive. The pursuit is long and exciting, and everyone's blood is roused by its ardour. The question arises whether the general well-being of the masses of the community will be advanced by an excessive indulgence in this amusement. The idea that prosperity can be wooed by chasing millionaires is one of the most common and most foolish popular delusions. The millionaire or multi-millionaire is a highly economic animal. He sucks up with sponge-like efficiency money from all quarters. In this process, far from depriving ordinary people of their earnings, he launches enterprise and carries it through – raises values and expands that credit without which on a vast scale no fuller economic life can be opened to the millions.

To hunt wealth is not to capture commonwealth.

This money-gathering, credit-producing animal can not only walk – he can run. And when frightened he can fly. If his wings are clipped, he can dive or crawl. When in the end he is hunted down, what is left but a very ordinary individual apologising volubly for his mistakes, and particularly for not having been able to get away? But, meanwhile, great propositions have crumbled to the ground. Confidence is shaken and enterprises chilled, and the unemployed queue up with ever-growing expense to the taxpayer and nothing more appetising to take home to their families than the leg or the wing of what was once a millionaire.

One quite sees that people who have got interested in this fight will not accept such arguments against their sport. What they will have to accept is the consequences of ignoring such arguments.

It is indispensable to the wealth of nations and to the wage and life standards of labour that capital and credit should be honoured and cherished partners in the economic system.

If this is rejected there is always, of course, the Russian alternative. But no one can suppose that self-reliant populations such as the United States, which cut down the forests and ploughed up the soil and laced the continent with railroads and carried wealth-getting and wealth-diffusing to a higher point than ever before reached by mankind, would be content for a week with the dull, brutish servitude of Russia.

There can never be good wages or good employment for any length of time without good profits, and the sooner this is recognised, the better.

There are elements of contrivance, of housekeeping, and of taking risks which are essential to all profitable activity. If these are destroyed the capitalist system fails, and some other system must be substituted.

No doubt the capitalist system is replete with abuses and errors and inequities, like everything else in our imperfect human life; but it was under it that the United States produced the greatest prosperity for the greatest numbers that has ever been experienced in human record. It is not illogical to say: 'Rather than condone these faults and these abuses we will sweep this system away, no matter what it costs in our material well-being. We will replace it by the only other system which enables large organisations and developments to be undertaken – namely, nationalisation of all the means of production, distribution, credit and exchange.'

It is, however, irrational to tear down or cripple the capitalist system without having the fortitude of spirit and ruthlessness of action to create a new Communist system.

If the capitalist system is to continue with its rights of private property, with its pillars of rents, interest and profit, and the sanctity of contracts recognised and enforced by the State, then it must be given a fair chance.

It is the same for us in the Old World. If we are to continue in the old leaky lifeboat amid stormy seas, we must do our best to keep it bailed, to keep it afloat and to steer for port.

If we decide to take to the rafts of a new system, there, also, we must be assured there is a chance of making land.

It is a very open question, which any household may argue to the small hours, whether it is better to have equality at the price of poverty, or well-being at the price of inequality.

Life is pretty rough anyhow. Whether we are ruled by tyrannical bureaucrats or self-seeking capitalists, the ordinary man who has to earn his living, and tries to make provision for old age and for his dear ones when his powers are exhausted, has a hard pilgrimage through this dusty world.

The United States was built upon property, liberty and enterprise, and certainly it has afforded the most spacious and ample life to the scores of millions that has ever yet been witnessed.

To make an irrevocable departure would be a serious step, and should be measured with fearless eye.

Although we are assured that the age of miracles is past, no one has suggested that the credulity of mankind has diminished. Everywhere we find the belief fondly held by millions that some great new world is going to open where work will do itself, or almost do itself, and where 'something for nothing' is the order of the day.

No doctrine is more unpopular, no counsel is more resented than the contradiction of these daydreams.

Nevertheless, I adhere to the school of those who believe that governments cannot make nations rich; that wealth is gathered only by individual exertion and enterprise; that State expenditure is almost always profligate and wasteful.

The more freedom enjoyed by the citizen and the less the interference of the State, the higher will be the standard of the public well-being.

This in no way detracts from the tireless and courageous rooting out of scandals and abuses. It in no way impugns vast State-aided and State-organised insurance schemes. It does not seek to limit compassionate legislation for the weak and poor, nor to relieve wealth from its obligations to the national exchequer.

We have achieved a very high degree of wealth taxation without too grievously hampering business or impairing enterprise. All our experience shows, however, that an attempt to take more than half the income and capital of citizens, however rich, defeats the very purpose of the tax collector. Other extravagant hopes are centred on the use of national credit.

When one sees how great is the power of a mighty modern State to manufacture credit and print money, no one can wonder that the idea of a limitless fountain of State-produced wealth should captivate the minds of the toiling millions.

I am a firm believer in manufacturing public credit to the highest extent possible without producing an evil reaction.

Wealth and credit are the draft horses of society, and they should be made to pull the national coach up the unending hill.

But beware you do not starve, maltreat or injure those invaluable animals, for without their aid we shall all slide back rapidly into the morasses of barbarism.

The inflationary expansion of credit has a part to play in every highly-organised economic State. It is like 'daylight saving'. And the world is now converted to this idea.

I remember how it was ridiculed, and how I myself was censured years ago for supporting it as President of the Board of Trade. But 'daylight saving' is nothing more or less than a refined adjustment of human activities to truth itself. We bring clock time into a more convenient relation with sun time, and real benefits result. But it is no good administering a double dose; for then you would get as much out of touch with reality as you were before the first dose was taken.

Inflation and deflation should be used to preserve a steady, even tenor. The idea that boundless riches can be liberated by currency manipulation is mischievous and vain.

These ideas of State-made wealth boil and bubble. One of the most obvious causes is the unwarranted dissatisfaction with the capitalist system, which has reared the majestic structure of American and European civilisation.

By it and in it we have been led into a scientific world which, with all its faults and injustices, is far beyond the brightest dreams of our ancestors. We have seen the immense expansion of population go hand in hand with the diffusion of comfort and culture, and of the elements of the good life for which there is no parallel in the past.

Confidence, courage, patience and the practice of the ordinary virtues in a State of freedom will unquestionably reopen the path from an amazing youth to a still more splendid maturity. Therefore, we must in times like the present beware of experiments and of fallacies which will undermine our economic foundations.

We must beware of trying to build a society in which nobody counts for anything except a politician or an official, a society where enterprise gains no reward and thrift no privileges. I say 'trying to build' because of all races in the world our people would be the last to consent to be governed by a bureaucracy. Freedom is their very life blood.

We have succeeded in keeping public thought free from wild, visionary aspirations because there is a very deep-seated and obstinate belief that there is no short cut to the millennium.

Some strange figures leaped upon the American scene, with doctrines and promises.

The assassination of Senator Huey Pierce Long did not stop the 'Share Our Wealth' agitation, which he launched to forward his ambitions. It sounds so easy to promise as he did 'to every deserving family' a motor-car, a radio, and £1,000, free of debt. When to this are added jobs for all, shorter hours of work, old-age pensions of £7 10s.

a month, it is easy to see how millions of people, struggling with keen and cruel difficulties, haunted by the memories of a recent prosperity, should be drawn into the eddies of such a gleaming whirlpool.

'Share Our Wealth' enthusiasts demand that a considerable part – in many cases a major part – of all the remaining great private fortunes should be liquidated. This is a plan which has often been tried before and will no doubt often be tried again. If it is, in the process all the good-will, thrift and contrivance of every business would be destroyed. There could be no resale of these impounded properties because there could be no purchasers.

The sharing of the wealth could only proceed if the Government were able to manage all these multifarious and haphazard assorted businesses in a manner more profitable than can their existing owners.

It is not so easy to mint the moonlight into silver and turn the sunshine into gold.

A figure slipped into the American political limelight – Father Coughlin. It was difficult for people in Britain to understand exactly what Father Coughlin wanted – perhaps he did not know himself. But when he talked on the iniquities of the financiers, and the evils of the profit system, he seemed to align himself with Socialists and Communists.

The idea that profits are unclean, that a profit is an evil, that profit-making is repugnant to moral sense, and should be branded as a crime is, of course, destructive of every form of prosperity. It removes from the whole of economic society every incentive to good housekeeping.

No one denies that a Government, invested with autocratic powers, can carry on every kind of business. But almost all are carried on at a loss compared with private enterprise. In Russia, where ruthless power is used, the managers of State concerns are imprisoned or even put to death for not achieving success and making the business pay. Capitalism, with no severer penalty than bankruptcy, produces a far higher economy.

Before we join with Father Coughlin in condemning the profit system, we should feel inclined to wonder what he would have put in its place, and whether the suggested alternative would give better results, not to any particular class or section, but to the community as a whole. It is the mass of the people who should be considered.

It might well be that measures which in the course of several years would vastly improve the economic position actually and relatively, and open broadly the high roads of the future, would be extremely unpopular, and that no single party, even if they possessed the secret, would be able to carry their policy in the face of opposition by the others. In fact it would probably be safe to say that nothing that is popular and likely to gather a large number of votes will do what is wanted and win the prize which all desire.

No doubt each political party picks out unconsciously from tables of economic law the tenets which they think will be most agreeable to the crowd that votes for them, or which they hope will vote for them. They ignore or transgress the others. They then proceed to plume themselves upon their orthodoxy. But the growth of public opinion, and still more of voting opinion, violently and instinctively rejects many features. No one, for instance, will agree that wages should be settled only by the higgling of the market. No one would agree that modern world-dislocation of industry through new processes, or the development of new regions, or the improvement of international communications, or through gigantic speculations, should simply be met by preaching thrift and zeal to the displaced worker. Few would agree that private enterprise is the sole agency by which fruitful economic undertakings can be launched or conducted. An adverse conviction on all these points is general, and practice has long outstripped conviction. The climate of opinion in which we live today assigns the highest importance to minimum standards of life and labour. It is generally conceded that the humble local toiler must be protected or insured against exceptional external disturbance.

Enormous expenditures have grown up for social and compassionate purposes. Direct taxation has risen to heights never dreamed of by the old economists and statesmen, and at these heights has set up many far-reaching reactions of an infrugal and even vicious character. We are in the presence of new forces not existing when the text-books were written. There are the violent changes in world prices and in the localities where the leadership of particular industries is situated. There is the power of vast accumulations of capital. There are the remarkable economies with their consequent competitive dominance which flow from scientific mass production. There is the vast network of cartels and trading agreements which has grown up irrespective of frontiers, national sentiments, and fiscal laws. These examples could be multiplied. It is certain that the economic problem is not adequately solved, indeed is not solved at all, by the teachings of the text-books, however grand may be their logic, however illustrious may be their authors.

But a harder task lies before us than the mere breaking up of old-established conclusions. It may well be indeed that these conclusions are sound, that they are the true foundations of the palace in which we seek some day to dwell. Our task is not to break up these foundations and use the fragments as missiles in party warfare. Our task is to build another storey upon them equally well-proportioned, symmetrical and unified.

If the doctrines of the old economists no longer serve for the purposes of our society, they must be replaced by a new body of doctrine equally well-related in itself, and equally well-fitting into a general theme. There is no reason that the new system should be at variance with the old. There are many reasons why it should be a consistent, but a more complex, secondary application. I cannot believe that the true principles will be discovered by our excellent Parliamentary and electoral institutions. We might have a General Election in which eight million voters were taught to sing in chorus, 'Make the foreigner pay', and eight million more to chant in unison, 'Give the rich man's money to the poor, and so increase the consuming power'; and five other millions to intone, 'Your food will cost you more'. We might have all this; we probably shall! But even so we may be none the wiser or the better off.

There are a few plain simple truths which can be proclaimed which may be a help.

First, panic is not only futile but pernicious. As we say in a disorderly meeting: 'Let everyone look after one.' If we all do our daily duties as good citizens of the world, in whatever station we occupy, we may be certain we shall get our daily bread.

Secondly, the downfall of values and prices must have its end. Whether the economists or statesmen take the right course or the wrong, the human race, having got thus far upon its journey, must be supplied with its necessities in food, clothing, and the materials to keep its structures in being. However great the production of science, however stunted the under-consumption of Fear, we are sure to reach a solid foundation.

Men must eat; fires must burn; trains and motor-cars must run; ships must sail, and crops will grow. We are straining after a far higher organisation than that. We are struggling with difficulties, but beneath them all there is an absolutely invulnerable foundation. Even reduced to primitive barter, the world could keep itself alive. In the existing state of the world we require more bone and fibre in our economic system. But our main difficulty is psychological. Everything is quite sound. But we lack focus. We lack grip. We have got to accept harder and stiffer rules of life and conduct. We have got to lay firmer hands upon the life we have so long enjoyed.

Beyond our immediate difficulty lies the root problem of modern world economics; namely, the strange discordance between the consuming and producing power. Is it not astonishing that with all our knowledge and science, with the swift and easy means of communication and correspondence which exist all over the world, the most powerful and highly organised communities should remain the sport and prey of these perverse tides and currents? Are we really to believe that no better adjustment can be made between supply and demand? Many attempts have been made, from the extremes in Russia to the extremes of Capitalism in the United States. Surely it is this mysterious crack and fissure at the basis of all our arrangements and apparatus upon which the keenest minds throughout the world should be concentrated? Are we not capable of evolving a united body of doctrine adapted to our actual conditions and requirements? Could not such a system of policy, when devised, be taken out of the political brawling and given a fair trial by overwhelming consent?

Many dangers threaten representative institutions. There are dangers from the right and dangers from the left. But the British Parliamentary system will not be overthrown by political agitation: for that is what it specially comprehends. It will pass only when it has shown itself incapable of dealing with some fundamental and imperative economic need.

It must be observed that economic problems, unlike political issues, cannot be solved by any expression, however vehement, of the national will, but only by taking the right action. You cannot cure cancer by a majority. What is wanted is a remedy. Everyone knows what the people wish. They wish for more prosperity. How to get it? That is the question.

All kinds of popular cries can be presented for an election, and each may contain some measure of the truth. None in itself will provide us with the key. If new light is to be thrown upon this grave and clamant problem, it must in the first instance receive examination from a non-political body, free altogether from party exigencies, and composed of persons possessing special qualifications in economic matters. Parliament would, therefore, be well advised to create such a body subordinate to itself, and assist its deliberations to the utmost. The spectacle of an Economic sub-Parliament debating day after day with fearless detachment from public opinion all the most disputed questions of Finance and Trade, and reaching conclusions by voting, would be an innovation, but an innovation easily to be embraced by our flexible constitutional system. I see no reason why the political Parliament should not choose in proportion to its party groupings a subordinate Economic Parliament of say one-fifth of its numbers, and composed of persons of high technical and business qualifications. I see no reason why such an assembly should not debate in the open light of day and without caring a halfpenny who won the General Election.

Parliament should create a new instrument specially adapted for the purpose, and delegate to that instrument all necessary powers and facilities.

We see our race drifting to and fro with the tides and currents of a deeply-disturbed ocean. The compass has been damaged. The charts are out of date. The crew have to take it in turns to be captains and every captain before every movement of the helm has to take a ballot not only of the crew but of an ever-increasing number of passengers.

No one can predict the immediate course of politics, but we may be quite sure that the virtues and sagacity of long-trained responsible peoples will in the long run give and endure, will do and dare all that may be necessary for welfare and survival. It will all end by our all trying our best, and by our all coming safely through our troubles.

CHAPTER 18

The Right To Strike

THE RIGHT TO strike is the foundation of the liberties of the labouring man. In it are involved all those things which matter most in his work-aday life; the right to choose and to change his employment or employer; the right to demand improved conditions, shorter hours, higher wages; the right to defend himself against petty tyranny or ill-usage. All these are bound up with the workman's right, either separately or in combination, to withhold his labour until his needs are satisfied.

The capitalist system on which our whole present civilisation is erected has grown up on the basis of the right to strike. Its main defence is that with all the inequalities and unfairnesses between man and man and class and class, with all the anomalies involved in the accidents of possession and inheritance, it has undoubtedly offered and offers an ever widening freedom to the individual worker with hand or brain in choosing how and where, under what conditions and what masters, he will earn his daily bread.

Just as the right to strike is the greatest glory of the capitalist system, so the denial of that right is the fatal defect of any system of Communism, or universal State ownership.

With all its practical defects, capitalism is founded on individual freedom. With all its fine theoretical ideals, socialism is founded on compulsion. We must therefore regard this right as one of the most precious enjoyed by human beings, and however much we suffer from its abuse we must understand that our civilisation is not only dignified by, but is dependent upon, its preservation.

Whereas we have seen over and over again other races of men in periods of upheaval aiming at unattainable standards of *equality*, the Anglo-Saxons have always prized personal *liberty* as the first of their political ideals.

In modern times, even while the franchise was very much restricted, Parliament has been steadfast and zealous in maintaining and making fully effective the right to strike; and a long series of laws enabling workmen to combine, to refuse their labour in combination, to conduct a strike in a practical, lawful and resolute way, find an honourable place on our Statute Book.

It is necessary from time to time that those who seem to think that money-making, or what is called production, is the only thing that matters, and who resent, as if it were an affront, every assertion of an independent status on the part of working men, should be reminded of the essential conditions of our free democratic society.

Even in the extraordinary stresses of the war, when we were fighting for our lives, strikes, although declared illegal, were in Great Britain dealt with only by persuasion, by concession, and by force of public opinion. The same is true, though to a lesser extent, of our Allies and even of our enemies.

It was reserved for Lenin and Trotsky, in their frantic applications of Communism, not only to deny the right to strike but to execute without mercy the leaders of the strikers and, as we are assured, send their carcases to the local Zoological gardens.

But a new set of circumstances has arisen in the world which all our citizens must take into very earnest consideration, and which it is vital for them to comprehend.

During the last hundred years the conditions of civilised life have altered more than they did in the previous thousand years. Our human nature has no doubt changed very little, but the system on which and by which scores of millions of people live has altered absolutely. At the end of the Napoleonic wars the British people lived, as it were, on the ground. Their conditions were harsh and crude, but they were simple. They were not capable of being shattered by any sudden shock or overturn. The people ate the food they grew; they worked where they lived; their industries were in their infancy; their cities and towns were fed from the surrounding districts. Being already on the ground they had not far to fall.

How different is the situation today!

We are hoisted up, scores of millions of us, on a vast artificial platform, thirty or forty storeys above the surface of the earth. The genius and industry of man have wrested from nature the means to accomplish this marvel.

On the high platform to which we have raised ourselves we not only enjoy comforts, amenities and securities utterly beyond the dreams of our great-grandfathers, we not only look out upon an almost limitless prospect, but, and this is the point which should specially be borne in mind, there are many millions more of us.

All these extra millions, be they rich or poor, exist on a purely artificial and scientific basis far removed from the natural life of man. Scientific civilisation has given these millions their chance of life. Without it they could never have come into the world, and if it were suddenly overturned or shattered they could not continue in the world.

All men and women must consider the indispensable and we will even say the sacred right to strike, and to strike in combination, on the one hand; and on the other hand the positively awful consequences which would fall upon all of us if we destroyed the structure or the processes with which our existence is bound up.

And at this point we observe that there has come into prominence a class of men who seem to think that because their hands are on the switches and the levers by which scientific civilisation lives they have only to stay them to be masters of the world. They claim that it is legitimate for those workers who deal with communications, transportation, and power in all its mechanical applications, to band themselves together and by a swift, sudden and secretly prepared blow lay the whole community at their mercy.

How very different is this kind of action from the ordinary exercise of the right to strike! It is, in fact, a gross and flagrant abuse of that right.

Whereas the foundation of the right to strike lies in the defence of personal liberties, in choosing or changing employment or bargaining with an employer for better wages and conditions, this abuse – the lightning strike of vital services – has nothing to do with the defence of personal freedom, but is, in fact, an unconstitutional and tyrannical attempt to seize the supreme control of the State.

And here the right to strike finds itself confronted with another right – *the right of the community to exist*, and for that purpose to defend itself by every conceivable means. In the great railway strike of 1911 the country was wholly unprepared; mechanical transport and the organising experience we have learned in the war did not exist. In consequence it became perfectly certain that had the strike continued another week or ten days several large cities in the North of England would have actually starved, and if then the strikers had relented, as no doubt they would, it would have been too late, for the food supplies could not have been replaced in time to prevent many thousands of people from dying of famine.

In a general railway strike arrangements were made which would have enabled the cities to be fed for a very considerable time, and during that time a great many things would have happened. Face to face with such a situation, there are no measures which a Government could take in defence of the lives of millions of helpless people in which it would not be supported by the overwhelming mass of the nation. Public opinion must inevitably rally to the Government with spontaneous force, and public opinion is a power which influences the mind of the striker as much as anyone else.

Therefore we believe that any attempt to subvert the State by means of a sudden general strike against the community by those employed in vital services would be bound to fail, although pushed to the utmost extreme on either side.

It stands to reason that the community as a whole must rally to those who are striving to feed it and against those who are striving to starve it; and the community, when roused, is an irresistible force.

But when we think of the loss and suffering which such great struggles and trials of strength among our own fellow countrymen must bring, we should surely ask ourselves whether there are not better ways of treating the matter.

Is it really so difficult after all to draw the line of distinction between the right to strike and the abuse of that right?

Is it too hard to define the industries in which men may leave their employment at the shortest notice, and separate them from those in which they cannot leave without giving adequate and ample notice?

Is it impossible to discriminate between strikes against the private employer and strikes against the community, between strikes in defence of personal liberty and strikes in pursuit of political domination?

If the community is, in fact, so utterly dependent upon the daily discharge of these vital services, it would surely be wise in the first place to make sure that the workers in them have no just cause of complaint, and that the wages and conditions of their employment are in no respect inferior to those of any other similar class of workers. Although agitators and wirepullers are always ready to foment quarrels, no great body of respectable men are likely to listen to them without some very genuine grievance.

But something more is needed. Those who enter these vital services must accept the fact that the abuse by them of the right to strike will be fought by the community and the Government with all their might. Would they not, therefore, be wise to consent to such restrictions upon their right to strike as are necessary to safeguard the life of the community, and to receive from the community in return and in compensation special privileges and advantages?

In short, the State should define the vital services; it should be responsible for the labour conditions in those services; it should devise and erect special machinery for settling disputes without recourse to striking; it should make a special contract with those who freely enter these services, in virtue of which they would consent voluntarily, and in return for exceptional advantages, not to quit their employment in such great numbers or at such short notice as to produce a general breakdown to the grave injury of the commonwealth.

Nothing but benefit will follow from the frank and manly discussion of these matters with a view to reconciling the rights of the individual with those of the community, and enabling men and women to work together to build up the prosperity of all.

The strength of a nation depends upon the spirit of its manual wage-earners.

Those who plough its fields, mine its coal, build its homes, operate its transport services, tend the machines in its factories and workshops, and perform the thousand and one tasks that are necessary to the smooth functioning of a complex civilisation, constitute, with their dependents, the vast majority of every community.

These millions of workers must be willing partners in the general Commonwealth. They must share in the prosperity that could not be created without them.

It would be suicidal selfishness that, in these days of mass production, would seek to deny to the workman his full reward.

These considerations must be borne in mind when we approach the thorny subject of unions.

The dangers in combinations of workmen have, for centuries, been portrayed. They may be captured by extremists. They sometimes make absurd and fantastic demands. They betray, on occasion, an alarming irresponsibility – and break without compunction agreements solemnly concluded. They tend to limit output and resist necessary change. But do these evils outweigh the resentment and bitterness engendered when unionism is suppressed and driven underground?

We regard the right of a workman to withhold his labour and enter into combinations with other workmen for that purpose as one of the fundamental principles of capitalistic society, and as differentiating it from all systems of tyranny, or the older naked forms of slavery.

Trade unionism passed, at the turn of this century, through a phase. A new, radical, combative unionism challenged the old respectabilities. It set out to enlist the unskilled workers and to secure 'a square deal for the under-dog'.

Among its leaders were a number of Socialist fire-brands. It used the strike weapon freely. There were riots and disturbances.

In the south of England labour had assumed a more menacing aspect; but Mr John Burns, the man who, more than any other, had shaped and led the new unionism, whose name had made nervous citizens tremble, sat, 20 years after Trafalgar-square riots, in the same Cabinet as myself.

Many other trade-union leaders developed in a similar way. They began as extremists. As experience brought new viewpoints and opened wider horizons, they mellowed. In the end they served not only their union, but the wider community.

The employer who will have nothing to do with unionism is playing into the hands of the extremists. He is creating the atmosphere in which they flourish and grow strong.

I believe that, in their own best interests, employers should place no obstacle in the way of their working people joining a labour union. And, as soon as a union can claim to speak for a substantial number of the workers in any undertaking, it is good policy to recognise it.

What, after all, does recognition mean? The only difference is this – that instead of making bargains with individual employees about wages and working conditions the management negotiates collective agreements.

I do not think that the growth of unionism entails any diminution of technical efficiency, or proves a bar to the employment of new inventions or improved methods of work. In so far as good relations are established with the unions it may even facilitate change.

Sane trade unionism, far from being revolutionary, is always much more interested in a good standard of life than in Socialist utopias. Government represents, and is responsible to, the whole of the people. Its relations with employers and trade unions are governed by that fact.

It does not take sides as between capital and labour. Labour Ministry conciliation machinery is always at the service of both the unions' and the employers' organisations. Work done in this way is invaluable, but it would be impossible if there were not general confidence in the impartiality of the Minister and the conciliation officers.

For the rest, trade union leaders are consulted equally with the representatives of the employers when questions relating to industry are under discussion.

The importance of the unions is thus amply recognised, and they are to some extent a privileged body. They enjoy immunity from actions for damages for loss or injury arising from strikes. That immunity was conferred upon them originally by an Act of 1871. Parliament then decided that combinations of employers could be sued, but not combinations of their working people.

It seemed intolerable to our grandfathers in England that funds accumulated by very poor people for purposes vital to the existence of their homes should be liable to be swept away as a result of a legal action arising out of a trade dispute.

Then, in 1900, there was an unofficial strike on the Taff Vale Railway. Union officials had tried to stop it, but the men were out of hand and there were rowdyism and intimidation. In the end the strike failed, as without union support it was bound to fail, and the beaten men crept back to work. But a legacy of resentment had been left behind. The Taff Vale Railway Company brought an action for damages against the Amalgamated Society of Railway Servants. It was claimed that though the society had not authorised the strike, it was responsible for the acts of its members.

The legal battle was carried through the Court of Appeal to the highest tribunal of all – the House of Lords. Here the decision was in favour of the company. It was ruled that as the Act of 1871 did not specifically declare the unions to be non-suable, the legal presumption was that they could be sued. The society had to pay about £20,000 in damages and double that amount in costs. Other legal judgments in a similar sense followed. It was obvious that the right to strike had become meaningless.

If damages of £20,000 could be awarded following an unofficial strike on a small branch railway, the union that called its men out in a major dispute faced almost certain ruin. No one, not even the lawyers, knew how far the liability of the unions might extend. Even the most impeccable acts, labour leaders were advised, might become actionable if they were committed on behalf of an association and if they injured another person financially.

Throughout the country trade unions saw the conditions under which they had lived for more than a generation threatened, and the organisations they had built to protect their interests paralysed or emasculated. They believed that the courts meant to break the unions, and they chafed under a deep sense of wrong.

These events led to the birth of the Labour Socialist Party of Britain. The decision drove the unions into politics.

At the next general election, the Labour Representative Committee secured the return of 29 candidates to Parliament. The Labour Party had arrived, and one of the first acts of the new Liberal Government was to restore to the trade unions the immunities the Taff Vale and other judgments had destroyed.

We discovered, as a result of a number of strikes against the community, that our existing legislation required further definition. A policy of political blackmail culminated in the general strike of 1926. It was broken, once and for all, by the Trade Disputes and Trade Unions Act of 1927. That Act, while leaving the unions free to forward the interests of their members by all lawful means, effectively prevents the grave evils apt to arise when power is divorced from responsibility. It discriminates between strikes of different characters. The immunities of *bona fide* trade disputes are not extended to strikes of a political nature. The sympathetic strike is permitted only within the trade or industry within which the original dispute arose. Otherwise it is illegal in all cases where, by inflicting hardship on the community, it seeks – or seems to seek – to coerce the Government. In similar circumstances, lock-outs by employers would also be illegal.

All union officials who take part in, or act in furtherance of, any illegal strike are liable to criminal prosecution. Individual workmen who act as strike pickets or in any other way actively support an illegal strike are also criminally liable. In addition to this unions may be sued in the courts.

Members of a union expelled for refusing to participate in an illegal strike may also claim damages which will be payable out of the union funds.

Municipal employees or the servants of any public authority who break their contracts of employment are liable to criminal prosecution as well as to civil action for damages. In this way a general strike has been made impossible.

I believe that a strong trade-union movement, free to pursue in its own way all legitimate purposes, is the bulwark against revolution.

The path to industrial democracy lies plain before us. We can achieve it by increasing collaboration of employers' and workers' organisations.

The standard and the conditions of life in Socialist Russia are such as no British worker would accept.

Yet here is a system whose supreme aim is the elimination of private profit and which has used the most ruthless measures to enforce its doctrines.

More and more people should be owners as well as earners. A continuing rise in the standard of living is the most practical answer to the mean-minded equalitarianism that grudges greater earnings to anyone but themselves. Incentive and opportunity must be the watchwords.

It is in the interest of the wage-earner to have many other alternatives open to him than service under one all-powerful employer called the State. He will be in a better position to bargain collectively and production will be more abundant; there will be more for all and more freedom for all when the wage-earner is able, in the large majority of cases, to choose and change his work, and to deal with a private employer who, like himself, is subject to the ordinary pressures of life and, like himself, is dependent upon his personal thrift, ingenuity and good-housekeeping.

The general march of industrial democracy is not towards inadequate hours of work, but towards sufficient hours of leisure. People are not content that their lives should remain mere alternations between bed and the factory; they demand time to look about them, time to see their homes by daylight, to see their children, time to think and read and cultivate their gardens – time, in short to live. To achieve this we know perfectly well that the trade-union movement ought to develop, ought not to be stereotyped, ought to have powers to enter a new field and to make new experiments. The unions must be free to develop their efforts, to build up a minimum standard of life and labour, and to secure the happiness of the people. But unions must realise that it is better for the strong to help the weak than for the weak to hinder the strong.

The production of new wealth is far more beneficial, and on an incomparably larger scale, than class and party fights about the liquidation of old wealth. We must try to share blessings and not miseries. The production of new wealth must precede common wealth, otherwise there will only be common poverty.

Low wages should be a thing of the past for there is no greater delusion than that low wages mean high profits. No labour is so dear as cheap labour, and the labour which costs nothing is the dearest of them all. Nevertheless, wage restraint is an economic necessity although, in asking for wage restraint, we do not in any way wish to limit the earnings of any section of the working population. The aim is to encourage the highest possible level of earnings in every industry, provided these swim upon increased output and efficiency. For example, the term 'differentials' provides recognition of extra skill, responsibility and effort, and is, therefore, one of the keys to progress. Industrial eminence owes much to craftsmanship. Rewards for extra skill or effort have had in the past, and still have, an important part to play in stimulating an increase in the volume and quality of output.

The Trade Unions are now a long established and essential part of national life. Like other human institutions they have their faults and weaknesses. At the present time they have more influence upon the Government of the country, and less control over their own members, than ever before. But we take our stand by these pillars of our society as it has gradually been developed and evolved itself, of the right of individual labouring men and women to adjust their wages and conditions by collective bargaining, including the right to strike; and the right of everyone, with due notice and consideration for others, to choose or change his occupation if he thinks he can better himself and his family.

Everyone knows, and I have been taught it all my public life, that employers are deeply thankful there is in existence a strong organised trade-union movement with which they can deal, and which keeps its bargains and which moves along a controlled and suitable path of policy.

I have always been a firm supporter of trade unionism. I believe it to be the only foundation upon which the relations of employers and employed can be harmoniously adjusted.

I am inclined to think, so far as any body of organised opinion can claim the right to speak for this immense portion of the human race, it is the trade-unions that, more than any other organisation must be considered the responsible and deputed representatives of Labour, although Labour is not necessarily Socialism.

Trade unions are the most highly organised part of Labour; they are the most responsible part; and they are from day to day in contact with reality. They are not mere visionaries or dreamers weaving airy

Utopias out of tobacco smoke. They are not political adventurers who are eager to remodel the world by rule-of-thumb, who are proposing to make the infinite complexities of scientific civilisation and the multitudinous phenomena of great cities conform to a few barbarous formulas which any moderately intelligent parrot could repeat in a fortnight.

The sphere of industrial and political activity is often indistinguishable, always overlaps, and representation in Parliament is absolutely necessary to trade unions, even if they confine themselves to the most purely industrial forms of action.

Although it may be very difficult to define in law what is or what is not a trade union, most people of common sense know a trade union when they see one. It is like trying to define a rhinoceros: it is difficult enough, but if one is seen, everybody can recognise it.

I support the principle of collective bargaining between recognised and responsible trade unions and employers, and include in collective bargaining the right to strike. But no man can be a collectivist alone or an individualist alone. He must be both an individualist and collectivist. The nature of man is a dual nature. The character of the organisation of human society is dual. Man is at once a unique being and a gregarious animal. For some purposes he must be collectivist, for others he is, and he will for all time remain, an individualist.

The trade unions have a great part to play but I think they should keep clear of Party politics. I have often said they should keep clear of both parties and devote themselves solely to industrial matters. They do useful work when they restrain featherheads, crackpots, vote-catchers, and office-seekers from putting the folly they talk into action.

Nor is it good for unions to be brought in contact with the courts. It is also not good for the courts. The courts hold justly a high and, I think, unequalled prominence in the respect of the world in criminal cases. And in Civil cases between man and man, no doubt, they deserve and command the respect and admiration of all classes in the community. But where class issues are involved, it is impossible to pretend that the courts command the same degree of general confidence. On the contrary, they do not, and a very large number of our populations have been led to the opinion that they are, unconsciously no doubt, biased.

Class hatred and class warfare, like national revenge, are the most costly luxuries in which anyone can indulge. Hate is a bad guide. I never considered myself at all a good hater – though I recognise that from moment to moment hate has added stimulus to pugnacity. You don't want to knock a man down except to pick him up in a better frame of mind . . . and you *may* pick him up in a better frame of mind.

Mouthing slogans of envy, hatred and malice spreads class warfare and divides a nation. Unfortunately, there is a class of people who use fine language about peace while all the time their hearts are filled with the spirit of class war.

It will not benefit the world if we succeed in banishing the old-fashioned wars of nations only to clear the board for social and doctrinal wars of even greater ferocity and destructiveness. This, indeed, is a growing danger. We were told that the old wars of religion had ended, but that is not much comfort if the wars of various kinds of secular religions or non-God religions are to begin and are to make Europe the arena of their hideous conflict, and if all that makes life worth living to the mass of the people is to be destroyed in the process.

Pessimists always assumed that the great mass of poorer people dwelling under the hard pressures of life would cast their votes for any party which promised a general overturn of the existing social and economic system. But this has not happened in Britain, nor in other democracies.

The failure of the red-hot men of the Left has involved a simultaneous failure of the white-hot men of the Right. Massive common sense has established a spacious and predominant middle zone within which the class adjustments of the nation can be fought out, and from which the extremists at both ends are excluded.

The programme that the State – that is to say, the politicians who have obtained a majority at an election – should have autocratic control of all the means of production, distribution, and exchange would never commend itself to the strong individualism of people. To have everybody made equal under boards of officials directed by politicians would be to destroy the whole sparkle and progress of life, without in any way raising the average.

To join in one fist the authority of the magistrate, of the employer, of the landlord, of the food purveyor, and of the legislator must be to reduce the ordinary wage-earner and his family, equally with more fortunate people, to an absolute subjugation.

Such doctrines might make their way in some semi-barbarous country, or in a nation ruined by defeat in war, but here, in our island, they have only to be presented under conditions of free politics and free criticism to be ignominiously repudiated.

The foremost to repudiate them – in fact, if not in form – are the great trade unions. Nothing can be more remarkable than the sober, resolute control of the theorists and doctrinaires which has been exercised by the responsible trade union leaders.

These leaders feel themselves responsible for securing better wages and conditions for the mass of their members. They have no intention of allowing their organisation to be made a vehicle for ambitious politicians.

In the main, they accept the existing social system, and mean to get as much out of it as they can for the working classes.

Trade-union leaders have felt it their duty to take a hard line against Communists on the grounds, chiefly, that they are the disturbers and hinderers of the material betterment of the wage-earning classes.

One of the greatest needs is political stability and tranquility, although many, in their mood of jealousy and spite and with their creed of lowering everything to the level of failure, are taking the shortest road to ruin and blight of prosperity. To vote for stability is to vote for prosperity. We must think of national interests, stand together, and study how best we can promote the fortunes, happiness and welfare of the people.

The history of many of our social services was first an experiment – a few tentative steps along an unknown road: perhaps a leap into darkness; then a period of gradual growth and development; finally, a custom which everyone takes for granted.

Values, conditions, and, above all, proportions changed. We entered upon a titanic period. The world around us has become gigantic. It is not that we are not growing ourselves in health, in wealth, in numbers, and in power; but others are growing faster than we are.

When we survey the progress of the civilised races during the first quarter of the new century as compared with our own, it was not without grave heart-searchings that we cast our minds forward and endeavour to compute what the balance of forces and masses will be when this formidable century comes to its close.

On the other hand, many evil hazards, of which our fathers and grandfathers were scarcely conscious, have been safely left behind.

The improvement in material conditions, the spread of education and political knowledge gave birth to new profound desires for comradeship and common action, not only among the leaders, but very widely throughout the masses of the various peoples.

There is no reason why new favourable tendencies should not

develop and spread their consequential effects with every year that the new century unfolds.

We cannot set limits to social services or to their development. Each generation is conscious of new needs, and must meet them in its own way.

There was a time when Disraeli aroused enthusiasm with the phrase: '*Sanitas sanitatum, omnia sanitas*' (Health and the laws of health).

It was the conception of the Ministry of Health. His critics had sneered: 'A policy of sewage.' But sewage was the essential then.

We have epidemics today, but they are no longer of the old intensity and virulence.

And now we confront new tasks.

We must not forget, however, in the pressure of new necessities, that old ones still exist.

We ought to be able to set up a complete ladder, an unbroken bridge, or causeway, as it were, along which the whole body of the people may move with a certain measure of security and safety against hazards and misfortunes. There are a great many people who will tell you that such a policy will not make our country stronger because it will sap the self-reliance of the working classes.

It is very easy for rich people to preach the sermon of self-reliance to the poor. It is also very foolish. There is no chance of making people self-reliant by confronting them with problems and with trials beyond their capacity to surmount. You do not make a man self-reliant by crushing him under a steam roller.

We must certainly make the most lavish compassionate contribution to the relief of distress in all its forms, and by the most honest and efficient administration system. What has not been done, so far, must be attempted with perseverance and, when occasion serves, with audacity. We cannot afford to have parasitic classes, crumpled homes, and abandoned communities.

Our social services are carried to the highest pitch, higher even than in America, so much has been done for the poor in this weary, over-burdened country.

To recount the achievements of the past is lawful; but to recount them for the purpose of denying the need of renewed effort would be shameful. Always the urge is forward.

We seek a free and varied society, where there is room for many kinds of men and women to lead happy, honourable and useful lives. We are fundamentally opposed to all systems of rigid uniformity, and we have grown by indulging tolerance, rather than logic. We know that control for control's sake is senseless.

Changes have been so unceasing, and at the same time so gradual, that many of those who have lived through them have hardly realised they were happening. It is only when from time to time we pause and look about us that we can appreciate the distance and the rate at which we have journeyed, and are still journeying.

The changes which have taken place in the social, moral, and religious spheres are less spectacular but equally serious and profound. The greatest social change is the arrival of women in almost every field of activity as the equals, the helpers and the rivals of men. One has only to read John Stuart Mill's essay upon 'The Subjugation of Woman', and compare those prescient thoughts with what we see around us every day, to realise how gigantic has been the enfranchisement which has occurred. One must regard it as one of the greatest enrichments and liberations that have ever taken place in the whole history of the world.

We speak of the improvement of modern machinery as 'labour saving'. What does 'labour saving' mean? Does it mean simply that some labourers are to work as long and as hard as ever, while millions of others are to be told that they will never be wanted again? If so, machinery and invention would be a curse to the wage-earning classes. But if 'labour saving' means that the wage-earning masses are, with the aid of machinery, to make the same amount of things for something like the same wage in a shorter time, and have more leisure, then indeed will machinery and invention be a gift and a blessing to mankind.

The energies of the country ought to continue to be devoted to the reorganisation and development of industries, and maintaining good relations between employers and employed. But we must not rest content with past achievements. Strange methods, huge forces, larger combinations – a Titanic world – have sprung up around us.

I believe that freedom can pay – and will pay – better dividends of health and happiness than any despotism. The British people have everything to gain from steady perseverance and progress. But they have more to lose in material well-being than any other people. If they listen to the advocates of violence and the class war, and turn their backs upon their ancient faith and ancient virtues, the whole enormous structure of the social services will be endangered.

Tireless perseverance, unresting, methodical, is what we need. There are no short cuts. There is no final goal. The task will never be finished. But if at each stage we have made a real march forward, and if at each our view expands over wider scenes, and if the light of hope still shines over the peaks in front of us, we shall have done our duty and gained, even in our time, an increasing reward.

Freedom of enterprise and freedom of service are not possible without elaborate systems of safeguards against failure, accident, or misfortune. We should not seek to pull down improvidently the structures of society, but to erect balustrades upon the stairway of life, which will prevent helpless or foolish people from falling into the abyss.

Establish a basic standard of life and labour and provide the necessary basic foods for all. Once that is done, set the people free, get out of the way, and let them all make the best of themselves, and win whatever prizes they can for their families and for their country.

CHAPTER 19

War And Peace

IT IS SO easy to launch a war. Somebody signs a paper or utters an ejaculation; someone presses a button, and terrible things begin. Where they end no one can say, least of all those who begin them.

The lesson of the World Wars was that those who fix the moment for the beginning of wars are not those who fix the hour of their cessation.

But war is not inevitable. It may be avoided. I believe that if a sufficient number of nations have the will to peace and the courage of their good intentions there will be no war. In the main, war consists of the same tunes, played through the ages, though sometimes only on a reed flute or bagpipe and sometimes through a full modern orchestra. And war is little more than a catalogue of mistakes and misfortunes.

Whole libraries have been written about the coming of war. Every government involved has laboured to prove its guiltlessness. Every people casts the odium upon some other. Every statesman has been at pains to show how he toiled for peace, but was nevertheless a man of action whom no fears could turn from the path of duty. Every soldier has found it necessary to explain how much he loved peace, but of course neglected no preparations for war.

It was the custom in the palmy days of Queen Victoria for statesmen to expatiate upon the glories of the British Empire, and to rejoice in that protecting Providence which had preserved us through so many dangers and brought us at length into a secure and prosperous age.

Little did they know that the worst perils had still to be encountered and that the greatest triumphs were yet to be won. Children were taught of the Great War against Napoleon as the culminating effort in the history of the British peoples, and they looked on Waterloo and Trafalgar as the supreme achievements of British arms by land and sea.

These prodigious victories, eclipsing all that had gone before seemed the fit and predestined ending to the long drama of our island race, which had advanced over a thousand years from small and weak beginnings to a foremost position in the world.

Three separate times in three different centuries had the British people rescued Europe from a military domination. Thrice had the Low Countries been assailed: by Spain, by the French Monarchy, by the French Empire. Thrice had British war and policy, often maintained single-handed, overthrown the aggressor.

Always at the outset the strength of the enemy had seemed overwhelming, always the struggle had been prolonged through many years and across awful hazards, always the victory had at last been won: and the last of all the victories had been the greatest of all, gained after the most ruinous struggle and over the most formidable foe.

Surely that was the end of the tale as it was so often the end of the book. History showed the rise, culmination, splendour, transition and decline of States and Empires. It seemed inconceivable that the same series of tremendous events through which since the days of Queen Elizabeth we had three times made our way successfully, should be repeated and on an immeasurably larger scale. Yet that is what happened.

The Great War differed from all ancient wars in the immense power of the combatants and their fearful agencies of destruction, and from all modern wars in the utter ruthlessness with which it was fought. All the horrors of all the ages were brought together, and not only armies but whole populations were thrust into the midst of them. The mighty educated States involved conceived with reason that their very existence was at stake. Germany having let Hell loose kept well in the van of terror; but she was followed step by step by the desperate and ultimately avenging nations she had assailed.

Every outrage against humanity or international law was repaid by reprisals often on a greater scale and of longer duration. No truce or parley mitigated the strife of the armies. The wounded died between the lines: the dead mouldered into the soil. Merchant ships and neutral ships and hospital ships were sunk on the seas and all on board left to their fate, or killed as they swam.

Every effort was made to starve whole nations into submission without regard to age or sex. Cities and monuments were smashed by artillery. Bombs from the air were cast down indiscriminately. The fighting strength of armies was limited only by the manhood of their countries. Europe and large parts of Asia and Africa became one vast battlefield on which after years of struggle not armies but nations broke and ran.

But nothing daunted the valiant heart of man. Son of the Stone Age, vanquisher of Nature with all her trials and monsters, he met the awful and self-inflicted agony with new reserves of fortitude. Freed in the main by his intelligence from mediaeval fears, he marched to death with sombre dignity. His nervous system was found in the twentieth century capable of enduring physical and moral stresses before which the simpler nature of primeval times would have collapsed.

Again and again to the hideous bombardment, again and again from the hospital to the front, again and again to the hungry submarines, he strode unflinching. And withal, as an individual, preserved through these torments the glories of a reasonable and compassionate mind.

In the beginning of the twentieth century men were everywhere unconscious of the rate at which the world was growing. It required the convulsion of war to awaken the nations to the knowledge of their strength.

Vast masses of warm-hearted human beings want to do their best for their country and their neighbours and long to build their homes and bring up their children in peace, freedom and the hope of better times for the young when they grow up. That is all they ask of their rulers and governors and guides. That is the desire in the hearts of all the peoples of mankind. How easy it ought to be, with modern science standing tiptoe ready to open the doors of a golden age, to grant them this humble, modest desire.

But then there come along tribes of nationalists, ideologues, revolutionaries, class warfare experts, and imperialists, with their nasty regimentation of academic doctrinaires, striving night and day to work them all up against one another so that the homes instead of being built, are bombed; and the breadwinner is killed, and the broken housewife left to pick the surviving children, maimed and scorched, out of the ashes.

To prevent a renewal of the horrors and waste of war is the dearest wish in every breast. In no class of society, in no political association is there really any difference of opinion upon the goal. The only question is 'What is the best course to take?' But upon this a babel arises.

Vague, pious truisms about peace and our love for it, endless, fruitless formulas of disarmament, ceaseless oscillations of nations have enshrouded policy with a fog. We are at once futile but entangled. It may not be heroic, but it is only natural to want to keep out of any trouble, although this may involve much greater troubles later on. The pity is that this attitude of caution may bring about the very evil it is designed to avoid.

Disarmament conferences in one form and another, have been the scenes of nauseating hypocritical manoeuvres. Every country tries to gain some military advantage for itself, and at the same time pose as the champion of peace and disarmament. Tireless ingenuity has been used in framing schemes which, while they steal a march on a rival Power, or have no chance of being accepted, can nevertheless be made the text for all kinds of fine and noble perorations.

What a cataract of misfortune opens upon short-sighted Governments and unfortunate peoples, who through mere incapacity to combine upon a broad international platform, let themselves become the prey to measureless tribulation!

It is the fear of ordinary men and women in many countries that their homes, their pleasures, their prudential thrift, their conceptions of right and wrong, their whole way of life and means of living, may be broken up by war. Between dwelling in a Fool's Paradise or in a Fool's Inferno there ought to be some middle space, be it only Purgatory for Fools.

It is one of the characteristics that distinguish man from the brute creation that man is prepared to kill or be killed for the sake of an idea. All ideas are, in a sense, explosive. But the idea which is independent of reasoning, which is held as an article of faith, is the most dangerous of all.

The old wars were decided by their episodes rather than by their tendencies. In modern war the tendencies are far more important than the episodes.

Those two 'imposters' Triumph and Disaster, never play their pranks more shamelessly than in war, and war is very cruel. It goes on for so long.

The Great War was incomparably the most prodigious manifestation of human strength that the world had seen. A hundred years almost to a year had passed since the end of the Napoleonic struggle.

There had been many small wars or colonial wars, but, broadly speaking, there had been a hundred years while the nations had been gathering their economic strength and charging their cells with latent power.

Steam, electricity, railways, in all their applications and consequences, had brought the nations to a pitch of prosperity and material force far exceeding anything of which the boldest minds had dreamed. Then, at the summit of this astonishing development, with all their slow-gathered patriotism, passion and resources, they fell upon one another in one frightful convulsion in which we seemed to recognise the Armageddon so long foretold by prophecy.

Although the Allies were throughout far more numerous, wealthy, and with the command of the sea better situated, they only by the skin of their teeth, after several horrible hazards, emerged victorious.

Whereas the cause of old wars are often obscure from lack of records, a vast fog of information envelops the fatal steps to the last Armageddon. A hundred reasons are offered to show why all the Governments acted as they did, and how good their motives were. But in this cloud of testimony the few gleaming points of truth are often successfully obscured.

In the mood of men, in the antagonisms between the Powers, amid the clash of interests and deep promptings of self-preservation or self-assertion in the hearts of races, there lay mighty causes. Then came the final explosion.

No one except the doers of these deeds bears the direct concrete responsibility for the loosing upon mankind of incomparably its most frightful misfortune since the collapse of the Roman Empire before the Barbarians. This vicious, fatal degeneration made the peace and civilisation of mankind dependent upon the processes of disintegration and spasms of recovery.

The campaign of 1916 on the Western Front was from beginning to end a welter of slaughter. Every man a volunteer, inspired not only by love of country but by a widespread conviction that human freedom was challenged by military and Imperial tyranny, our men grudged no sacrifice however unfruitful and shrank from no ordeal however destructive.

Struggling forward through the mire and filth of the trenches, across the corpse-strewn crater fields, amid the flaring, crashing, blasting barrages and murderous machine-gun fire, conscious of their race, proud of their cause, they seized the most formidable soldiery in

Europe by the throat, slew them and hurled them unceasingly backward.

Having lived through war, people feel they can live through anything. But even persons of the meanest intelligence or the least excitable imagination are aware that a third world war could certainly break civilisation.

The world which greeted the awful twentieth century was brilliant, hopeful, and sure of itself. But Armageddon liquidated not only empires, banking houses, and social conventions, but the very principles of thought among men, which became fluid as never before in the human story. People became habituated to the idea of a world in flux. Nothing was solid; nothing was lasting; earthquake was the order of the day.

The old ideas, the old systems of government, morals, and economics were discredited or cast aside, and nothing coherent was put in their places. At the same time, in spite of the catastrophe, perhaps in consequence of it, the world's affairs grew in scale.

A sense of the helplessness of Man amid the current of Destiny steals numbingly over the mind. Our vaunted progress – why should it continue? How many times, perhaps long before the dawn of history, has humanity attained a high development and the consciousness of glorious possibilities? How many times has it been swept back into chaos, so that everything has had to grow up again, slowly, painfully, blindly, from the beginning?

No doubt in the days of the Roman Empire when human intellect stood at least as high as it does today, and when the Christian revelation had already come, very able men – princes, commanders, magnates – often met together to discuss the approaching catastrophe and to make plans based on long experience to ward it off. The depressing fact is that they never could get together enough power and wisdom to master that deep overflow of events which we call destiny.

They talked and argued as we talk and argue; they were borne along as we are borne along. They and all they stood for perished, as may yet be our own fate.

Nevertheless, I shall continue to proclaim that it is still in our power to ward off war, to curb barbarism, to preserve liberty and to avert our doom.

There are heaving, thrusting, pulsating organisms which think and act with purpose. Before them expostulates a war-weary, peace-interested, territorially-satisfied throng of countries great and small. But the profound antagonisms of great Powers do not comprise the whole danger. Immense forces exist to restrain even the fiercest of the leading nations from actually giving the signal for a world war. But side by side with them and their clamant grievances and fears there exist a number of minor states equally embroiled with one another, and even more inflammable.

It is indeed foolish to suppose that armaments in themselves make wars or that the lack of armaments prevents them. Wars come through the quarrels of nations, and as long as the nations are fairly evenly matched they can be fought out whether they are armed or not.

It is not the weapons but the grievances which we should endeavour to reduce. End the quarrels and the weapons would soon be laid aside. Moral disarmament should be the aim. The rest will follow. Indeed, it may be argued that in many cases strong armaments and modern scientific weapons make not for war, but for peace; and that the lack of them would lead to war.

Scientific armament, indeed, gives the power to smaller nations to defend themselves more effectively against a mass invasion by huge barbarous neighbours. And most of all is the danger of war brought nearer when the peace-loving, peace-interested powers disarm while those who are dissatisfied and wish to alter the situation are vigorously arming.

The story of the human race is War. Except for brief and precarious interludes, there has never been peace in the world; and before history began, murderous strife was universal and unending.

But up to the present time the means of destruction at the disposal of man had not kept pace with his ferocity. Reciprocal extermination was impossible in the Stone Age. One cannot do much with a clumsy club. Besides, human legs could only cover a certain distance each day. With the best will in the world to destroy his species, each man was restricted to a very limited area of activity.

As tribes, villages, and governments evolved, War became a collective enterprise and the technique of slaughter was improved. Yet always, on balance, the life-forces kept a lead over the forces of death.

It was not until the dawn of the twentieth century of the Christian era that War really began to enter into its kingdom as the potential destroyer of the human race. The organisation of mankind into great States and Empires and the rise of nations to full collective consciousness enabled enterprises of slaughter to be planned and executed upon a scale and with a perseverance never before imagined. Science unfolded her treasures and her secrets to the desperate demands of men and placed in their hands agencies and apparatus almost decisive in their character.

In consequence many novel features presented themselves. Whole nations were subjected, or sought to be subjected, to the process of reduction by famine. The entire population in one capacity or another took part in the War; combatants and civilians were equally the object of attack. The Air opened paths along which death and terror could be carried far behind the lines of the actual armies, to women, children, the aged, the sick, who in earlier struggles would perforce have been left untouched.

Marvellous organisations of railways, ships, and motor vehicles placed and maintained tens of millions of men continuously in action. Healing and surgery in their exquisite developments returned them again and again to the shambles. Nothing was wasted that could contribute to the process of waste. The last dying kick was brought into military utility.

But all that happened in the four years of the Great War was only a prelude to what was preparing for the fifth year. The campaign of 1919 would have witnessed an immense accession to the power of destruction. Had the Germans retained the *morale* to make good their retreat to the Rhine, they would have been assaulted in the summer of 1919 with forces and by methods incomparably more prodigious than any yet employed. Thousands of aeroplanes would have shattered their cities. Scores of thousands of cannon would have blasted their front.

Arrangements were being made to carry simultaneously a quarter of a million men, together with all their requirements, continuously forward across country in mechanical vehicles moving ten or fifteen miles each day. Poison gases of incredible malignity, against which only a secret mask (which the Germans could not obtain in time) was proof, would have stifled all resistance and paralysed all life on the hostile front subjected to attack.

No doubt the Germans, too, had their plans. But the hour of wrath had passed. The signal of relief was given, and the horrors of 1919 remain buried in the archives of the great antagonists.

The War stopped as suddenly and as universally as it had begun. The world lifted its head, surveyed the scene of ruin, and victors and vanquished alike drew breath. In a hundred laboratories, in a thousand arsenals, factories, and bureaux, men pulled themselves up with a jerk, turned from the task in which they had been absorbed. Their projects were put aside unfinished, unexecuted; but their knowledge was preserved; their data, calculations, and discoveries were hastily bundled together and docketed 'for future reference' by the War Offices of every country.

The campaign of 1919 was never fought; but its ideas marched along, in every Army, explored, elaborated, refined under the surface of peace, should war come again.

In a survey of the general situation thus created, certain sombre facts emerged, solid, inexorable, like the shape of mountains from drifting mist.

Henceforward whole populations would take part in war, all doing their utmost, all subjected to the fury of the enemy. It was established that nations who believed their life at stake would not be restrained by pledges or conventions from using any means to secure their existence. It was probable – nay, certain – that among the means next time at their disposal would be agencies and processes of destruction whole-sale, unlimited, and perhaps, once launched, uncontrollable.

Mankind had never been in this position before. Without having im-proved appreciably in virtue or enjoying wiser guidance, it had got into its hands for the first time the tools by which it could unfailingly accomplish its own extermination. That is the point in human destinies to which all the glories and toils of men had at last led them.

Death stands at attention, obedient, expectant, ready to serve, ready to shear away the peoples *en masse*; ready, if called on, to pulverise, without hope of repair, the whole fabric of civilisation. He awaits only the word of command. He awaits it from a frail, bewildered being, long his victim, now – for one occasion only – his master.

It was evident that whereas an equally contested war might work the ruin of the world and cause an immeasurable diminution of the human race, the possession by one side of some overwhelming scientific advantage would lead to the complete enslavement of the unwary party. Not only are powers now in the hand of man capable of destroying the life of nations, but for the first time they afford to one group of civilised men the opportunity of reducing their opponents to absolute helplessness.

In barbarous times superior martial virtues – physical strength, courage, skill, discipline – were required to secure such a supremacy; and in the hard evolution of mankind the best and fittest stocks came to the fore. But no such guarantee exists today. There is no reason why a base, degenerate, immoral race should not make an enemy far above them in quality the prostrate subject of their caprice or tyranny, simply because they happened to be possessed at a given moment of some new death-dealing or terror-working process and were ruthless in its employment. The liberties of men are no longer to be guarded by their natural qualities, but by their dodges; and superior virtue and valour may fall an easy prey to the latest diabolical trick.

Such, then, is the peril with which mankind menaces itself. Means of destruction incalculable in their effects, wholesale and frightful in their character, and unrelated to any form of human merit; the march of Science unfolding ever more appalling possibilities.

But, in spite of the fires of hatred burning deep in the hearts of some of the greatest peoples in the world, and fanned by continual provocation and unceasing fear, nations have a chance to control their destinies and avert what may well be general doom. Surely, if a sense of self-preservation still exists among men, if the will to live resides not merely in individuals or nations but in humanity as a whole, the prevention of the supreme catastrophe ought to be the paramount object of all endeavour. Its structure, airy and unsubstantial, framed of shining but too often visionary idealism, is in its present form incapable of guarding the world from its dangers and of protecting mankind from itself.

It may be through the United Nations alone that the path to safety and salvation can be found. To sustain and aid the United Nations is the duty of all. To reinforce it and bring it into vital and practical relation with actual world-politics by sincere agreements and understanding between the Great Powers, between the leading races, should be the first aim of all who wish to spare their children torments and disasters compared to which those we have suffered will be but a pale preliminary.

As we go to and fro with decent orderly people going about their business under free institutions, and with so much tolerance and fair play in their laws and customs, it is startling and fearful to realise that we are no longer safe. For nearly a thousand years England has never seen the camp fires of an invader. We preserved our life and freedom through the centuries.

> A thousand years scarce serve to form a State,
> An hour may lay it in the dust.

Many people think that the best way to escape war is to dwell upon its horrors, and to imprint them vividly upon the minds of the younger generation. They flaunt grisly photographs before their eyes. They fill their ears with tales of carnage. They dilate upon the ineptitude of generals and admirals. They denounce the crime and insensate folly of human strife.

All this teaching ought to be very useful in preventing us from attacking or invading any other country, if anyone outside a madhouse wished to do so. But how would it help us if we were attacked or invaded ourselves? That is the question we have to ask.

Only a few hours away by air there dwells a nation which abandoned all its liberties in order to augment its collective might. There is a nation which with all its strength and virtues is in the grip of a group of ruthless men preaching a gospel of intolerance unrestrained by law, by Parliament or by public opinion.

Now these are facts – hard, grim indisputable facts – and in face of these facts, what are we to do? There are those who say 'Let us ignore the continent of Europe. Let us leave it with its hatreds and its armaments to stew in its own juice, to fight out its own quarrels. Let us turn our backs upon this scene. Let us fix our gaze across the oceans.'

Now there would be much to be said for this plan, if only we could unfasten the British islands from their rock foundations and could tow them three thousand miles across the Atlantic Ocean, and anchor them safely upon the smiling coasts of Canada. I have not yet heard of any way in which this could be done. No engineer has come forward with any scheme. Even our best scientists are dumb. But is it prudent, is it possible, however we might desire it, to turn our backs upon Europe and ignore whatever may happen there? Everyone can judge this question for himself, and everyone ought to make up his mind about it. It lies at the heart of our problem. For my part I have come to the conclusion – reluctantly I admit – that we cannot get away. Here we are and we must make the best of it. We cannot detach ourselves from Europe. For our own safety and self-preservation we are bound to make exertions and run risks for the sake of keeping peace.

Nations which allow their rights and liberties to be subverted by tyrants must suffer heavy penalties for those tyrants' crimes. Tyranny is our foe. We do not war with races as such, but against tyranny, whatever trappings or disguise it wears, whatever language it speaks, be it external or internal, we must for ever be on our guard, ever mobilised, ever vigilant, always ready to spring at its throat. Dictators and those who immediately sustain them cannot quit their offices with the easy disdain – or more often relief – with which an American President or a British Prime Minister submit themselves to an adverse popular verdict. For a dictator the choice may well be the Throne or the Grave. The character of men who have raised themselves from obscurity to positions of fierce, dazzling authority does not permit us to believe that they would bow their heads meekly to the stroke of Fate. One has the feeling they would go down or conquer fighting, and play the fearful stakes which are in their hands.

The policy of appeasement can appease, or stimulate a tyrant's more ferocious appetite. What we have to give, what we are made to give, may cost us dear, but it may not be enough. We have to take care that what is called disarmament does not in fact mean leaving us where we can be blackmailed out of our skin.

Civilised nations of the world receive consideration principally on account of the armaments they possess, and are able to pay for. The contentment of their people, the freedom of their institutions, the impartiality of their courts, their ancient traditions, their standard of comfort, their philosophy, poetry and art, will not count very much for fame in this degraded age. Arms and the men to use them are the criterion by which hungry aggressive States measure their steps and small countries their behaviour. Aggression, fully armed, grows bolder with easy successes.

Everyone would be glad to see the burden of armaments reduced in every country. But history shows on many a page that armaments are not necessarily a cause of war and that the want of them is no guarantee of peace. If, for instance, all the explosives all over the globe could by the wave of a magic wand be robbed of their power and made harmless, so that not a cannon or a rifle could fire, and not a shell or a bomb detonate, that would be a measure of world disarmament far beyond brightest dreams. But would it ensure peace? On the contrary, war would begin almost the next day when enormous masses of fierce men, armed with picks and spades or soon with clubs and spears, would pour over the frontiers into the lands they covet, and would be furiously resisted by the local populations and those who went to their aid. This truth may be unfashionable, unpalatable, unpopular. But it is the truth. The story of mankind shows that war was universal and unceasing for millions of years before armaments were invented or armies organised. Indeed the lucid intervals of peace and order only occur in human history after armaments in the hands of strong governments have come into being. And civilisation has been nursed only in cradles guarded by superior weapons and discipline. To remove the causes of war we must go deeper than armaments, we must remove grievances and injustice, we must raise human thought to a higher plane and give a new inspiration to the world. But what sign of this is there now?

The cause of disarmament will not be attained by Mush, Slush, and Gush. It will be advanced steadily by the harassing expense of fleets, armies and armaments, and by the growth of confidence in peace. It will be achieved only when, in a favourable atmosphere, half a dozen great men, with as many first class Powers at their back, are able to lift world affairs out of their confusion.

Great wars usually come only when both sides think they have good hopes of victory. Peace must be founded upon preponderance. There is safety in numbers. If there were five or six on each side there might well be a frightful trial of strength. But if there were eight or ten on one side, and only one or two upon the other, and if the collective armed forces of one side were three or four times as large as those of the other, then there will be no war. The practical arrangements which are appropriate to one peril, and to one region of the world, may be repeated elsewhere in different combinations for other dangers and in other scenes. And it might well be that gradually the whole world would be laced with international insurances against individual aggressors and that confidence and safety would return to mankind.

Wars do not always come when all the combatants are ready. Sometimes they come before they are ready, sometimes when one nation thinks itself less unready than another, or when one nation thinks it is likely to become not stronger, but weaker, as time passes. And one of the oldest rules of war is that to try to be strong everywhere is to be strong nowhere. To try to make everyone safe is to make nobody safe, and, moreover, to endanger the State.

O, horrible war! Amazing medley of the glorious and the squalid, the pitiful and the sublime! If modern men of light and leading saw your face closer, simple folks would see it hardly ever!

How to stop war surely is the supreme question which should engage the thoughts of mankind. Compared to it all other human interests are petty and other topics trivial.

Except for a few handfuls of ferocious romanticists, or sordid would-be profiteers, war spells nothing but toil, waste, sorrow and torment to the vast mass of ordinary folk in every land. Why should this horror, which they dread and loathe, be forced upon them? How is it that they have not got the sense and the manhood to stop it? Nowadays the masses have the power in all democratic countries. Even under dictatorships they could easily resume the power, if any large proportion of the individuals of whom these masses are composed singled this issue out among all others and thought, spoke and acted about it in a resolute, and if need be, a self-sacrificing manner.

'How was it,' the historians of the future will, perhaps, ask, 'that these vast, fairly intelligent, educated, and on the whole virtuous communities were so helpless and futile as to allow themselves to become the victims of their own processes, and of what they most abhorred?'

The answer will be, 'They had no plan.' The thinking people in the different countries could not agree upon a plan; the rest continued to gape and chatter vacuously at the approaching peril until they were devoured by it. They were amused from day to day by an endless flow of headlines about trifles amid which they could not, or did not take the trouble to, discern the root of the matter.

Sentiment by itself is no good; fine speeches are worse than useless; short-sighted optimism is a mischief; smooth, soothing platitudes are a crime. And here at the outset is a mocking paradox, which seems to rob our collective thought of its logic. No plan for stopping war is of any value unless it has behind it force, and the resolve to use that force. Mere passive resistance by some nations would only precipitate disaster if others, or their leaders, stood ready to take advantage of it. It is easy to deride the pacifist who is ready to fight for peace. None the less, safety will only come through a combination of pacific nations armed with overwhelming power, and capable of the same infinity of sacrifice, and indeed of the ruthlessness which hitherto have been the attributes of the warrior mind. The scales of Justice are vain without her sword. Peace must have her constables.

To bring the matter to an agate point, there must be a Grand Alliance of all nations who wish for peace against the Potential Aggressor, whoever he may be. Let nations and States be together upon a simple, single principle: 'Who touches one, touches all.' Who attacks any, will be resisted by all, and resisted with such wrath and apparatus, with such comradeship and zeal, that the very prospect may by its formidable majesty perhaps avert the crime. Surely there is no other saving thought in the world but this? But how to convert it into reality?

It must be observed that the Potential Aggressor presents himself in different forms to different countries – some fear one, some fear another; that some in each case are near to danger, others some distance from it, others again far off. But if war breaks out, who shall say when and where it will stop?

Therefore a speedy and genuine organisation of the maximum force against Potential Aggressors offers us the sole hope of preventing war or of preventing, if war should come, the ruin of those who have done no wrong.

People have had their lessons; they also have the power. They have formed a very clear opinion, and they loathe the idea of war. They wish to do everything in their power to prevent it. If the world polled tomorrow and every grown man and woman recorded their opinion, ninety-nine out of a hundred would declare their desire for peace. There never was so immense a volume of resolve for peace among hundreds of millions of thinking folk in every land. So why does the moth go to the candle? Its wings have been singed already: it has felt the bite of the flame, it would no doubt like to live its brief life. And yet it flies to the burning candle with universal, almost automatic resignation.

Such a contrast between the will of man and his actions seems to spring only from madness or from a seizure of herd passion.

We all hate and fear war. Let me tell you why in my opinion, and it is only an opinion, not a prophecy, let me tell you why a third world war seems unlikely to happen. It is because, among other reasons, it would be entirely different in certain vital aspects from any other war that has ever taken place. Both sides know that it would begin with horrors of a kind and on a scale never dreamed of before by human beings. It would begin by both sides suffering in the very first stage exactly what they dread the most. It would also be different from other wars because the main decisions would probably come in the first month or even in the first week. The quarrel might continue for an indefinite period, but after the first month it would be a broken back war in which no great armies could be moved over long distances by land. Governments dependent upon long distance communications by land might well find that they had quite soon lost their power to dominate events. These are only a few of the grave facts which rule our destinies.

We also dwell in times where there is danger not only of national wars, but of social or civil wars.

There would not be much use in preventing wars of strong nations, raging against each other for territory, trade and dominance, if this had no other result than to clear the board for wars of political creed and doctrine as savage as the old wars of religion.

Violent hatred arising from social stresses can also grow inside a nation. The vehicle of Parliamentary discussion can no longer carry the load, and it breaks down. A society speechless with anger can only express itself by war – civil war. There are moments in the story of every country when catastrophic frenzy may sweep all men off their feet. Then comes the sword. The tolerances of life take flight; thousands fall in battle; thousands of others are shot against the wall, or basely murdered in the ditch. Feuds innumerable are lighted; scores are added up which never can be paid. But at length regular armies come into the field. Discipline, organisation grips in earnest both sides. They march, manoeuvre, advance, retreat, with all the valour common to the leading races of mankind. New structures of national life are erected upon blood, sweat and tears, which are not dissimilar and therefore capable of being united.

This is what happened in Spain. None ever meant this hideous thing to come upon their country. It burst upon them with all the astounding force of an explosion. After that everyone had to choose his side, bend his head, and butt into the storm.

There is nothing that men and women cannot do if they work together in peace and freedom. The last war effort could not have been achieved if the women had not marched forward in millions and undertaken all kinds of tasks and work for which any other generation but our own – unless you go back to the Stone Age – would have considered them unfitted; work in the fields, heavy work in the foundries and in the shops, very refined work on radio and precision instruments, work in the hospitals, responsible clerical work of all kinds, work throughout the munition factories, work in the fighting Services. The bounds of women's activities were definitely, vastly, and permanently enlarged.

One would have thought that in the days of peace the progress of women to an ever larger share in the life and work and guidance of the community would have grown, and that, under the violences of war, it would be cast back. The reverse was true. War was the teacher, a hard stern efficient teacher. War taught us to make these vast strides forward towards a far more complete equalisation of the parts to be played by men and women in society.

In the vast tumultuous world which towers up around us, under the shadow of the nuclear age, no single country can control its destiny alone. The revolution in the science of destruction has profoundly changed the factors and values by which men have hitherto been guided – or misguided. This is not primarily because particular localities or bases are more vulnerable than they were, though that is no doubt the case. It is because the entire character and timetable of any future war has undergone a cataclysmic change, the like of which has never been known to mortal man.

Warfare is now classified into conventional and unconventional forms and these have become the official expressions of armies. These hitherto harmless, inoffensive terms, now strike a knell in our hearts.

Another great war, especially an ideological war, fought as it would be not only on frontiers but in the heart of every land with weapons far more destructive than men have yet wielded, would spell the doom, perhaps for many centuries, of such civilisation as we have been able to erect since history began to be written.

The more the human is enriched and occupied and the conditions of our life are improved and our capacities enriched, the greater is the chance that unconventional weapons, as these hideous apparitions are called, will lead not to general annihilation, but to the outlawry of war which generation after generation has hitherto sought in vain.

But there is no reason why the free world should die. On the contrary, it has only to remain united and progressive and prudent and far-seeing in order not only to survive, but to preserve its right to live without the need of another hideous world catastrophe.

The disproportion between the quarrels of nations and the suffering which fighting out those quarrels involves; the poor and barren prizes which reward sublime endeavour on the battlefield; the fleeting triumphs of war; the long, slow rebuilding; the awful risks so hardily run; the doom missed by a hair's breadth, by the spin of a coin, by the accident of an accident – all this should make the prevention of another great war the main preoccupation of mankind. It has been stripped of glitter and glamour.

The angel of peace is unsnubbable. Well was it written. 'Agree with thine adversary quickly whilst thou art in the way with him.'

Let me close with a thought which may appeal to all.

On Christmas Day, 1914, the German soldiers on the Western Front ceased firing. They placed small Christmas trees on their trenches and declared that on this day there should be peace and good will among suffering men. Both sides came out of their trenches and met in the blasted No-Man's Land. They clasped each other's hands, they exchanged gifts and kind words. Together they buried the dead, hitherto inaccessible and deprived of rites which raise man above brute.

Let no man worthy of human stature banish this sublime inspiration from his mind, and though it will probably never come in my time, I still hope that a gentler, more generous, more life-giving breeze will blow upon this weary earth, and that all the men in all the lands will become more serviceable to one another.

CHAPTER 20

Great Fighters Of Lost Causes

A PERSISTENT FASCINATION is inherent in Lost Causes. What is the explanation of this psychological fact? Why should a lost cause live so hardily in the future when it has failed in the past? That answer may be that mankind is more sentimental than successful. Many people can more easily imagine themselves being noble in a lost cause than in sharing the faded triumphs of arrogant complacent victors. Moreover, the success of all the winning causes has not yet led the world out of misery and confusion. Great advances have been made; but they are not in many cases attributable to the decision of the famous struggles of history. Other unseen, unnoticed, intangible forces and tendencies have seemed to shape the destinies of man more powerfully than his conscious definite choices. The lost cause passes into the sanctity of the tomb, free for evermore from new reproach. The winning cause is saddled with the responsibilities of the future. History is replete with examples of the failure of success; and how often underneath the passing splendours of victory and domination have forces re-gathered which have in the long run effected the success of failure!

'Victrix causa Diis placuit, sed victa Catoni.' 'The gods are for the winning, but Cato for the Lost Cause.' This line of Lucanus has carried comfort to many proud wounded bosoms.

Freed from the world's unrelenting cares and misfortunes, imagination may build Valhallas in which lost causes reign in airy serenity over brighter and better worlds than that in which we toil and blunder.

The figure of the valiant champion of a lost cause faithfully struggling to the end against irresistible odds, 'greatly falling with a falling State', appeals to our romantic sentiments. But more, it stirs those profound instincts upon which stand the grandeur and dignity of the human race. We rejoice that there were great unyielding souls who fought their quarrels out to the end. Even when the winning cause seems to have been indisputably the best for the world, we feel we owe them a debt scarcely less than that which we have so amply paid to the prosperous warriors. Their lives, their deeds, their agonies, are gazed upon with emotion and honour by countless generations who are quite glad their heroes did not have their own way.

Let us then turn haphazard the pages of the past, and glance at some of the personages recorded in the lists of failure.

We do not know enough of the disputes between Cain and Abel to judge this long-decided issue impartially. Undoubtedly Cain killed Abel; but Abel – if we knew the whole story – may have been very provoking. He may have been a pitiless usurer who got Cain into such a position that flesh and blood could stand it no more. For years he may have ground him down and bled him white. Finally, he may have presented him with some demand which left him no choice but ruin for his loved ones or a violent blow. Which was the lost cause here? Abel died and Cain conquered. He conquered only to gain a curse.

How little we can foresee the consequences either of wise or unwise action, of virtue or malice. Without this measureless and perpetual uncertainty, the drama of human life would be destroyed.

We must descend to personages about whom we have some fuller information. There is no lack. Hector, Demosthenes, Hannibal, Mithridates, Jugurtha, Sulla, Cicero, Vercingetorix, the Emperor Julian, Stilicho, the Cid, Harold, Charles the Bold, Thomas More, Guatemotzin, Atahualpa, Charles V, Mary Tudor, Charles I, Constantine, Palaelogus, George III, Marie Antoinette, Metternich, Napoleon, Wellington, Lee, Ludendorff. But any reader can add competitors to this list.

Take Demosthenes. He had made for himself an ideal out of the Greek past for which there was really no defence except in his oratory. He strove to maintain an Athens floating in a divine hegemony, the Queen of the Hellenic commonwealths, binding her daughters to her, not by the rods of Empire, but by a sublime culture. Greek must not oppress Greek. All were to flourish in harmony, all were to present a solid front against the barbarian. And then Philip of Macedon began to trouble these ideal conditions. All Greeks were equal, equally glorious, but unfortunately Macedon was more up-to-date in military tactics, nay, also in the slow craft of diplomacy. Macedon advanced upon the Greeks alike with Phalanx and with Fraud. Demosthenes felt passionately that tyrants, even good tyrants, were un-Greek. Against the pitiless encroachments of Philip and the vain intrigues of the Greek Senate he delivered the magnificent Orations. Philip kept jogging and edging along.

Demosthenes was the first great lawyer to enter politics, and was thus gradually sucked into the whirlpools of action. Sooner or later all good thinking is challenged by better thinking or more often by sharper action. Sharper action often wins. Philip forged ahead and gradually enslaved the Greek world. Demosthenes met his intrigues and force of arms with eloquence, but the sword beat the word. The word was potent enough to unite Thebes and Athens, but Philip broke both Thebes and Athens. Demosthenes saw from the beginning the weakness of his side. Fighting Philip, he said, was like pitting amateurs against professional boxers. The amateurs were knocked out. But are we to say 'It served them right'? Perhaps we ought to. Still, how much poorer was the world when the idea of pan-Hellenic freedom, culture, and mutual inter-dependence perished. The dominant forces in human history have come from the perception of great truths and the faithful pursuance of great causes.

The argument of Demosthenes and the resistance of Athens became the anvil upon which the sword of Alexander the Great was whetted. The liberal conception – noble, although unconsciously founded upon domestic slavery – was cast down. Imperialism strode in disdainful pride and majesty through the world. Demosthenes was driven into prison and exile. Hunted in his sanctuary, he found escape only by poison. Still, his glory matches that of his conqueror Alexander. The surge of his orations stirs men's minds today, while who cares for the victories of Alexander?

Hannibal was a loser of a different type. He lived in the realm of action. He has left us scarcely a fragment of his mind. We can only gape at the prodigy of his deeds. Any records which he or his people left have been expunged. We only know of him from the pages of his foes. But it is from the Roman, marked across the generations by the sense of fear and tragedy, that the greatness of Hannibal emerges. Hannibal's cause was not only that of Africa but of Europe against the coming power of Rome. Perhaps it was even wider – whether the

Mediterranean and all that centred around it, should be ruled by an Aryan or Semitic race.

The picture of Hannibal, and, indeed, Carthage, has been drawn for us only by the victors in their days of merciless triumph, and they have engraved the now well-recognised war propaganda of Punic cruelty and perfidy upon the stones of history. They have destroyed all others. But surely the figure of this man, bound from infancy by his father to implacable war on Rome, breaking in upon Italy from the north, waging war invincibly for fifteen years, destroying every army that met him in the field, until finally recalled to Africa to save the homeland, is without its equal in martial achievements of men. We know so little of his character. It is only by the dints and splinterings of the shields he smote that we can imagine the weight and sharpness of his sword. Still, here and there we have a glimpse of the human being behind these terrible manoeuvres.

It is the morning of Cannae. Hannibal is riding along the lines of his army. An officer upon his staff or in his entourage, named Gisco, gazing across the plain at the enormous masses of eighty thousand Romans in battle array, expresses inopportunely his awe at their great numbers. 'Yes, Gisco,' says Hannibal turning in his saddle with gleaming sardonic eye, his whole being poised for its impending supreme function, 'but there is something more wonderful still. Not one of them is called Gisco.' We can almost hear the laughter of the fierce group of Carthaginians.

The fibre of this man bearing up victorious against every misfortune, with stinted slender resources, with mere levies replacing professional troops betrayed and undermined from home, and the sure, natural, nascent strength of Rome lapping him on every side, must have been tenser than any we have been told about. Poison for him too was the last manoeuvre. We all rejoice that Rome beat Carthage. The Roman records make it clear that we should do so. But in all that supreme drama, it is Hannibal who bears the palm.

Personally, I have also always been much attracted by the elephants, plodding ponderously through the blizzards and avalanches of the Alpine passes, playing their part faithfully in so many battles, at last tested too hard and put to flight like tanks turning against their own army. One hopes that they did not suffer too much. There are so few elephants and so many men. They terrified the elephants with the hideous blare of metallic noises; they cut their soft trunks with swords, they stuck javelins in scores into their unprotected stomachs, and the elephants tried very hard to be faithful, but the limit was reached for the elephants. And here also there was a lost cause. The men won.

Someone ought to write well about these battles and make us see exactly what happened and why. They are much more interesting than the battles of the Great War, which were mainly shells and bullets lashing and whipping up the mud for years on end, and every now and then destroying drenched crouching men.

We must have an opinion between Right and Wrong. We must have an opinion between Aggressor and Victim. Questions which have to be settled are not always questions between what is good and bad; very often it is a choice between two very terrible alternatives.

The Emperor Julian, called the Apostate, contended in another sphere. Bred a Christian, he set himself to restore the old indolent poetic dreams and mysteries of pagan mythology and folk lore. Not by tortures or butcheries did he oppress the new religion; he sought to make it unfashionable, unprofitable, inconvenient. Rather heavier taxes, some disabilities in public office, shafts of ridicule and satire, vulgar prejudice, governmental disfavour coldly applied – these were his weapons. He was master of the world, and a formidable antagonist. But the world was very miserable. The great majority of men were slaves. In their sorrows they sought consolation. The old gods had nothing to send them from Olympus. The nymphs and fauns, the deities of every spring and dell and grotto gave back only echoes and murmurs, the passionate gasps of suppressed pain which loaded the air. The world needed a creed of facts, and the most astonishing array of facts ever propounded to human minds were already before them.

Over all this scene the philosophers spread their cobwebs of speculation. But who cared for them? There are times when the world rests on speculation for its religion, but this was a time when it hungered for facts. In the whole pagan mythology there was not a single fact which could contend either with the philosophers or with that pure and humble religion which made the slave in spirit the equal of the Emperor; which turned suffering into joy; which vanquished hate by love; which made torment bliss, and death a glorious immortality.

When Julian died in battle against the Parthians he was only thirty-two. His profoundly-conceived social and political measures against the Christians had not had a full trial. They had undoubtedly produced far more adverse effects upon the new religion than the brutalities and bestialities of other persecutions. But the ancient gods he loved so well must not have loved him less. They withdrew their champion from a forlorn contest. He was an uncertain symbol in an age of change. He combined Roman virtues with Greek graces. Ruler, warrior, aesthete, philosopher, his day was done. Still, he was the most redoubtable opponent encountered by Christianity in the Roman world.

Where there is great power there is great responsibility, where there is less power there is less responsibility. Only where there is no power there can, I think, be no responsibility. There is always error in all human affairs – error of conception, error of statement, error of manner, error of weakness, error of partisanship.

We ought at this point to say a word about Canute, who championed the lost cause of trying to stop the tide from coming in. His line is by no means extinct today, but Canute was only teaching foolish courtiers a lesson.

All causes that were not the causes of Rome were destined to be lost. The central power once dominant could only grow; and all the outside forces could only shatter themselves against Rome as enemies, or augment the strength of Rome as vassals. Several great dim figures loom up through the shadow of eclipse. Here again we can only judge of the anti-Roman cause from the Roman tale. Jugurtha delivered Numidia from the Roman yoke; and for a space defended Numidian freedom. The pen of Sallust has preserved his memory, no doubt distorted by the prejudices of the conqueror. The scornful gibes which Jugurtha uttered as the swelling Roman tides gathered about his country have survived and endured. He labelled Rome 'urbem venalem' – a city for sale, but Rome, her strength and corruption growing together, disposed of him so effectually that only this one taunt has remained to make the quarrel.

Vercingetorix has gained a larger fame. The cause of Numidia was soon dead. The cause of the Celt stirs the world today. Usually beaten, never conquered, unsuccessful and irrepressible, stricken but immortal, the Celtic race contend today in every field. Vercingetorix was the only Celt who drew together in one nation-conscious organisation against Caesar and his legions all the blue-eyed, red-haired warriors of Gaul. It is written of the Celts in those days that they always marched to battle and they always fell. Caesar's dry-as-dust dispatches record the destruction of successive Gallic armies. When we summon to our minds the picture sculptured by Romans on their triumphal arches of these nomadic, shaggy and trousered warriors, with their herds of cattle and heavy ox-drawn waggons formed into fortified camps within which men, woman, and children faced the worst that fortune had in store, we ask ourselves 'Had they a cause?'

The Romans esteemed it as nothing. They regarded the Gauls as mere barbarians, the easy prey of disciplined forces, fit only to be subjugated or despoiled, and if recalcitrant, mutilated or enslaved.

What Europeans have done in Africa in the last two generations Rome did to the Gauls. How could tribalism, however valiant, prevail against the legions, with good finances and a coherent civilised State behind them? Caesar subdued them tribe by tribe, almost village by village. Suddenly a princely rescuer arose. Vercingetorix by prowess and eloquence persuaded all Gaul to stand together. For eight years they waged war as a nation. It was a desperate war; almost as hard and as cruel as any fought out on the globe. It culminated in the long siege of Alesia, in which Vercingetorix had fortified himself. Caesar reduced Alesia; the garrison with all their families perished by famine or the sword, or became the human chattels of their captors. Enthusiasm and devotion were proved to be almost helpless when pitted against good drill and a superior theme.

Here again no literature survives to tell us how the Celts viewed their cause. Of course, they wished to live free, happy, and glorious in the good lands into which they had found their way, and for this they fought to the death. But the idea behind them meant only a Europe inhabited in isolated sections. Each tribe could enjoy and glorify the arts of primitive warfare, could display chivalrous prowess and yield to the intoxications of poetry and ale. There was rude culture sustained by Bard and Druid and recorded in letters. But the nomadic cause was lost and rightly lost. Vercingetorix, preserved to be a feature in Roman triumph, was strangled at the foot of the Capitol. There was nothing more to be gained from him, not even the exhibition of his misery. But his soul and the souls of Gaul were marching along. Under the Roman rule Gaul became France, and France today is a leader of Europe. The lost cause has been retrieved.

It takes too poor a view of man's mission here on earth to suppose that he is not capable of rising – to his material betterment – far above his day-to-day surroundings. What is this force, this miracle which makes peoples cast aside all their fears, and set themselves up to aid a good cause? You must look deep into the heart of man, and then you will not find the answer unless you look with the eye of the spirit. Then it is that you learn that human beings are not dominated by material things, but by ideas for which they are willing to give their lives or their life's work.

What Vercingetorix was to the French, Boadicea was to the British. Her statue, chariot-borne, stands opposite Big Ben today. Sarcasm about this monument complained that Boadicea held no reins with which to drive her horses, and remarked that if the rest of her tactics were upon this level, no wonder her armies suffered defeat. There is no doubt that efficiency counts for a lot. The poets take their revenge upon it after they have been conquered; and the victors read the poetry, enjoy it thoroughly, incorporate it in the system, and believe they wrote it themselves.

I have always had great sympathy for King Harold. The problems which awaited him when he ascended the throne were almost insoluble; but bold was the bid he made for life and power. In an island defended only by local militias and the Royal Guards, a country open at every point to invasion from the seas, a country which had no speedy means of internal communications, Harold in 1066 had to await two separate invasions. In the north the Norsemen were assembling their galleys and transports. In the south Duke William and the Norman chivalry prepared their descent. Harold seems to have taken every step with prudence, valour, and sound strategy. He exhorted the local militias of the threatened counties to take the field and put themselves into the best posture of defence. He remained himself in a central position with his famous house-carles. The first regular troops that England had ever produced – these house-carles were mounted infantry. They marched on ponies and they fought on foot. They may have numbered six or seven thousand men. Their marches were remarkable. When the news of the Norwegian invasion arrived they hastened, with Harold at their head, to Yorkshire, where they animated and directed the local militias.

In the battle of Stamford Bridge on the 25th September, the house-carles with their battle-axes, hewed the Danes to pieces. Harold gained his first and last decisive victory. There was no time to celebrate it. The Normans had landed in the south. Swift then, house-carles, on the road from York to Pevensey! Sometimes there was a road – often there were only tracks. But the house-carles covered the distance of 270 miles in less than three weeks. Harold arrived in time to confront the second invasion at Hastings on the 14th October.

The British people have abandoned all partisanship about the Battle of Hastings. I think their hearts ought to be on the side of Harold. I am all for Harold in battle and defeat. Still, I could not bring myself to say, 'I wish he had won.' Such an assertion would challenge the foundations of a history with which present inhabitants of the United Kingdom may well rest content. Harold's cause was a dull one. England might have remained a stolid country without romance, without ecclesiastical drama, without the spirit of adventure, without all those refinements which the French tongue already carried. At the Battle of Hastings, the advanced culture had the better tactics.

Harold had only infantry and battle-axes. The Normans had archery, cavalry, and manoeuvre. History gives loud cheers for the primitive territorials who stood with unyielding house-carles all day long against mailed missile-hurling adventurers. However, it was just as well they got the worst of it. But here again losing a cause had its 'come-back'. Intermarriage was the unconscious strategy of the vanquished. Once again Venus asserted her authority over Mars. One could not expect Harold to have either the foresight or detachment for views of this kind in the tumultuous hours at Hastings which preceded his receiving an arrow in the eye. The hours were tragic and terrible.

Whoever studies faithfully the scroll of history becomes conscious, in the end, of a pattern that persists and of a pattern that changes. Men and women are for ever moved by the same desires – repeat, from age to age, the emotions and the problems of their ancestors. But the codes and standards by which they judge these emotions and problems vary.

In some respects, at least, the moral law to which priests and preachers appeal is fluid, not fixed. It is no nearer finality today than when Columbus sailed into the sunset to seek a new route to the Indies, or when Julius Caesar first gazed upon the chalk cliffs of Britain.

The evolution of morals is, in fact, in ceaseless progress, and all the great struggles of history have been won by superior will-power wresting victory in the teeth of odds or upon the narrowest of margins.

It would be pleasant to write about the Jacobites and the fall of the House of Stuart. They never seemed to fit the English requirements. We review them all. James I, odious but crafty; Charles I, eyeing his judges with unaffected scorn; Charles II, restored his dynasty, given a second chance, up-borne by the love of his people, spending it all with ladies and lap dogs; James II, ready to run all risks, make all sacrifices, inflict all punishments to compel Protestant England to cleave again to Rome; they none of them suited England.

Modern historians attribute the troubles of these reigns largely to the influence of currency questions. Precious metals had become more plentiful. The value of money declined and prices continued to rise. The poor Kings had to conduct the administration and defence of the country on a fixed-income basis. They could not make both ends meet. The Parliaments could not understand how monetary conditions had altered the entire economic and financial situation. In measuring out the King's allowance they took no account of the rise in prices. They invited their Monarchs to 'live of their own'. These ill-starred functionaries found this very difficult. So the House of Stuart was eradicated from British soil and the Hanoverians reigned in their stead. Then in our time came all sorts of modern improvements like big business and market speculation; and Jacobitism and its league became for ever a lost cause.

As always, everyone has his day, and some days last longer than others.

In many ways General Robert E. Lee presents one of the noblest instances of the champion of the lost cause. History, impressed by his military genius and exalted personal character, gazes with puzzled and disdainful eyes upon his cause. We know that the Confederate soldiers who fought so bravely for the South were convinced that they defended the freedom and sovereign rights of their States. We know that the abolition of slavery was never demanded by the North until the war had lasted for more than two years. Nevertheless, the outstanding issue of that celebrated struggle was and must ever be the eradication of slavery from the North American continent. So here we have, in conjunction with this glorious, victorious, heroic figure, fighting with repeated success against enormous odds, a cause judged to be odious and squalid among men. Nevertheless, as time has passed, the fame of Lee and of his great lieutenants has outshone that of the victors. Their cause has vanished, their country has been incorporated in the strong life of the American union; but their names gleam and glisten in the human story, and are among the dearest treasures of the United States.

We must learn to draw from misfortune the means of future strength. It is a crime to despair. And it is always a comfort in times of crisis to feel that you are treading the path of duty according to the lights that are granted to you. At all times it is no use saying, 'We are doing our best.' You have got to succeed in doing what is necessary.

The sense of drama in history calls for structure, proportion, and completeness in the lives of its great figures. Their struggles, their rise, their triumph, their reign, their fall – these are the chapters into which the story usually divides itself. The Muse seeks at once the culminating point, the main achievement, the great period for which the hero of her tale will ever be remembered. When this is passed and done with she is apt – inconstant jade! – to glide swiftly off to other topics. But life does not in practice yield very readily to this treatment.

History consists unhappily mainly in the struggles and tribulations of mankind. She averts her eyes from the inevitable period of exhaustion or the dull years of recovery.

In order to have the correct perspective and proportion of events, it is necessary to survey the whole chain of causation. No one is compelled to serve great causes unless he feels fit for it, but nothing is more certain than that you cannot take the lead in great causes as a half-timer. Those who serve high causes need no reward. Strength is granted to us all when we are needed to serve great causes. The human race cannot make progress without idealism. We draw from the heart of suffering itself the means of inspiration and survival.

These words of Walt Whitman are appropriate:

'Now mark me well, it is written in the essential nature of things that from any fruition of success, however full, shall come forth something to make a greater struggle necessary.'

We must go forward with unrelenting and unwearying efforts through every living minute that is granted to us.

CHAPTER 21

Why Are We Here?

THE SOVEREIGN QUALITY of Man is his adaptability. The sharpest contrast exists between the circumstances of one generation and the next. The river of Life flows on unstayed. The properties of its waters are constant, but its course lies through ever-changing scenes. Now it glides almost imperceptibly forward through the long shining reaches of fertile plain; now it plunges thundering in a cataract; now it swirls and roars along the jagged channel of a dark ravine; presently it may be silently spreading itself in some vast expanse of sand or marsh.

Our history is in these years running through the rapids. We are flung this way and that way against boulders and precipices, over ledges and around whirlpools. To keep our frail barque of Government and Society from being dashed to pieces on the rocks or overwhelmed by the foaming waters is a task of enormous difficulty. When we look back we see the distant panorama of the falls, with the rainbows of splendour shining on clouds of spray, glorifying the terrors of that awful passage. As we peer anxiously forward nothing but the foaming torrent and the black walls of its gorge confront our gaze and offer us no certain prospects, except of turning at no great distance some new, sudden corner, and plunging farther into the unknown and unforeseeable.

There never was a time of which it is more true to say: 'Nothing happens but the unexpected.' Where were we this time last year? When we cast our minds back we seem almost to have forgotten it. Prospects which often seem so sure, vanish like cloud shapes in a windy autumn sky. At the same time, all our lives we see things happen that everyone had taught us were impossible.

It takes too poor a view of man's mission here on earth to suppose that he is not capable of rising – to his material betterment – far above his day-to-day surroundings.

History unfolds itself by strange and unpredictable paths. We have little control over the future; and none at all over the past.

There have been men and women in the world for probably a million years; but nothing began to be written down about the human race until four or five thousand years ago. All we know about these countless bygone generations is that *they* thought life worth while; otherwise we should not be here. Yet the conditions under which they lived must, judged by our standards now, have been indescribably terrible.

Naked, always nearly starving, hunting each other, hunted by wild beasts almost as cruel and crafty as themselves, living from day to day and from hand to mouth, without one scrap of security or comfort, with no more learning, law, or faith than a pack of prowling wolves, they rejoiced in the gift of Life, fought desperately to preserve it, and to hand down to others the torch which lights the world today.

Then, when we come to recorded history, the tale of this poor four or five thousand years of which we have such scanty and misleading accounts, we see that a new hope had dawned upon the human race. The creature suffered more than his rude forefathers; his life had become more complicated; the old simple, almost animal, existence, with its primordial pleasures of hunting, eating, loving, and fighting, had passed away. In its place came innumerable tyrannies less easy to bear than the crude privations and speedy death of prehistoric times.

We see Man gathered into nations, drilled into armies, governed by laws, oppressed by superstitions, yet no longer naked, and with a little more to eat. But upon the countenance of historic Man was stamped a look of care, and already his eyes asked the question which so many ask today:

'Why are we here?'

To him, as to us, came the answer welling from the very depths of his being:

'We are here on our way to something far better.'

This was the new hope which made life still tolerable and sometimes glorious to the dark, dim ages of the earliest civilisations, and which alone enabled them to bear the pangs of growing knowledge and increasing artificial restraints.

Great empires rose and fell, letters and learning spread, noble religions and philosophies of life cheered and encouraged the weary wayfarer. Confucius wrote his books of wisdom. Mahomet fled from Mecca to Medina. Buddha looked down upon Damascus. Christ was born in Bethlehem. All in different languages to different audiences and under every sky and climate told one secret:

'Man is a spirit; his home is not here, but somewhere beyond time and space; beyond these scenes of imperfection are higher forms of existence. There is a land awaiting us far off where each may have his heart's desire.'

There is no limit to human demand, and there is no limit to the power of mankind to meet that demand. For hundreds of years, in the Middle Ages, the laws of supply and demand were stationary. Everything worked, year after year, at a uniformly low level, and all the populations lived miserably. Then, on a sudden, wages began to rise, enterprise began to quicken, all kinds of new articles and utensils appeared in the cottages and dwellings of the working people. All kinds of new luxuries and comforts opened to the rich and middle classes. The laws of supply and demand suddenly began to work on a much larger and expanding scale.

What had happened? A few small ships had come back across the Atlantic Ocean full of gold and silver, and a gradual, subtle process of inflation had set in. It could not have been the trade of the New World which had refreshed the Old. These poor little ships could only bring spoonfuls of merchandise, and every voyage took over half a year. What they brought was the precious metals which altered, in the sense of expanding, the standards of value throughout the world, and made in those generations expansions in the good living of the human race which has never since been lost.

We come somewhat abruptly to the modern age. It only began at the very earliest a hundred years ago. Man had long been groping and fumbling for science and machinery. In the nineteenth century he got them in his hands. Every year saw great leaps forward. Every invention opened the path to others. Tremendous discoveries were made about the physical universe around us. Mighty powers were harnessed to the service of our material needs. The pace of scientific discovery is growing faster and ever faster.

There is a choice before mankind, of science and the humanities on the one hand which, combined, opened up vistas of splendour never seen before, and on the other hand, collapse in hatred and confusion and, it might well be, obliteration. We must therefore resolve to work with patience and courage for the days when men could overcome the dark suspicions which some have inherited and others have created.

There never will be enough of everything while the world goes on. The more that is given the more there will be needed. That is why life is so interesting. Formidable powers now rest in the hands of man, or are about to be seized by him. Clearly, if things go on as they are, the human race is about to be subjected to processes of change more rapid and more fundamental than anything that has occurred in all history.

Mankind is now making greater progress in mastering and applying natural forces than in the last million years or more. That is a fearsome thought, and the first question we must ask ourselves is, 'Are we fit for it? Are we worthy of all these exalted responsibilities? Can we bear this tremendous strain?'

Hitherto everyone has eagerly welcomed scientific discovery. We see the masses enjoying so many comforts and facilities of which the rich and powerful never dreamed a hundred years ago, and naturally, we have sat grateful to science for these inestimable gifts which increase the pleasures and reduce the pains of human existence.

But science does not only concern itself with beneficent discoveries. The whole apparatus of scientific slaughter on a vast scale is being perfected and expanded day by day.

When we reflect upon the shocking possibilities we may not feel so proud and happy about all that science has done and is going to do.

The achievements of science in the nineteenth and twentieth centuries were not necessary to the happiness, virtue, or glory of mankind. Endless possibilities of moral and mental improvement were open to us without any of the blessings or conveniences which we now enjoy.

It is above all essential that the man and woman of today should realise upon how much lower a plane science stands than that of manners and morals.

It is far more important, for instance, to speak the truth oneself than to possess the most wonderful radio or television set. It is much better to be kind and merciful than to whirl about in our fastest cars. It is far more splendid to keep one's word and be considerate towards other people than to be able to fly.

Justice ranks far above steam. An upright, fearless judge renders a more exalted service than the cleverest inventor. Freedom is worth far more than electricity. The rights of the individual, a happy home and family, such as have existed even under hard, bleak conditions, are incomparably more precious than any amount of wonderful organisation.

In so far as we can have both these sets of alternatives which I have contrasted, let us rejoice; but we shall fall indeed on evil days if we are forced to lose the old for the sake of the new.

All this terrific material progress is really only valuable in so far as it liberates the innate goodness of the human heart. It would be not a blessing but a curse if it rolled forward uncontrolled by the moral principles of simple decent men and women.

It can never be our salvation. It may be our doom.

Take the wonderful conquest of the air. Men able to fly! The dreams of thousands of years realised! The magic carpet of the Arabian Nights in full activity at reasonable prices.

We are forced to ask this question – Will the aeroplane end war, or will it end civilisation?

Are we the children of a glorious epoch advancing into the fullness of our inheritance, or are we simply a gang of squalid mischievous urchins who have got hold of firearms and raided the local laboratory for some tubes of typhus bacilli?

Are we moving forward into a paradise of earthly delights where there will be enough for all, or are we simply plunging into a senseless hell where all the treasures and joys of ordinary life will be calcined?

Broadly speaking, this is the supreme issue which confronts us. We ought to think about it.

Is it in our power to decide? In my browner hours I sometimes doubt it. But then, one must always hope; for there is nothing so useless and so cowardly as despair. One must always try.

It may not be in our power to decide the immediate future of the world, but it is our right and duty to choose – and to choose well.

Of all the achievements of modern science none is more wonderful than the conquest of the air. For 40 centuries man has longed to fly. In our age he has gained his heart's desire. Yet how often results belie expectation!

The Sphinx of ancient legend devoured those who failed to solve her riddles. But the air may be equally fatal to the generation which has guessed right.

It was because Icarus soared too near the sun that he crashed into the sea.

And now that, thousands of years later, we have at last discovered the glory of wings, it may be that we, too, have sealed our own fate.

Man has wrested this great secret from Nature and Science.

Is he worthy of it?

If not, it will destroy not only his science, but his civilisation. It will deprive him of all that he has elaborated for centuries in a struggle for freedom, law and peace.

Unless we are worthy to use the weapons of science they will destroy us. None but Ulysses can bend the bow of Ulysses.

In this case, not to be worthy is not merely to be incapable of using the weapon, but to perish by it.

One is reminded of the 'Arabian Nights' story of the fisherman who uncorked the genii from the bottle which spread over the whole heavens and threatened to annihilate him. Whether this genii we un-corked will treat us kindly or whether we will one day wish we had persuaded him to re-enter his bottle is a question confronting mankind.

A quotation from Walt Whitman occurs to me:

'Now mark me well, it is written in the essential nature of things that from any fruition of success, however full, shall come forth something to make a greater struggle necessary.'

The aeroplane, like every modern method of locomotion, makes the world continually smaller for its inhabitants. The globe is shrinking rapidly.

We see the advantages, but do we see the disadvantages? Much mystery has been taken out of the world by aviation. In my youth, Africa was called 'the Dark Continent'. Sir Henry Rider Haggard wrote fascinating books on wealthy white civilisations which might lie in the large unexplored areas. We knew it was only fiction – but those remote fastnesses held many secrets.

It was still possible to dream, to weave romances, to plan adventures into the unknown. We had a fine, large world to roam about in, with a sense of limitless space and of enormous possibilities.

Nowadays we have reduced the world to a fraction of the size it was 100 years ago. People can rush about frantically through the air. They certainly do not see the beauties of the world, and it is surely their responsibility to show that they make it better.

Reading and reflection at home, agreeable conversation with an intelligent friend, a long walk or ride through the forest or over the moor, where all the charm of Nature can be seen and enjoyed, and beneficial exercise attends the diversion – these long ago furnished to what we think were our *benighted* ancestors everything that life has to offer.

As for the advantages of travel, they may be greatly exaggerated. In order to know anything about a country you must walk through it, or ride on horseback. You must sleep on its soil; pluck its foliage with your fingers.

You must light your fires by its fords and streams, and watch the dawn break beyond strange mountains. Such travel instructs and illuminates.

But the modern gadabout tourist who hurries through a country, rarely looking even at the surface and never beneath it, gazing vacuously at the monuments and cities the guide-books proclaim and ticking them off as 'done' in the time-table, is probably a more narrow-minded person than a man or woman who is playing a real part in the village debating society, or developing the gifts of civilised social intercourse by acts of kindness and good humour.

We live in an age where the mood decides the fortunes of peoples rather than the fortunes decide the mood. If the human race wishes to have a prolonged and indefinite period of material prosperity, they have only got to behave in a peaceful and helpful way towards one another, and science will do for them all that they wish and more than they can dream.

If it is, of course, their wish to be quarrelsome and think it fun to bite one another hard and all the time, there is no doubt that every day they can kill each other in a quicker and more wholesome manner than ever before. The choice is theirs and ours.

Man is becoming increasingly master of his own fate, increasingly uncertain of what is going to be and, I think, he is beginning to understand this fact better than he has ever done before.

And it looks as if the races of Christendom are diminishing while on the other hand, vast floods of Asiatic and semi-Asiatic life are pouring forth to occupy the globe.

Survival is very important, because if a race does not survive other breeds occupy its possessions, and live where it was accustomed to live.

Some people will say: 'Well, what does that matter? If we peter out, others will take our place, and everything will go on all right.'

But then there is a view held by other folk that a race, long welded together, with a great body of history, tradition and achievement behind it, has a message to give to the world full of help and full of hope.

It is a message of fair play, common sense of law, and of freedom, of government, of tolerance, and good will lighting the path of many nations.

If for one moment we acquiesce in our race dying out gradually in the future, then evidently our life-thrust is exhausted. Our task is done. Our tale is told.

We shall have joined the gloomy assemblage of vanished peoples that have been blotted out from the light of the sun.

All the great story of history, of rise and expansion, for which great men schemed and conquered, and brave men fought and died, will be only as a tale that was told.

One may say, of course, that this will happen one day or other to every earthly system and every branch of the human family.

Scientists predict with great assurance a period when our planet itself will swing cold and lifeless around a dying sun, but this is so far off that it does not really come into our present discussion.

When we talk of survival we mean survival, at any rate, for a good long time – perhaps another thousand years or more, and a great and beneficent shaping of world destiny within that period.

To be easily reconciled to the idea of race extinction is to be morbid. It is contrary to the life spirit of the world and neglectful of the purposes of the Creator or of the creative force.

I am on the side of those who wish to see our race last as long as possible, and help guide the world away from harm and evil through long sunshine centuries.

My hope is that the civilisation and mission which have arisen out of our life, with all the glories of its language and literature, should have a long continuity, and pass away only when the human race as a whole has risen to heights far above any that we can now discern.

What is the use of living, if it be not to strive for noble causes and to make this muddled world a better place for those who will live in it after we are gone? How else can we put ourselves in harmonious relation with the great verities and consolations of the infinite and the external? Humanity will not be cast down. We are going on – swinging bravely forward along the high road – and behind the distant mountains is the promise of the sun.

Those who have no care for the future, no knowledge of the past, may be content to live out their little day; but men and women who feel that their work in the world contributes towards some large future unity and ideal will deem it their inexorable duty to take every step in their power to prevent it being cast away.

But do not let it be cast away for small thoughts and wasteful recriminations and memories which, if they are not to be buried, may ruin the lives of our children and our children's children. Let us make sure that we play our part in turning thought into action and action into fame.

There was a time when the Age of Faith endeavoured to prevent the Age of Reason, and another time when the Age of Reason endeavoured to destroy the Age of Faith. Tolerance was one of the chief features of the great liberalising movements which were the glory of the latter part of the nineteenth century, by which states of society were reached where the most fervent devotion to religion subsisted side by side with the fullest exercise of free thought. We may well recut to those bygone days, from whose standards of enlightenment, compassion, and hopeful progress the twentieth century has fallen so far.

Man has emerged in greater supremacy over the forces of nature than has ever been dreamed of before. He has it in his power to solve quite easily the problems of material existence. There lies before him, if he wishes, a golden age of peace and progress. All in his hand. He has only to conquer his last and worst enemy – himself.

There is more material difference between today and the beginning of this century than between the beginning of this century and the beginning of history. It is no wonder that all this intense, furious progress, with its waves of knowledge and half knowledge surging round the world, should have shaken human life to its foundations. It is no wonder we live in a gasping and bewildered generation. For while our powers of knowledge have grown at such prodigious speed, our wisdom and our virtues have remained almost stationary.

All the inventions and all the discoveries have given us no better answer to the question which any child or the rudest savage can ask:
'Why are we here?'

Indeed, the collective movement of the human mind, and the very spreading of science and philosophy, have seemed to destroy in many men and women the old answers without putting anything in their place. When faith in survival after death, faith in a better world where all will be put right, dies in a human heart its owner is a prey to anxieties and stresses harder to bear than those of his rugged, savage ancestors of the Stone Age.

Gone for ever are the halcyon days of Queen Victoria. They are as far from us as those of Queen Anne or Queen Elizabeth. We look back upon the scene, enchanted by distance, as a traveller watches from the steamer the land he loves fade out of sight. When I was young, in the eighties and nineties, everything seemed settled or moving safely along the high road to improvement. The British race led the world, Britannia ruled the waves. English Parliamentary institutions were a pattern being hastily and hopefully imitated by all civilised countries.

The Victorians believed devoutly that they had got the answers to all mundane problems, or would get them agreeably, surely, and in good time. Liberalism – not the party creed, but the prevailing temper in politics; Free Trade in economics; the Gold Standard – administered by London in the interests of the British Empire where nearly all the gold was found – as the medium of exchange; the sanctity of the marriage tie; even the party system, all seemed permanent principles and institutions. Where are they all today?

The younger generation – the generation that escaped the scythe of the last world war arrived eager, fearless, and quite undisciplined upon the scene of action. They ask a hundred questions which their fathers cannot answer – questions not so much of politics, but of finance, economics, social laws, and morals, to which the cut-and-dried answers which were so confidently given years ago no longer seem – to put it mildly – entirely adequate. There is a boundless producing power and an insatiable consuming power; but no one can tell how to join them together.

The problems of the world are increasingly incapable of being solved except by the concerted action of many great states.

At a time when only the freest interchange of services between men in all lands on an ever-increasing scale can rid us of the unemployment nightmare, no nation should wall itself in its own pen, feverishly digging up its back garden for a vegetable patch.

Everyone longs for peace and preaches peace, yet nations arm and prepare for wars more horrible than what we have experienced.

The bulk of Asia is like China – plunged in anarchy or frozen under Communism.

We are ceaselessly disturbed or amused, at any rate occupied, by fleeting superficial sensations. The old books are unread or undigested. The churches are empty. And the younger generation ask us:

'What are we to do?'

Still there are some very simple things that can be said.

Do not be frightened. Do not despair. Keep your head. The trees do not grow up to the sky. Strength will be given as it is needed, and guidance will come to nations that deserve it. Do the right and simple thing according to your conscience and honour in your own sphere. You know quite well what that is. Search diligently but resolutely for practical solutions. Conquer or go down fighting. No one can do more.

It is not impossible, but it seems unlikely that the human race will be mastered and destroyed by the great powers it has wrested from Nature. It seems unlikely that the nations will commit mass suicide in another world war. It seems unlikely we shall starve, because plenty is within our reach. It ought not to be impossible to reconcile love of home and country and readiness to die in their defence with a comprehension of the wider duties and larger groupings required from a citizen of the world. The perplexities and tribulations of our age may well be but the birth-throes of a new harmony.

Do not let us meanwhile cast away the substance of greatness. Let us not break up the solid structure of power founded upon kindliness, and freedom, for dreams which may some day come true but are now only dreams. We are, perhaps, more capable of bearing shocks and strains – especially long strains. Our institutions are capable of changing with time and circumstances. We ought to weather any storm that blows, at least as well as any other existing system of human government. It may well be that the most glorious chapters of our history are yet to be written.

How strange it is that this vast scenario of life unfolds itself year by year since the beginning of the world, and yet there is never repetition! Infinite unguessable variety characterises this non-stop performance. Always the unexpected takes the most prominent part. How poor a guide are the years that are passed to the year that is to come!

Samuel Butler in 'Erewhon' describes life as a journey down a long, dark passage. As we advance the conductor throws open windows one after another; but this bright light only makes the darkness before us more intense.

How vain then to speculate upon the fortunes that await us all!

Neither western or eastern groups can be wholly indifferent to the fate of the other. Science and machinery are capable of multiplying the wealth of the world so quickly that the whole mass of mankind can look forward to an era in which hours of labour would be continually shortened, and the ever-growing hours of leisure enriched with comforts and pleasures which hitherto have been granted to the few.

We need the efforts of everyone, and these efforts can only be evoked by a policy known to be inspired solely by noble ideals of brotherhood and equity between nation and nation. We must lay aside every impediment and cleanse our hearts from all vainglorious pride and ambition. We must not grudge either our services or our money. If taxes have to be increased we must pay them cheerfully.

Nor should we be in doubt where our efforts should be made. They should be made first of all upon ourselves. Each one must arm himself or herself with a strong theme of personal philosophy and discipline. Never mind if it does not answer all the questions. It will answer some, and those the ones that matter most to everyone.

The second effort should be upon those who are nearest us and with whom we come in contact. Do right by them. Everyone, however lowly his station or simple his gifts, can be a rock for others to cling to, and many who may never be heard of in the newspapers can be captains and princes spreading justice and protection around their path. After these tasks are done others will be more obvious and more easy.

Many people say the expense and consequences of social reforms are a direct weakening of the power of the community. They say that men and women ought to be self-reliant; that they should practise thrift and self-denial, and store up from their wages savings which will carry them through periods of misfortune. But this altogether overlooks the real conditions of the modern age.

Suppose a man's employment is taken away from him by world causes? Suppose some subtle change takes place in currency which wipes out the staple employment of a township! Suppose there is a new invention and no one wants the old stuff any more!

What is the use of preaching to the humble bread-winner the virtues of thrift and self-denial? All the thrift and self-denial he can practise in a lifetime would be of no avail in such collapses. The pillars of his house would be shattered. Like Shylock, he might exclaim:

> No! No! Take all; for you do
>   take my life
> When you do take the means
>   by which I live!

There should be renewed, spontaneous ebullient effort to lift to a higher ledge the social conditions of the age. We have laid heavy burdens on wealth, but we have secured a vast set of solid bulwarks and balustrades which protect the bulk of people from the worst strokes of fortune.

We ought not to be afraid of running risks. Since when have we learned that we are entitled to security in this transitory world of chance and illusion? The only way to avoid risks is never to have lived at all. Choosing a career is a risk. Marrying is a risk. Childbirth is a risk. All around the most careful man – every breath he draws, every step he takes, every mouthful he eats – are hazards that may be mortal. And certainly anyone worth his salt would rather live in one of the great periods of shock and change in world history than merely vegetate for a brief span in an aeon of stagnation.

The very problems and dangers that encompass us ought to make men and women of this generation glad to be here at such a time. When we think of all we owe to our forefathers, of whose toils and struggles we are the heirs, whose exertions and forethought gained us the noble and splendid position we still hold among the nations, and which in our lifetime we have maintained in the greatest wars that ever raged, we ought to rejoice at the responsibilities with which Destiny has honoured us.

We ought to be proud that we are guardians of our country in times when so much is at stake; and as long as we do our duty and do our best, there is nothing we need fear in this state of existence or in any other we may be called upon to encounter.

We have come through fires welded and tempered as never before. No peril, no difficulties of the future can be greater than those already triumphantly overcome. We have only to be sure of ourselves to accomplish our duty and to hold our own.

Almost the chief mystery of life is what makes one do things. Look back over the path you have travelled and examine searchingly and faithfully the reasons, impressions, motive, occasions which led you to this or that decisive step on your career. Sometimes you will find that people who impressed you least influenced you most.

Small people, casual remarks, and little things very often shape our lives more powerfully than the deliberate solemn advice of great people at critical moments. Men and women as often as not address themselves to serious emergencies with resolution and with a conscious desire to choose the best way. But usually in our brief hazardous existence some trifle, some accident, some quite unexpected and irrelevant fact has laid the board in such a way as to determine the move we make.

We have always to be on our guard against being thrown off our true course by chance and circumstance, and the glory of human nature lies in our seeming capacity to exercise conscious control of our own destiny. In a broader view, large principles, a good heart, high aims, a firm faith, we may find some charts and a compass for our voyage.

Still, as we lean over the stern of the ship and watch the swirling eddies in our wake, the most resolute of us must feel how many currents are playing their part in the movements of the vessel that bears us onward.

CHAPTER 22

Divided We Fall

ONE GETS QUITE tired of saying things which are first mocked at and then adopted, sometimes, alas, too late. No idea is so outlandish that it should not be considered with a searching but at the same time with a steady eye.

Ideas are born as the sparks fly upward. They die from their own weakness; they are whirled away by the wind; they are lost in the smoke; they vanish in the darkness of the night.

Someone throws on another log of trouble and effort, and fresh myriads of sparks stream ineffectually into the air.

Men have always tended these fires, casting into them the fruits of their toil – indeed, all they can spare after keeping body and soul together.

Sometimes at rare intervals something exciting results from their activities.

Among innumerable sparks that flash and fade away, there now and again gleams one that lights up not only the immediate scene, but the whole world.

So when the idea of 'The United States of Europe' drifted off upon the wind and came in contact with the immense accumulation of muddle, waste, particularism and prejudice which had long lain piled up in the European garden, a new series of events opened.

Never before have three hundred and eighty millions of the strongest, most educated, and most civilised parent races of mankind done themselves so much harm by their quarrels and disunion as have the great nations of Europe during the present century.

Never had they more reason to be discontented with the condition to which they reduced themselves, and never could they see more clearly at once the cause of their misfortunes and its remedy. They had only to look around to see the fair regions they inhabit impoverished by the greatest of all wars, disturbed by hatreds and jealousies which the conflict only aggravated.

But this idea of European unity, so novel to untutored ears, was no more in fact than a reversion to the old foundation of Europe. Why should it appear startling to its inhabitants? Why should Europe have feared unity? As well might a man fear his own body. It was clearly evident that such a development would be beneficial.

In so far as the movement towards European unity expresses itself by the vast increase of wealth which would follow from it, by the ceaseless diminution of armies which would attend it, by ever-increasing guarantees against the renewal of war, it bodes no ill to the rest of the world. On the contrary, it can only bring benefits to every nation whose interests are identical with the general interests of mankind.

We can express our purpose in a single word – 'Europe'. At school we learned from the maps hung on the walls, and the advice of our teachers, that there is a continent called Europe. I remember quite well being taught this as a child, and after living a long time, I still believe if is true. However, professional geographers tell us that the Continent ot Europe is really only the peninsula of the Asiatic land mass. I must tell you in all faith that I feel that this would be an arid and uninspiring conclusion, and for myself, I distinctly prefer what I was taught when I was a boy.

In Europe lie most of the causes which led to the two world wars. In Europe dwell the historic parent-races from whom our western civilisation has been so largely derived. Here is the fairest, most temperate, most fertile area of the globe. The influence and the power of Europe for centuries shaped and dominated the course of history. Here the story descends from the ancient Roman Empire, Christendom, the Renaissance, and the French Revolution. From the hatreds and quarrels of Europe catastrophes of the whole world have sprung. The sons and daughters of Europe have gone forth and carried their message to every part of the world. Religion, law, learning, art, science, industry, throughout the world all bear, in so many lands, under every sky and in every clime, the stamp of European origin, or the trace of European influence.

When asked what I meant by a United States of Europe, my answer is that we have lit a fire which will either blaze or go out. Or perhaps the embers will die down and then, after a while, begin to glow again. We are not making a machine: we are growing a living plant.

We are nearly all of us agreed, in the unity and restoration of Europe as a great hope for the future.

There are linked together the three circles. First, the British Commonwealth. Secondly, the irrevocable association of the English-speaking world. Thirdly, the safety and revival of Europe in her ancient fame and long-sought unity. In all these circles we, in this hard-pressed but unvanquished island, have a vital part to play; and if we can bear the weight, we may win the crown of honour.

Many years have passed since I first wrote about 'The United States of Europe'. I described the unhappy and dangerous plight of the Continent, torn by ancient quarrels, stirred by modern Nationalism, divided and hampered by a maze of tariff-walls, overshadowed by the Hitler-Mussolini Axis, exhausted and drained by one Great War, and oppressed by fear of another. Now here tonight in my same old room at Chartwell I am writing on the same subject.

When I first began writing about the United States of Europe years ago, I wondered whether the U.S.A. would regard such a development as antagonistic to their interest, or even contrary to their safety. But all that has passed away. American opinion is favourable to the idea.

Years ago I thought the argument was unanswerable. But it proved utterly vain. Europe was plunged in a war more awful in its devastation than any ever waged by man, and – more than that – once more the European quarrel dragged America from its isolation, once more it involved the whole world. It almost seems an evil omen.

Certainly the scene we surveyed in the autumn of 1946 bore many uncomfortable resemblances to that of 1938; in some respects, even darker. The peoples of Europe fallen immeasurably deeper into the pit of misery and confusion. Many of their cities in ruins. Millions of homes destroyed. They had torn each other into pieces with more ferocity on a larger scale and with more deadly weapons than ever before.

But is the brotherhood of mankind any nearer? Has the Reign of Law returned? Alas, many of the old hatreds burn on with undying flame. Skeletons with gleaming eyes and poisoned javelins glare at each other across the ashes and rubble-heaps of what was once the august Roman Empire and later a Christian civilisation.

Is there never to be an end? Is there no salvation here below? Are we to sink through gradations of infinite suffering to primordial levels:

> A discord. Dragons of the prime,
> That tare each other in their slime:

or can we avoid our doom?

There is the old story of the Spanish prisoner pining for years in his dungeon and planning to escape. One day he pushes the door. It is open. It has always been open. He walks out free. Something like this opportunity lies before the peoples of Europe. Will they grasp it? Will they be allowed to grasp it? Will they have time?

The heart of an old man goes out to all these poor ordinary folk. How good, how kindly they are; how helpful and generous to one another in their village life; how capable of ceaseless progress and improvement. And here on their cottage thresholds stand Science, Invention, Organisation, Knowledge – aye, and Power, too. Not only are they offered the simple joys which, or the hopes of which, have cheered the pilgrimage of Man – food, warmth, courtship, love, marriage, a home, little children playing by the fire, the fair fruits of honest toil, rest and serenity when life's work is done. They are offered far more; a wider, more agreeable form of existence, conscious and responsible citizenship, the career open to talent, a richer and more varied dietary, fun, amusements, happy, genial intercourse with one another.

President Roosevelt declared the Four Freedoms. Of these the chief was 'Freedom from Fear'. This does not mean only fear of war or fear of the foreign invader. Even more poignant is the fear of the policeman's knock; the intrusion upon the humble dwelling; the breadwinner, the son, the faithful friend, marched away into the night with no redress, no trial by jury, no rights of man, no justice from the State.

A horrible retrogression! Back to the Dark Ages, without their chivalry, without their faith.

Yet two or three hundred millions of people in Europe had only to wake up one morning and resolve to be happy and free by becoming one family of nations, banded together from the Atlantic to the Black Sea for mutual aid and protection. One spasm of resolve! One single gesture! The prison doors clang open. Out walk, or totter, the captives into the sunshine of a joyous world.

It is a very simple act, not even a forward bound. Just stand erect, but all together.

It is no use espousing a cause without having also a method and a plan by which that cause may be made to win. There must be vision. There must be a plan, and there must be action following upon it.

There is demanded of us a moral and intellectual impulse to unity and a clear conception and definition of joint purpose. Can we produce that complete unity, or must we fall into jabber, babel and discord? All must stand together or all will fall. We must aid each other, we must stand by each other. This is no new problem in the history of mankind. Very often have great combinations almost attained success and then, at the last moment, cast it away. Very often have the triumphs and sacrifices come to naught. Very often the eagles have been squalled down by the parrots. Very often, people, indomitable in adversity, have tasted the hard-won cup of success only to cast it away.

I selected France as the land from which the signal should come; first because it involved a finer self-conquest for the French than for any other great people to take the lead. It was for France to take the Germans by the hand and lead them back into the brotherhood of man and the family of nations.

I was encouraged by a famous voice from the past. At the National French Assembly in Bordeaux on March 1, 1871, while the French Republic and Germany were still at war, Victor Hugo said:

'And one will hear France cry, "It is my turn. Am I your enemy? No! I am your sister. I have retaken all, and I give it all back on one condition; that is that we shall be but one united people, but one single family, but one Republic. I will demolish my fortresses. You will demolish yours. My vengeance, it is fraternity. No more frontiers, the Rhine for all! Let us be the same Republic. Let us have the United States of Europe, let us have Continental federation, let us have European freedom!"'

It was difficult then. The prophetic message was rejected. The poet's inspiration died. Events took a different course. Germany flaunted the laurels of victory and France for more than 40 years brooded upon revenge. We had two World Wars, in the first of which France was bled white, and in the second laid low and conquered; and in both of which Europe and the whole world were convulsed and shattered.

The only worth-while prize of victory is the power to forgive and to guide.

The Cause or Question points itself at the United States in a remarkable manner. Isolationism is no more. The Atlantic Ocean is no longer a shield. The Pilgrim Fathers could now cross it in a day; but the troubles from which they fled and the tyrannies against which they revolted can follow just as quick. Not content with tearing their own Continent into shreds, the quarrels and hatreds of Europe have now laid their claws upon the New World.

Americans should realise that they must seek the root of these evils. Prevention is better than cure. Why be ravaged every 25 years with pestilences bred in Europe? Would it not be reasonable prudence to use the power which has come to the New World to sterilise the infection-centres of the Old? Prolonged and careful study of Europe and courageous, tireless action to prevent the recurrence of war-pestilence would seem to be a prime interest of every thoughtful American, enjoined upon him by prudence as well as virtue.

The peace and safety of the United States of America requires the institution of a United States of Europe. It is better to face, in an orderly fashion and from on high, the remote potential antagonism of two Continental groupings than to be dragged for certain into one toil and horror after another by chronic degeneration and the blind convulsions of chance.

The United Nations Organisation is the hope of mankind and the expression in American minds of these ideas and arguments. The shape of the United Nations has changed greatly from its original form and from the intention of its architects. The differences between the Great Powers have thrown responsibility increasingly on the Assembly which has been vastly swollen by the addition of new nations. We wish these new nations well, indeed, we created many of them, and have done our best since to ensure their integrity and prosperity. But it is anomalous that the vote or prejudice of any small country should affect events involving populations many times its own numbers and affect them as momentary self-advantage may direct. This should be improved.

Justice cannot be a hit-or-miss system. We cannot be content with an arrangement where our system of international laws applies only to those who are willing to keep them.

The mere creation of international organisations does not relieve us of our individual responsibilities. It falls to the righteous man individually to do what he can and to form with his friends alliances that are manifestly crowned with justice and honour.

Regional organisms or federations under the supreme world-organisation are foreseen and encouraged in the San Francisco Charter. It is agreed they are not detrimental to the main structure. It has now to be realised as a fundamental practical truth that without them the central structure cannot stand or function.

Let me use the military modes and terminology with which our sad experience has made us all only too familiar. When a great Army is formed by a nation or band of allies it has its General Headquarters; but who would pretend, with our experience, that any General Headquarters could deal directly with a mob of brigades and divisions, each headed by their colourful commander, each vaunting the prowess of their own recruiting district or home State, each pleading the particular stresses of their own task and station?

Unless the intermediate organisms are provided, the World Peace Organisation will either clatter down in ruin or evaporate in empty words. What could be more vain and futile than a crowd of little States, with a few big ones pushing about among them, all chattering about world unity, all working for their separate interests, and all trying to sum up their decisions by votes!

In fact, however, great progress has been made in the creation of these mighty, secondary organisms, the main pillars of the world-structure are already towering up as realities before our eyes.

There is the United States of America within its larger association of the Western Hemisphere. There is the Soviet Union, with its Slavonic fraternities. There is the British Commonwealth of Nations spread all over the globe united by sentimental loyalties which glow in the flame and emerge stronger every time the furnace becomes incandescent.

We must undoubtedly contemplate an Asiatic grouping cherishing the spirit of Asia. The enormous populations of the Far Eastern world will find a coherent expression.

There should be a place, and perhaps the first place – if she can win it by her merits – for Europe, the Mother Continent and fountain source not only of the woes but of most of the glories of modern civilisation.

Here is an aspect which must be observed. Not only do three at least of the pillars of the world Peace Temple stand forth in all their massive strength, but they are already woven together by many ties of affinity, custom and interest.

The United States of America, as the most powerful country in the modern age, is the guardian of the Western Hemisphere and has connections which are growing everywhere. The vast mass of Soviet Russia in Europe and Asia, with its Slavonic attachments, can only give an improved life to its many peoples through the vivifying but no doubt disturbing tonic of world-wide trade and contacts.

The British nation, lying in the centre of so many healthy and beneficent networks, is not only the heart of the Commonwealth of Nations, and an equal partner in the English-speaking world, but it is also a part of Europe and intimately and inseparably mingled with its fortunes. All this interlacement strengthens the foundations and binds together the World Temple.

All the people living in the Continent called Europe have to learn to call themselves Europeans, and act as such so far as they have political power, influence or freedom. Once the conception of being European becomes dominant among those concerned, a whole series of positive and practical steps will be open.

The Council of Europe must look always forward rather than back. Secondly, it must seek the most free and fertile trade between all its members. It must strive for economic harmony as a stepping-stone to economic unity.

Next, the Council of Europe must reach out towards some common form of defence which will preserve order among, and give mutual security to, its members, and enable Europe to take an effective part in the decisions of the Supreme United Nations Organisation.

Inseparably woven with this is the approach to a uniform currency. As we have to build from chaos this can only be achieved by stages. Luckily coins have two sides, so that one side can bear the national and the other the European superscription. Postage stamps, passports, trading facilities, European social reunions for cultural, fraternal and philanthropic objects will all flow out naturally along the main channel opened.

We are told this conception of a free living, regenerated Europe is anti-Russian or, to speak more exactly, anti-Soviet in its character, intention and effect.

This is not true. The many peoples of Russia and Asia who are comprised in the Union of Socialist Soviet Republics, and who occupy one-sixth of the land surface of the globe, have nothing to fear and much to gain from a United States of Europe, more especially as both these groupings must be comprised within the World Organisation and be faithful to its decisions.

We are also told that International Communism will be hostile; and it may well be that the devotees of this anti-God religion in every country will be enjoined to raise their voices in favour of keeping

Europe divided, helpless, impoverished, or even starving. Such conditions, they may argue cogently, are an essential preliminary to world Communist domination. All this may be so.

But Europe and the great world around it must find their own way through their troubles and perplexity. They must not let themselves be deterred from what is right and beneficial for their own policy and interests by any arbitrary veto.

We must have the four great entities and contributors to world Government all playing their part and bearing their proper weight in the World Organisation. We must hope, indeed, that China will make a fifth. No one party or section of mankind must bar the grand design of a united Europe. It must roll forward, and within its proper limits it will roll forward, righteous and strong.

I read in a newspaper:

'The real demarcation between Europe and Asia is no chain of mountains, no natural frontier, but a system of beliefs and ideas which we call Western Civilisation.

'In the rich pattern of this culture there are many strands: the Hebrew belief in God, the Christian message of compassion and redemption; the Greek love of truth, beauty and goodness; the Roman genius for law. Europe is a spiritual conception, but if men cease to hold that conception in their minds, cease to feel its worth in their hearts, it will die.'

These sentiments are so beautiful, and their expression so fine an example of English prose, that I venture to quote them.

It seems a shocking thing to say that the Atomic Bomb in the guardianship of the United States is the main safeguard of humanity against a third world war. In the twentieth century of the Christian era, with all the march of science and the spread of knowledge, with all the hideous experiences through which we have passed, can it be that only this dread super-sanction stands between us and further measureless misery and slaughter?

Nevertheless, I believe the fact is true. Greater divergencies have opened among men than those of the religious wars of the Reformation, or of the political and social conflicts of the French Revolution, or of the Power-struggle just concluded with Hitler's Germany. The schism between Communism on the one hand and Christian ethics and Western Civilisation on the other is the most deadly, far-reaching and rending that the human race has known.

Behind Communism lies the military power of Soviet Russia.

This power is in the firm grasp of thirteen or fourteen extremely able men in the Kremlin. We cannot measure the internal pressures to which they are subjected, nor can we tell how far they may be swayed by crude ambitions of world-conquest.

We are confronted at once by a Theme and a Sword. If the issues in the world were capable of being decided by the strength of ground armies, the outlook for the Western Democracies and for modern Civilisation would be indeed forlorn.

The Atomic Bomb is the balancing factor. Everyone knows it will not be used except in self-defence against mortal injury and provocation. No one can be sure whether it is a final and decisive method of war. Air power, however manifested and armed, may decide a war; but alone it cannot hold a front on land. Still, of all the deterrents against war now acting upon the minds of men, nothing is comparable to this frightful agency of indiscriminate destruction.

There is no reason why all questions between State socialism and individual enterprise should not be settled gradually and peacefully by the normal workings of democratic and Parliamentary machinery. The pyramid of society may become more solid and stable when its top is melted down to broaden its base.

Few things are more important and potentially decisive than that Europe should cease to be a volcano of hatred and strife and should instead become one of those broad upland regions upon which the joy, the peace and glory of millions may repose.

And that great prize – the moral leadership of Europe – still stands before the statesmen of all countries, but it is not to be achieved merely by making speeches of unexceptionable sentiments. If it is to be won by any nation it will only be by an immense amount of wise restraint and timely, discreet action which, over a period of years, has created a situation where speeches are not merely fine exhortations but record the unity and conciliation which have been achieved.

I believe myself to be what is called a good European, and deem it a noble task to take part in restoring the true greatness of Europe and reviving its glories and happiness. Europe can only be united by the heartfelt wish and vehement expression of the great majority of all the peoples in all the freedom-loving countries. There can be no hope for the world unless the peoples of Europe unite together to preserve their freedom, their culture and their civilisation.

Everything that tends to make Europe more prosperous and more peaceful is conducive to British interests.

We are bound to further every honest and practical step which the nations of Europe may make to reduce the barriers which divide them and to nourish their common interests and their common welfare. We would rejoice at every diminution of internal tariffs and the martial armaments of Europe. We could see nothing but good and hope in a richer, freer, more contented European commonalty.

But we have our own dream and our own task. We are with Europe, but not of it. We are linked, but not combined. We are interested and associated, but not absorbed.

And should European statesmen address us in the words which were used of old – 'Shall I speak for thee to the King or the Captain of the host?' – we should reply with the Shunamite woman: 'Nay, Sir, for we dwell among our own people.'

The conception of a 'United States of Europe' is right. Every step taken to that end which appeases the obsolete hatreds and vanished oppressions, which makes easier the traffic and reciprocal services of Europe, which encourages its nations to lay aside arms or precautionary panoply, is good in itself, good for them and good for all.

It is, however, imperative that there should be a proportionate growth of solidarity throughout the Commonwealth, and also a deepening self-knowledge among the English-speaking peoples. Then without misgiving and without detachment, we could watch and aid their sure and sound approach to mass-wealth being very conscious that every stride toward cohesion which is beneficial to the general welfare will make us a partner in their good fortune.

Across our course there flows the ever-changing stream and tide of world events. It is not necessary, indeed it would not always be possible, for us to pronounce upon every episode of international affairs as it occurs.

The fleet in which we are sailing may sometimes be scattered by a gale, and may be driven for the time being to different points of the compass, but as long as every captain on his ship, however situated, however circumstanced, is steadfastly steering towards the same harbour, we may be sure that we shall keep on drawing together until, finally, the whole armada is once again in force.

We look forward across the confusion and darkness to a far broader relationship and to a far surer foundation for every nation in the world, and it is essential that we should deal with realities and not with shams. Mere words, pious sentiments and good intentions, dearly cherished hopes, by themselves are of no avail. No country can be expected or ought to be asked to undertake the responsibility for the protection of the rights and interests of others, unless it obtains simultaneously for itself compensating security and protection necessary to make up for the addition to its risks.

Let us rise then to the level of events and to the height of noble themes. Let us rise while there is time. Let us lay aside every impediment of pride or sloth. Let us trifle no more on the edge of the abyss. Let us act with fidelity and decision. Let us embrace the sacrifices and discipline of mind and body which the cause requires, and on these lines of advance you will find the surest path to safety and peace.

CHAPTER 23

We Miss Our Giants

CAN WE DO without great men? Can we dispense with hero-worship? Do we really need giants?

Must the march of events be ordered and guided by eminent men, or do our leaders merely fall into their places at the heads of moving columns?

Is human progress the result of great resolves and great deeds by individuals, or are these resolves and deeds only the outcome of time and circumstances? Is history the chronicle of famous men and women, or only of their responses to the tides and tendencies of their age?

Do we owe the ideals and wisdom that make our world to the glorious few, or to the patient anonymous innumerable many? The question has only to be posed to be answered. We have but to let the mind's eye skim back over the story of nations, or indeed to review the experience of our own small lives, to observe the decisive part which accident and chance play at every moment. If this or that had been otherwise, if this instruction had not been given, if that blow had not been struck, if that horse had not stumbled, if we had not met that woman, or missed or caught that train, the whole course of our lives would have been changed; and with our lives the lives of others, until gradually, in ever-widening circles, the movement of the world itself would have been affected.

And if this be true of the daily experience of ordinary average people, how much more potent must be the deflection which the master teachers, thinkers, discoverers, commanders have imparted at every

286

stage! True, they required their background, their atmosphere, their opportunity; but these were also the leverages which magnified their power.

I have no hesitation in ranging myself with those who view the past history of the world mainly as the tale of exceptional human beings whose thoughts, actions, qualities, virtues, triumphs, weaknesses, and crimes have dominated the fortunes of the race. But we may now ask ourselves whether powerful changes are not coming to pass, are not already in progress, or indeed far advanced? Is not mankind already escaping from the control of individuals? Are not our affairs increasingly being settled by mass processes? Are not modern conditions hostile to the development of outstanding personalities, and to their influence upon events; and lastly, if this be true, will it be for our greater good and glory? These questions merit some examination from thoughtful people.

It is an error to believe that the world began when any particular party or statesman got into office. It has all been going on quite a long time, and many movements and parties will rise and decline, and I trust many politicians will catch the fleeting glint of popular acclaim before the continuity of our life is cut asunder or fades away.

I have always taken the view that the fortunes of mankind in its tremendous journey are principally decided for good or ill – but mainly for good, for the path is upward – by its greatest men and its greatest episodes.

There are many tests by which we may try to measure the greatness, and one of them is the favourable influence exerted upon the fortunes of mankind. The price of greatness is responsibility.

Certainly we see around us today a marked lack of individual leadership. John Morley, statesman and philanthropist, man of letters and man of affairs, years ago, towards the close of his life, delivered an oration in which he drew attention to the decline in the personal eminence of the leaders in almost all the important spheres of thought and art. He contrasted the heads of the great professions in the early twentieth century with those who had shone in the mid-Victorian era. He spoke of 'the vacant thrones' in Philosophy, History, Economics, Oratory, Statecraft, Poetry, Literature, Painting, Sculpture, Music which gaped on every side. He pointed – as far as possible, without offence – to the array of blameless mediocrities who strutted conscientiously around the seats of the mighty decked in their discarded mantles and insignia. The pith and justice of these reflections were unwelcome, but not to be denied. They are no less applicable to the United States. With every natural wish to be complimentary to our own age and generation, with every warning against 'singing the praises of former times', it is difficult to marshal today in any part of the English-speaking world an assembly of notables which, either in distinction or achievement, can compare with those to whom our grandfathers so gladly paid attention and tribute.

It must be admitted that in one great sphere the thrones are neither vacant nor occupied by pigmies. Science in all its forms surpasses itself every year. The body of knowledge ever accumulating is immediately interchanged and the quality and fidelity of the research never flags. But here again the mass effect largely suppresses the individual achievement. The throne is worthily occupied; but by a throng.

In part we are conscious of the enormous processes of collectivisation which are at work among us. We have long seen the old family business, where the master was in direct personal touch with his workmen, swept out of existence or absorbed by powerful companies, which, in their turn, are swallowed by mammoth trusts. We have found in these processes, whatever hardships they may have caused to individuals, immense economic and social advantages. The magic of mass production has carried all before it. The public have a cheaper and even better article or a superior service, the workmen have better wages and greater security. More painful still, and scarcely so needful, is the continuous obliteration of the small independent shops and their replacement by chain stores, or vast emporia. No one can doubt that this process will grow continually, and that the public will be the gainer.

The results upon national character and psychology are more questionable. We are witnessing a great diminution in the number of independent people who had some standing of their own, albeit a small one, and who, if they conducted their affairs with reasonable prudence, could 'Live by no man's leave underneath the law'. They may be better off, as the salaried officials of great corporations; but they have lost in forethought, in initiative, in contrivance, in freedom, and in effective civic status.

These instances are but typical of what is taking place in almost every sphere of modern industrial life, and of what must take place with remorseless persistency, if we are to enjoy the material blessings which scientific and organised civilisation is ready to bestow in measureless abundance.

In part again, these changes are unconscious. Public opinion is formed and expressed by machinery. The newspapers do an immense amount of thinking for the average man and woman, and so does radio and television. In fact, they supply him or her with such a continuous stream of standardised opinion, borne along upon an equally inexhaustible flood of news and sensation, collected from every part of the world every hour of the day, that there is neither the need nor the leisure for personal reflection. All this is but a part of a tremendous educating process.

But it is an education which passes in at one ear and out at the other. It is an education at once universal and superficial. It produces enormous numbers of standardised citizens, all equipped with regulation opinions, prejudices, and sentiments, according to their class or party. It may eventually lead to a reasonable, urbane, and highly-serviceable society. It may draw in its wake a mass culture enjoyed by countless millions, to whom such pleasures were formerly unknown.

We must not forget the enormous circulations at cheap prices of the greatest books of the world, which is a feature of modern life in civilised countries, and nowhere more so than in the United States. But this great diffusion of knowledge, information, and light reading of all kinds may, while it opens new pleasures to humanity and appreciably raises the general level of intelligence, be destructive of those conditions of personal stress and mental effort to which the masterpieces of the human mind are due.

It is a curious fact that the Russians, in carrying by compulsion mass conceptions to their utmost extreme, seem to have lost not only the guidance of great personalities, but even the economic fertility of the process itself. The theme aims at universal standardisation. The individual becomes a function; the community is alone of interest; mass thoughts dictated and propagated by the rulers are the only thoughts deemed respectable. No one is to think of himself as an immortal spirit, clothed for a space in the flesh, but sovereign, unique, indestructible. No one is to think of himself even as that harmonious integrity of mind, soul, and body which, take it as you will, may claim to be 'the epitome of the Universe'. Sub-human goals and ideals are set before these millions. The Beehive! No, for there must be no queen and no honey, or, at least, no honey for others. In Soviet Russia we have a society which seeks to model itself upon the ant. There is not one single social or economic principle or concept in the philosophy which has not been realised, carried into action, and enshrined in immutable laws a million years ago by the white ant.

But human nature is more intractable than ant-nature. The explosive variations of its phenomena disturb the smooth working out of the laws and forces which have self-subjugated the white ant. It is at once the safeguard and the glory of mankind that they are easy to lead and hard to drive. So Communism, having attempted to establish the most complete form of mass-life and collectivism of which history bears records, have lost the distinction of individuals. We have not much to learn from them, except what to avoid.

Mass effects and their reactions are, of course, more pronounced in the leading nations than in more backward and primitive communities. In Great Britain, the United States, Germany, France, the decline in personal pre-eminence is much more plainly visible than in societies who have less wealth, less power, less freedom. The great emancipated nations seem to have become largely independent of famous guides and guardians. They no longer rely upon the hero, the commander, or the teacher as they did in bygone rugged ages, or as the less advanced peoples do today. They wend on their way ponderously, unthinkingly, blindly, but nevertheless surely and irresistibly, towards goals which are ill-defined and yet magnetic.

Is it, then, true that civilisation and democracy, when sufficiently developed, will increasingly dispense with personal direction; that they mean to find their own way for themselves, and that they are capable of finding the right way? Or are they already going wrong? Are they off the track? Have they quitted the stern, narrow high-roads which alone lead to glorious destinies and survival? Is what we now see in the leading democracies merely a diffusion and squandering of the accumulated wisdom and treasure of the past? Are we blundering on together in myriad companies, like innumerable swarms of locusts, chirping and devouring, towards the salt sea, or towards some vast incinerator of shams and fallacies? Or have we, for the first time, reached those uplands whence all of us, even the humblest and silliest equally with the best, can discern for ourselves the beacon lights?

'The more things change, the more they are the same,' say the French.

Certainly, the efforts at human government attempted by the various nations of the world very largely confirm this profound and challenging paradox.

Out of anarchy, indefinite, intolerable, and threatening to become interminable, sprang kings, given all power and almost God-like status. Of course, the kings governed well, or misgoverned, according to their circumstances and their characters. At any rate, they seemed far better than the hitherto unending anarchy and terror which had preceded them.

But the risk of entrusting the entire fortunes, not merely of a group of tribes, but of the great nations which developed under the kings to the accident of an individual birth, weighed heavily upon the spirit of mankind.

At one period Pericles or Augustus, at another Draco or Caligula!

After the old primeval anarchy had been suppressed society set itself to try to restrain their kings. They invented constitutions of many different types, designed to average the risks. Here they might hamper a great law-giver, a prophet, a true leader of the race; there, on the other hand, they fitted a strait-waistcoat on a monster, a crack-pate, an idiot, or perhaps only a worm.

Still, this doctrine of averaging risks by means of constitutions, and of keeping kings without returning to anarchy, became deeply engrained in the people of our island. Out of it arose by many painful processes the famous Parliamentary system and monarchy. Under this the king gathers and preserves all that is best in the nation. By a profound clairvoyance power was divided and sub-divided by Councillors of State and Parliamentary assemblies. The concept, wrought from the Magna Carta spread over wide portions of the globe. The forms were often varied, but the idea was the same. Sometimes, as in the United States, through historical incidents, an elected functionary replaced the hereditary king.

All over Europe, we saw Parliamentary systems coming into being, either crowned or uncrowned, which restrained the rulers and kept officials of all kinds in their place compared to the ordinary citizen, ploughman, artisan, artist, or thinker.

In the days of Queen Victoria it looked as if the world was going to settle down into a highly cultivated, peaceful society, capable of bringing home the full reward of modern science, and under whose sway there would be a continuous process of self-improvement and higher social organisation. This process was accompanied by gigantic expansion both of population and wealth. However, underneath there had grown up an immense mass of people who were highly discontented at the slow progress which they were making into the happier future, and the sinister twentieth century dawned in unrest.

Then came terrible wars laying nations low, sweeping away old ideas with a scourge of molten steel, but what is extraordinary about these wars is that the world emerged from them and all their waste of human life and treasure far larger and more vehemently active than ever before. The wars fanned the wings of science, and science brought to mankind a thousand blessings, a thousand problems, and a thousand perils.

New idols were worshipped in the shrines of Europe. New un-shackled war lords imposed themselves upon its peoples. Every violent demagogue was always afraid of being outbid by some other agitator who would go further and cared little if his country fared worse. If one declared he would turn the world upside down, another could cap him by promising to turn it inside out. Progressive society got on to the slippery slope. Great thinkers assumed far too readily that progress could only take place in one direction: from Liberalism to Radicalism; from Radicalism to Socialism; from Socialism to Communism, and so on to the highest ranges of sterile, destructive thought.

And modern conditions do not lend themselves to the production of the heroic or super-dominant type. On the whole, they are fatal to pose. The robes, the wigs, the ceremonies, the grades that forti-fied the public men and ruling functionaries of former centuries have fallen into disuse in every country. Even the divinity that 'doth hedge a king' is considered out of place except on purely official occasions. Sovereigns are admired for their free and easy manners, their readiness to mingle with all classes, their matter-of-fact, work-aday air, their dislike of pomp and ritual. The Minister or President at the head of some immense sphere of business, whose practical decisions from hour to hour settle so many important things, is no longer a figure of mystery and awe. On the contrary, he is looked upon, and, what is more important for our present purpose, looks upon himself as quite an ordinary fellow, who happens to be charged for the time being with a peculiar kind of large-scale work. He hustles along with the crowd in the public conveyances, or waits his turn upon the golf links.

All this is very jolly, and a refreshing contrast to the ridiculous airs and graces of the periwigged potentates of other generations. The question is whether the sense of leadership and the commanding attitude towards men and affairs are likely to arise from such simple and unpretentious customs and habits of mind; and further, whether our public affairs will now, for the future, run on quite happily without leaders who, by their training and situation, no less than by their abilities, feel themselves to be uplifted above the general mass.

The intense light of war illuminates as usual this topic more clearly than the comfortable humdrum glow of peace. We see the modern commander entirely divorced from the heroic aspect by the physical conditions which have overwhelmed his art. No longer will Hannibal and Caesar, Turenne and Marlborough, Frederick and Napoleon sit their horses on the battlefield, and by their words and gestures direct and dominate between dawn and dusk the course of a supreme event. No longer will their fame and presence cheer their struggling soldiers. No longer will they share their perils, revive their spirits, and restore the day. They will not be there. They have been banished from the fighting scene, together with their plumes, standards, and breast-plates. The lion-hearted warrior, whose keen eye discerned the weakness in the foeman's line, whose resolve outlasted all the strains of battle, whose mere arrival at some critical point turned the tide of conflict, has disappeared. Instead, our Generals are to be found on the day of battle at their desks in their offices fifty or sixty miles from the front, anxiously listening to the tinkle of the telephone, for all the world as if they were speculators with large holdings when the market is disturbed. All very right and worthy! They are at their posts. Where else, indeed, should they be? The tape machine clacks on, recording the blood-red ink that railways are down or utilities up, that a bank has broken here, and a great fortune has been captured there. Calm sits the General – he is a high-souled speculator. He is experienced in finance. He has survived many market crashes. His reserves are ample and mobile. He watches for the proper moment, or proper day – for battles now last for months – and then launches them to the attack. He is a fine tactician, and knows the wiles of bull and bear, of attack and defence, to a nicety. His commands are uttered with decision. Sell fifty thousand of this. Buy at the market a hundred thousand of that.

Ah! No, we are on the wrong track. It is not shares he is dealing in. It is the lives of scores of thousands of men. To look at him at work in his office you would never have believed that he was fighting a battle in command of armies ten times as large and a hundred times as powerful as any that Napoleon led. We must praise him if he does his work well, if he sends the right messages, and spends the right troops, and buys the best positions. But it is hard to feel that he is a hero. No, he is not the hero. He is the manager of a stock-market, or a stock-yard.

The obliteration of the personal factor in war, the stripping from high commanders of all the drama of the battlefield, the reducing of their highest function to pure office work will have profound effects upon sentiment and opinion. Hitherto the great captain has been rightly revered as the genius who, by the firmness of his character and by the mysterious harmonies and inspirations of his nature, could rule the storm. He did it himself; and no one else could do it so well. He conquered there and then. Often he fell beneath the bolts and balls, the saviour of his native land. Now, however illogical it may seem, and even unjust, his glamour and honours will not readily descend upon our calculating friend at the telephone. This worthy must assuredly be rewarded as a useful citizen, and a faithful, perspicacious public servant; but not as a hero. The heroes of modern war lie out in the crater fields, mangled, stifled, seared; and there are too many of them for exceptional honours. It is mass suffering, mass sacrifice, mass victory. The glory which plays upon the immense scenes of carnage is diffused. No more the blaze of triumph irradiates the helmets of the chiefs. There is only the pale light of a rainy dawn by which the batteries recommence their fire; and another score of divisions flounder to their death.

The wars of the future will be even less romantic and picturesque. There will not be much glory for the General in this process. My gardener exterminated seven wasps' nests. He did his work most efficiently. He chose the right poison. He measured the exact amount. He put it stealthily in the right place, at the right time. The entire communities were destroyed. Not even one wasp got near enough to sting him. It was his duty and he did it well. But he was no hero.

So if some spectacled 'brass hat' of a future world-agony extinguishes London or Paris, Tokyo or San Francisco, by pressing a button, or putting his initials neatly at the bottom of a piece of foolscap, he will have to wait a long time for fame and glory. Even the flashlights of the photographers in the national Ministry of Propaganda will be only a partial compensation. Still our Commander-in-Chief may be a man of exemplary character, most painstaking and thorough in his profession. He may only be doing what in all the circumstances someone or other would have to do. It seems rather hard that he should receive none of the glory which in former ages would have been the attribute of his office and the consequences of his success. But this is one of the mass effects of modern life and science. He will have to put up with it.

From this will follow one favourable reaction. The idea of war will become loathsome to humanity. The military leader will cease to be a figure of romance and fame. Youth will no longer be attracted to such careers. Poets will not sing nor sculptors chisel the deeds of conquerors. It may well be that the chemists will carry off what credit can be found. The budding Napoleons will go into business, and the civilisation of the world will stand on a surer basis. We need not waste our tears on the mass effects of war. Let us return to those of peace.

So, can modern communities do without great men? Can they provide a larger wisdom, a nobler sentiment, a more vigorous action, by collective processes than were ever got from the Titans? Can nations remain healthy, can all nations draw together in a world whose brightest stars are film stars and whose gods are always in the gallery? Can the spirit of man emit the vital spark by machinery? Will the new problems of successive generations be solved successfully by 'the common sense of most'; by party caucuses; by Assemblies whose babble is no longer heeded? Or will there be some big hitch in the forward march of mankind, some intolerable block in the traffic, some vain wandering into the wilderness; and will not then the need for a personal chief become the mass desire?

There is only one duty, only one safe course for a leader, and that is to try to be right and not to fear to do or to say what he believes to be right. That is the only way to deserve and to win the confidence of people.

It is no use leading others up the garden and then running away when the dog growls.

It is said that leaders should keep their ears to the ground. All I can say is that a nation would find it very hard to look up to leaders detected in that somewhat ungainly posture.

Yes, we miss our giants. We are sorry that their age is past. There is a sense of vacancy and of fatuity, of incompleteness.

Since the time of Caesar, the best historians have been those who themselves helped to shape destinies of nations. Even Gibbon, when he wrote of Roman wars and Roman politics, was drawing on personal experience of camp and parliament, and a sense of safety, a pride in the rapidly opening of avenues of progress, a confidence that boundless blessing would reward political wisdom and social virtue, were the accepted basis upon which the eminent Victorians lived and moved.

By singleness of purpose, by steadfastness of conduct, by tenacity and endurance, by these and only these, can we discharge our duty to the future of the world and to the destiny of man. People who are not prepared to do unpopular things and to defy clamour are not fit to lead.

The general levels of intelligence and of knowledge have risen. We are upon a high plateau. A peak of ten thousand feet above the old sea level is scarcely noticeable. There are so many eminences that we hardly bother about them. The region seems healthy; but the scenery is un-impressive. We mourn the towering grandeur which surrounded and cheered our long painful ascent. Ah! if we could only find some enormous new berg rising towards the heavens as high above our plateau as those old mountains down below rose above the plains and marshes!

We want a monarch peak, with base enormous, whose summit is for ever hidden from our eyes by clouds, and down whose precipices cataracts of sparkling waters thunder. Unhappily the democratic plateau or platform does not keep that article in stock. Perhaps something like it might be worked up by playing spot-lights upon pillars of smoke or gas and using the loud-speaker apparatus. But we soon see through these pretences.

No, we must take the loss with the gain. On the uplands there are no fine peaks. We must do without them while we stay there. Of course, we could always if we wished go down again into the plains and valleys out of which we have climbed. We may even wander thither unwittingly. We may slide there. We may be pushed there. There are still many powerful nations dwelling at these lower levels – some contentedly – some even proudly. They often declare that life in the valleys is preferable. There is, they say, more variety, more beauty, more grace, more dignity – more true health fertility than upon the arid highlands. They say this middle situation is better suited to human nature. The arts flourish there, and science need not be absent. Moreover, it is pleasing to look back over the plain and morasses through which our path has lain in the past, and remember in tradition the great years of pilgrimage. Then they point to the frowning crag, their venerated 'El Capitan' casting its majestic shadow in the evening light, and ask whether we have anything like that up there. We certainly have not.

CHAPTER 24

If I Lived My Life Again

HOW AM I to live my life over again? Under what conditions is this prodigy to be accomplished, or this trial to be endured? Am I just to set out on life from infancy or boyhood on the chance of my taking different decisions from time to time? If so, why should I take different decisions or act otherwise than I did?

I am a being composed in a certain manner, equipped with certain impulses and inhibitions, moving amidst circumstances which create themselves around me at every moment, and evoke from me certain action or neglect of action. If I had to live my life over again in the same surroundings and meet the same events, why should I do anything different from that which I have done?

No doubt I should have the same perplexities and hesitations; no doubt I should have my same sense of proportion, my same guiding lights, my same onward thrust, my same limitations; and if these came in contact with the same external facts, why should I not run in fact along exactly the same grooves?

Of course, if the externals are varied, if accident and chance flow out through new uncharted channels, I shall vary accordingly. But then I should not be living my life over again, I should be living another life in a world whose structure and history would, to a large extent, diverge from this one.

Events are the final rulers and time is needed for them to make their pronouncements clear.

If, for instance, I went to Monte Carlo and staked my money on red, as I usually do, having a preference for the optimistic side of things, and the spinning ivory ball had fallen into a red slot in the roulette board instead of falling, as it nearly always did on these occasions, into a black slot, I might have made a lot of money. If I had invested this money in plots of land on the lake-shore at Chicago and had never gone to Monte Carlo any more, I might be a multi-millionaire. On the other hand, if, fired by my good luck, I had continued to gamble, I might have become an habitué of the tables and should now be one of those melancholy shadows we see creeping in the evening round the gaming and so-called pleasure resorts. Clearly two processes are at work – the first dictating where the ivory ball is to come to rest, and the second what reaction it produces from me.

If both these are to vary, their interplay becomes too intricate for us even to catch one glimpse of what might have been! Therefore, let us suppose that the march of events and its freaks and accidents remain as we now know them, and that all that happens is that I have another choice.

But now I must ask a further question. Do I have my new choice *with my present knowledge* of what has actually happened? Or am I to have nothing better in health, character, knowledge, and faith to guide me next time than what I had before? If the latter, our argument comes very quickly to a dead end. If the same choice and the same environment were at any given moment to be repeated, and I were the same person, I should infallibly take the same step. If, for instance I were the sort of person who would spin a coin to settle whether he should take a journey, or buy a house, or open a lawsuit, or join a Government, and the coin in fact came down 'tails up' as it had before, I should certainly act as I did. Unless, indeed, I were the sort of person who, having obtained a decision from the spin of the coin, would decide that it was unworthy to be swayed by such trifles and, therefore, did the opposite. For the purpose of this argument, either alternative is the same, everything flowing out just as we know now it has flowed out.

If, then, there is to be any reality in the new choice offered to me to live my life over again, I must have foreknowledge. I must carry back with me to this new starting point the whole picture and story of the world and of my own part in it, as I now know them. Then, surely, I shall know what to make for and what to avoid; then, surely, I shall be able to choose my path with certainty. I shall have success in all my dealings. Thus armed I shall be able to guide others, and, indeed, guide the human race, away from the follies in which they wallow, away from the errors to which they are slaves, away from the endless tribulations in which they plunge themselves.

But wait a minute. All that I was offered was one choice, to live my life over again. I take back with me to that moment all that I know today. But once I have exercised my choice, my present picture of existing world's history and all my own life story is out of date, or, rather, it will never happen. Of course, if I use my foreknowledge only in some trifling matter, that will very likely not make much appreciable difference in the currents of cause and effect. A very small tadpole waggling its tail this way or that, swimming up towards the sunlight or down into the green mysterious depths, does not make much commotion in a good-sized pond. Foreknowledge of where he would find food, and how he would avoid danger, might give him a good deal better chance of survival, without the people who owned the estate in which the pond lay ever noticing that he possessed the sublime gift of prescience. Everything that we do, even the most casual action, may conceivably be of profound consequence. Happily, in practice, a very good deal of what we do passes away without becoming noticeably a part of the chain of causation.

I might, for instance, use my foreknowledge to back the winner of the Derby at the first moment that I began to live my life over again without markedly altering the economy of the universe. But my foreknowledge would give me no assurance about the next Derby. True, that in the life of the world as it has worked out, I know the name of the horse who won. But now something new has happened. I have won such an enormous stake that several important bookmakers have defaulted. One of their richest clients was ruined in the crash. In despair he jumped into a pond – perhaps it was the same pond in which our tadpole had been swimming (squashing the tadpole). But this is by the way. The client happened to be the owner of the horse that was going to win the Derby the following year. His untimely death, of course, disqualified his horse. Under the existing rules it was struck out of the race, and I, proceeding to Epsom next year with all my foreknowledge, found myself the most ignorant man on the Downs about what was going to happen. I was so cluttered up with all my recollections of the way the other horses had run in the world as it would have been, that I made the most foolish speculations about what would now happen in the new world that my supernatural intuition had made.

Indeed, my knowledge would not give me certainty even about the first Derby. The mere fact of the heavy bets I made might cause unscrupulous people to dope or sabotage the horse, so that it did not win the race, once I had altered the conditions.

Thus we may say that, if one had the chance to live one's life over again, foreknowledge would, in important decisions, be only fully effective once. Thereafter I should be dealing with a continually diverging skein of consequences which would increasingly affect my immediate environment. Indeed, I should be puzzled and put wrong by trying to apply my foreknowledge of what I remembered had happened to the new unknowable series of events which were now actually unfolding. It is hard enough to decide when we do not know what the future will contain. Fancy having to decide, hampered at every moment by the memories of a future which could now never come to pass!

Foreknowledge, in fact, could never be exercised more than once; and that only in a negative sense. It could only say 'Don't'. It could never say 'Do'. The very fact of its exercise would create different conditions, and perhaps prevent my ever doing for the first time, and once only, the act I had planned.

If these thoughts are true about small personal matters, consider how much more potent and how final would be the disturbance arising from a new choice with foreknowledge upon some great or decisive issue. When my armoured train was thrown off the rails by the Boers in the South African War and I had to try to clear the line under fire, I had to keep getting in and out of the cab of the engine, which was our sole motive power. I, therefore, took off my Mauser pistol, which got in my way. But for this I should, forty minutes later, have fired two or three shots at twenty yards at a mounted burgher named Botha, who summoned me to surrender. If I had killed him on that day, 15th November, 1899, the history of South Africa would certainly have been different, and almost certainly would have been less fortunate. This was the Botha who afterwards became Commander-in-Chief of the Boers and later Prime Minister of the South African Union. But for his authority and vigour, the South African rebellion which broke out at the beginning of the Great War might never have been nipped in the bud. In this case, the Australian and New Zealand army corps, then sailing in convoy across the Indian Ocean would have been deflected from Cairo to the Cape. All preparations to divert the convoy at Colombo had actually been made. Instead of guarding the Suez Canal, it would have fought with the Boer insurgents. In this case both the Australian and South African points of view would have been profoundly altered. Moreover, unless the Anzacs had been available in

Egypt by the end of 1914, there would have been no nucleus of an army to attack the Gallipoli Peninsula in the spring, and all that tremendous story would have worked out quite differently. Perhaps it would have been better, perhaps it would have been worse. Imagination bifurcates and loses itself along the ever-multiplying paths of the labyrinth.

But at the moment when I was climbing in and out of the cab of that railway engine in Natal, it was a thoughtless and unwise act on my part to lay aside the pistol, upon which my chances of escape from a situation in which I was deeply compromised might, in fact, in a very short time depend. No use to say, 'But if you had known with your foreknowledge that he was not going to shoot you, and that the Boers would treat you kindly, and that he would become a great man who would unite South Africa more strongly with the British Crown, you need not have fired at him.' That is not conclusive. Many other things would have been happening simultaneously. If I had kept my pistol I should have been slower getting in and out of the engine, and I might have been hit by some bullet which otherwise missed me by an inch or two, and Botha, galloping forward in hot pursuit of the fugitives from the wreck of the train, might have met – not me with my foreknowledge – but some private soldier with a rifle who would have shot him dead, while I myself, sent with the wounded into the unhealthy Intombi Spruit hospital at Ladysmith, would probably have died of enteric. A double loss, which, so far from being avoided, would have been entailed by foreknowledge and prudent action upon that knowledge!

If we look back on our past life we shall see that one of its most usual experiences is that we are often helped by our mistakes and injured by our most sagacious decisions. I suppose if I had to relive my life I ought to eschew the habit of smoking. Look at all the money I have wasted on tobacco. Think of it all invested and mounting up on compound interest year after year. I remember my father in his most sparkling mood, his eye gleaming through the haze of his cigarette, saying, 'Why begin? If you want to have an eye that is true, and a hand that does not quiver; if you want never to ask yourself a question as you ride at a fence, don't smoke.' I remember Lord Roberts, the dapper and famous Field-Marshal, in 1902, stopping me as I walked down St James's Street puffing a large cigar, echoing the same advice. 'Don't smoke,' he said. 'It is so easy not to incur the habit. I am sure your father injured his health by oversmoking. Give it up now and live long in full vigour and activity. Let me give you this piece of advice as an old man.' Of course, I ought to have taken it. Of course, I ought to put that down as one of the things to do if I lived my life over again.

But consider! How can I tell that the soothing influence of tobacco upon my nervous system may not have enabled me to comport myself with calm and with courtesy in some awkward personal encounter or negotiation, or carried me serenely through some critical hours of anxious waiting? How can I tell that my temper would have been as sweet or my companionship as agreeable if I have abjured from my youth the goddess of Nicotine? Now I think of it, if I had not turned back to get that matchbox which I left behind in my dug-out in Flanders, might I not just have walked into the shell which pitched so harmlessly a hundred yards ahead? (Here I will pause, unrepentant, to light another cigar.)

So far as my own public course has been concerned, I have always acted in politics as I felt I wanted to act. When I have desired to do or say anything and have refrained therefrom through prudence, sloth-fulness, or being dissuaded by others, I have always felt ashamed of myself at the time; though sometimes afterwards I saw that it was lucky for me I was checked. I am sure that in my early days I acted in accordance with my deepest feeling and with all that recklessness in so doing which belongs to youth, and is, indeed, the glory of youth and its most formidable quality, and if I had to live my early years over again I would not do otherwise than as I did.

I would not withdraw anything I have said in the past, still less apologise for it.

When the Great War broke out and I started with the enormous prestige of having prepared the Fleet in spite of so much opposition, and of having it ready, according to the science of those days, almost to a single ship at the fateful hour, I made the singular mistake of being as much interested in the military as in the naval operations. Thus, without prejudice to my Admiralty work, I was led into taking minor military responsibilities upon my shoulders which exposed me to all those deadly risks on a small scale which await those in high stations who come too closely in contact with action in detail. I ought, for instance, never to have gone to Antwerp. I ought to have remained in London and endeavoured to force the Cabinet and Lord Kitchener to take more effective action than they did, while I all the time sat in my position of great authority with all the precautions which shield great authority from rough mischance.

Instead, I passed four or five vivid days amid the shells, excitement, and tragedy of the defence of Antwerp. I soon became so deeply involved in the local event that I had in common decency to offer to the Government my resignation of my office as First Lord of the Admiralty, in order to see things through on the spot. Lucky indeed it was for me that my offer was not accepted, for I should only have been involved in the command of a situation which locally, at any rate, had already been rendered hopeless by the general course of the war. In all great business very large errors are excused or even unperceived, but in definite and local matters small mistakes are punished out of all proportion. I may well have lost all the esteem I gained by the mobilization and readiness of the Fleet, through getting mixed up in the firing lines of Antwerp. Those who are charged with the direction of supreme affairs must sit on the mountain-tops of control; they must never descend into the valleys of direct physical and personal action.

It seems clear now that when Lord Kitchener went back upon his undertaking to send the Twenty-ninth Division to reinforce the Army gathering in Egypt for the Dardanelles expedition, and delayed it for nearly three weeks, that I should have been prudent then to have broken off the naval attack. It would have been quite easy to do so, and all our arrangements were made upon that basis. I did not do it, and from that moment I became responsible for an operation the vital control of which had passed to other hands. The fortunes of the great enterprise which I had set on foot were henceforward to be decided by other people. But I was to bear the whole burden in the event of miscarriage. Undoubtedly I might have obtained a far larger measure of influence upon the general course of the war, if I had detached myself in the Admiralty from all special responsibility and made the ships sail away once the troops were fatally delayed. However, it must not be forgotten that the land attack upon the Gallipoli Peninsula, costly and unsuccessful as it was, played a great part in bringing Italy into the war in the nick of time, kept Bulgaria in awed suspense through the summer of 1915, and before it was finished broke the heart of the Turkish army.

One of the most curious features of our lives is the way in which sometimes we make mistakes and judge wrongly of events, and yet find that those very errors turn to great good fortune. In 1923, a dozen Liberal constituencies pressed me to be their candidate. Manchester was for every reason the battle-ground on which I should have fought. A seat was offered me there, which, as it happened, I should in all probability have won. Instead, for some obscure complex, I chose to go off and fight against a Socialist in Leicester, where, being also attacked by the Conservatives, I was of course defeated. On learning of these two results in such sharp contrast, I could have kicked myself. Yet, as it turned out, it was the very fact that I was out of Parliament, free from all attachment and entanglement in any particular constituency, that enabled me to make an independent and unbiased judgment of the situation when the Liberals most unwisely and wrongly put the Socialist minority Government for the first time into power, thus sealing their own doom. Thus I found myself free a few months later to champion the anti-Socialist cause in the Westminster by-election, and so regained for a time at least the goodwill of all those strong Conservative elements some of whose deepest feelings I share and can at critical moments express, although many never liked or trusted me. But for my erroneous judgment in the General Election of 1923 I should never have regained contact with the great party into which I was born and from which I was severed by so many years of bitter quarrel.

Observe how swiftly fortune can change the scene and switch on the lights!

It is a strange and formidable experience laying down responsibility and letting the trappings of power fall in a heap to the ground. A sense not only of psychological but of physical relaxation steals over one to leave a feeling of relief and of denudation. There is no purpose in living when there is nothing to do. Life is sensation; sensation is life.

It is surely a proof of the greatness of a man so to have handled matters during his life that the course of after events is continuously affected by what he did.

To have lit beacon fires which still burn; to have sounded trumpet calls whose challenge still calls.

It is a tragedy which robs the world of all the wisdom and treasure gathered in a great man's life and experience, and hands the lamp to some impetuous and untutored stripling, or lets it fall shivered into fragments upon the ground.

Only faith in a life after death in a brighter world where dear ones will meet again – only that and the measured tramp of time can give consolation.

Some men when they die after busy, toilsome, successful lives leave a great store of securities, of acres or factories, or the goodwill of large undertakings. But some simply bank treasure in the hearts of friends.

This forms a real possession, and they will cherish his memory till their time is come.

If actors in great events ever revisit, from beyond the grave, the scenes of their struggles and successes, who shall say what they would do given a second chance?

The only guide to a man is his conscience; the only shield to his memory is the rectitude and sincerity of his actions. It is very imprudent to walk through life without this shield, because we are so often mocked by the failure of our hopes; but with this shield, however the Fates may play, we march always in the ranks of honour.

The life of man does not depend upon the external conditions to which he is subjected, provided, of course, that they are compatible with the maintenance of his existence.

To live modestly, to walk soberly in the sunshine of fortune, to shun external adventures, to avoid entangling commitments, to enforce frugality upon Governments, to liberate the native genius of the country, to let wealth fructify in the pockets of the people, to open a career broadly and freely to the talents of every class – these were the paths so clearly marked for me, and it was so wise and pleasant to tread them.

I recall Adam Lindsay Gordon's lines –

> Life is mostly froth and bubble,
> Two things stand like stone –
> Kindness in another's trouble,
> Courage in our own.

If I could re-live one year of my life, I would choose 1940.

June the 6th, 1940, was one of the most fertile days of my life. I put down on paper everything that we should need for a successful invasion of France. I did this two days after Dunkirk.

But when I survey the scene of my past life as a whole, I have no doubt that I do not wish to live it over again. Happy, vivid, and full of interest as it has been I do not seek to tread again the toilsome and dangerous path. Not even an opportunity of making a different set of mistakes, and experiencing a different series of adventures and successes, would lure me. How can I tell that the good fortune which attended me, upon the whole with fair constancy, would not be lacking at some critical moment in another chain of causation?

Let us be contented with what has happened to us, and thankful for all we have been spared. Let us accept the natural order in which we move. Let us reconcile ourselves to the mysterious rhythm of our destinies, such as they must be in this world of space and time. Let us treasure our joys but not bewail our sorrows. The glory of light cannot exist without its shadows.

Far off, on the skyline, we see the peaks of the Delectable Mountains. But we cannot tell what lies between us and them. We know where we want to go; but we cannot foresee all the stages of the journey.

The span of mortals is short, the end universal; and the tinge of melancholy which accompanies decline and retirement is in itself an anodyne. It is foolish to waste lamentations upon the closing phase of human life. Noble spirits yield themselves willingly to the successive falling shades which carry them to a better world or to oblivion.

Life is a whole, and luck is a whole, and no part of them can be separated from the rest. The journey has been enjoyable and well worth making – once.

Sources

ALTHOUGH I HAVE explained in the Preface the origins of this book and how the material was compiled and edited, listed on this page are many more invaluable key sources I used. I realise that some may criticise me for not indicating and dating sources on every page, but in a book designed to reach the widest readership, I did not wish to interrupt the emotional flow of Winston's words with continual cross-references to footnotes, and I therefore felt it would be inappropriate to turn it into a text-book by giving elaborate source references throughout. Apart from which, a considerable proportion of the material was derived from individuals, unpublished texts, and records of personal discussions with Churchill. The list of Acknowledgments identifies the most important of these contributors and contributions.

One of the greatest mines of information was the Conservative and Unionist Central Office archives with its extensive records of local constituency meetings and speeches, pamphlets and booklets. Part of these archives have been transferred to the London School of Economics.

Almost every chapter theme was created by combining quotes on each subject from many sources, but at all times Winston's words appear exactly as written or spoken by him. I also remained totally true to his developing thoughts on each subject, and in no way upset the balance of his arguments. The topical force of what he has to say becomes all the more extraordinary when one remembers that so much of it was recorded before the 1939 war.

The following newspapers and magazines provided material:

ANSWERS*
COLLIER'S*
DAILY EXPRESS
DAILY GRAPHIC*
DAILY MAIL

DAILY TELEGRAPH AND MORNING POST
EDINBURGH EVENING NEWS
ENGLISH LIFE*
ESSEX WEEKLY NEWS
EVENING NEWS
EVENING STANDARD
THE GUARDIAN
ILLUSTRATED SUNDAY HERALD*
THE LISTENER
MANCHESTER DAILY DISPATCH*
MANCHESTER GUARDIAN (now The Guardian)
NASH'S MAGAZINE*
NASH'S PALL MALL*
THE NATION*
THE NEW COMMONWEALTH SOCIETY JOURNAL
NEWS OF THE WORLD
NOW (Conservative Party Magazine)
OBSERVER
PEARSON'S MAGAZINE*
PICTORIAL WEEKLY*
STRAND MAGAZINE*
THE STUDENT (Edinburgh University Magazine)
SUNDAY CHRONICLE*
SUNDAY DISPATCH*
SUNDAY EXPRESS
SUNDAY GRAPHIC*
SUNDAY PICTORIAL (now Sunday Mirror)
SUNDAY TIMES
THE TIMES
TORY CHALLENGE (Tory Party Magazine)
VITAL SPEECHES OF THE DAY*
WEEKLY DISPATCH*
WESTERN DAILY NEWS*
WEST HAM EXPRESS*
WORLD JEWRY
YORKSHIRE POST

Pamphlets and Booklets consulted included:

BOLSHEVISM: A DISEASE

COUNTRY BEFORE PARTY
INTERNATIONAL ADVERTISING CONVENTION
LIBERAL PUBLICATIONS
ON HUMAN RIGHTS (*The United Committee for the Taxation of Land Values*)
THE PEOPLE'S RIGHTS (*Lancashire Speeches*)
THE PILGRIM'S SOCIETY
POLITICAL JOURNAL OF THE CONSTITUTIONAL CLUB
UNITED EUROPE MOVEMENT
REASON AND REALITY
THE STATE OF THE NATION (*Conservative Party Central Office*)
THIS IS FREEDOM!

(Newspapers or magazines marked with an asterisk are no longer published.)